Race, Culture, and Portuguese Colonialism in Cabo Verde

by

Deirdre Meintel

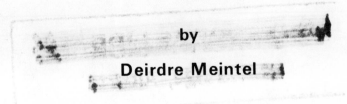

Foreign and Comparative Studies/African Series XLI
Maxwell School of Citizenship and Public Affairs
Syracuse University
1984

Library of Congress Cataloging in Publication Data

Meintel, Deirdre, 1946-
    Race, culture, and Portuguese colonialism in
Cabo Verde.

    (Foreign and comparative studies. African series ; 41)
    Bibliography: p.
    Includes index.
    1. Cape Verde--Race relations. 2. Cape Verde--History.
3. Slave-trade--Cape Verde--History. I. Title.
II. Series.
DT671.C242M44 1984   305.8'00966'58   84-23405
ISBN 0-915984-66-0

CONTENTS

Acknowledgments v

Preface vii

Map xi

Chapter

I. The Field Work 1
Introduction--Field Work in Cape Verde--Conclu-
sion and Prologue

II. African Islands in the Atlantic: The Physical
Setting 15
Islands--African Islands of the New World

III. A Society Built on the Slave Trade: An Historical Outline 31
Discovery--A 'Maritime Crossroads'--Cape Verde
at Mid-nineteenth Century--Conclusion

IV. The *Crises*: Drought and Its Social Consequences. 55
Introduction--Drought and *Crises*--The Specter of
Famine

V. Slavery: The Living Past 73
A Racial System--Lusotropicalism--Land Tenure
and Slavery in Cape Verde--Abolition--Conclusion

VI. Race Relations under Colonialism: The Post-
Slavery Period 93
Introduction--The Living Past--Race and 'Culture'

VII. Colonizers and Colonized: Cape Verdeans in the
Empire 127
The *'Indigenato'* Policies--Cape Verdeans as
Assimilados--Education in Cabo Verde: Myth and
Reality--Cultural Controls: 1930-1974--Race and
Group Identity--Epilogue

VIII. Race and Culture in Colonial Cape Verde: A Comparative View 159
Racial Categories and Race Relations: Brazil
and Cabo Verde--From Cabo Verde to America

Appendices 171

Glossary 173

References 179

Index 195

Note on the Author 202

For all who made this book possible,
especially António

ACKNOWLEDGMENTS

This book is the product of many years of collaboration and friendship with a great number of individuals, only a few of whom are mentioned here. Needless to say, none of them are responsible for any errors of fact or interpretation in these pages.

Funding for the research in Cabo Verde was provided by the National Institute of Mental Health. Research on Cape Verdean-Americans, and the writing of the doctoral thesis on which this book is partly based, were made possible by the Center for Urban Ethnography, University of Pennsylvania, where John Szwed, in particular, gave useful advice and suggestions.

At Brown University, several friends and professors played important roles in nurturing this work from its inception, most of all George Hicks, my thesis director, and Philip Leis and Robert Jay, all of the Department of Anthropology. Nelson Vieira and George Monteiro of the Center for Portuguese and Brazilian Studies gave encouragement and practical assistance at many points in the development of this project. I thank all of them, as well as Lois Monteiro, of the Departments of Sociology and Bio-Medicine, for their help and support.

Peter Gutkind, my colleague for the several years I spent in the Department of Anthropology at McGill University, merits thanks for his interest in the study and his help in finding publishing outlets for the results. Professor Jack Goody, director of the Department of Social Anthropology at the University of Cambridge, and his colleagues, graciously allowed me a year of stimulating fellowship as a Visiting Academic while I was making revisions on the manuscript.

To enumerate the many Cape Verdeans who were important sources of assistance in the research is impossible, so I confine myself to mentioning but a few individuals by name. At the beginning of the project, Belmira Miranda Lopes and the late Charles Fortes opened many doors for me in the Cape Verdean-American community in the Providence area. The friendship and help I have received in the succeeding years from Raymond Almeida, Tony Ramos, Virginia Gonçalves and Yvonne Smart have been invaluable.

In Cabo Verde, several families extended kind hospitality, most notably Chico Feijo and his wife Tibia in Brava, Nesy, Yolanda and Joao Brito in Fogo, and the Martins family of São Vicente. I also thank Felix Monteiro for generously sharing the insights he has developed over a lifetime of research on the folklore and history of the islands, and Dr. Baltasar Lopes, educator and linguist, for the congenial and enlightening hours I spent with him and his wife Teresa. Thanks are also due Dr. Arnaldo França for his assistance with research in Praia. I feel a special admiration and gratitude toward certain individuals who stood by me at the difficult moments of the last several months of the field work, especially Nhô Djessa and the several persons who ensured the safe transport of field materials.

Three individuals contributed to this book to such a degree that I believe it could not have been possible without them. António Nobre Leite, then pastor of the Church of the Nazarene, gave moral support when it was crucially needed and made possible many contacts and acquaintances that otherwise would have been inaccessible. He and his wife Corsinia, and their children, were such delightful company that my work in their extensive library became something of an alibi for enjoying time spent among them. António Carreira of the Museu de Etnologia das Antigas Colonias has, from the well-remembered moment of our first meeting, selflessly shared his awesomely detailed knowledge of the history of Cabo Verde. His enthusiasm for the subject has constantly rekindled my own. Without the faithful correspondence and timely advice of George Brooks, this work might have remained a closet production. To these three individuals I will always remain deeply indebted.

Several of the persons closest to me have been part of this book: Nuno Machado, who kindly drew the map of Cabo Verde and who is present on these pages in many other ways as well; Asen Balikci, who provided me with an ideal personal context for bringing this project to completion; and my family, especially my parents George and Pat Meintel and my sister Mary Kay, for encouraging me from the very beginning.

PREFACE

In these pages, I have set out to give an account of a society that, in certain important aspects, no longer exists. The Cape Verde Islands, where I carried out anthropological research from late 1971 through most of 1972, were then a Portuguese colony. To my knowledge, I was the first social scientist allowed a lengthy stay in the islands, and it seemed apparent that I would be the last for a long time to come. Many aspects of Cape Verdean life were already changing, due to the increased Portuguese military presence spurred on by the wars on the African mainland. Also, large-scale emigration dating back more than a century had done much to bring the islands into the orbit of the world cash economy. Still, no one then anticipated the sudden end to the Caetano regime in Portugal, which took place on April 25, 1974. On July 5, 1975, following a popular referendum, the islands became the Republic of Cabo Verde. Thus, the study presented here comprises a partial record of a society now being transformed into something new.

The ten islands that make up the archipelago, located 283 miles off Africa's western coast at the nearest point, were never more than a backwater of Portugal's empire. Small, with a surface area of 1,556.4 square miles, and afflicted by frequent drought, they were a disappointment to the first European settlers, who arrived in 1462. During certain periods, the geographical position of the Cape Verdes became strategically important for Portuguese commercial or military endeavors; in the last decade or so of colonial rule, they were ascribed a certain ideological significance as a supposed "racial paradise" while serving as a military springboard to Africa. In economic importance, though, the Cape Verdes were eclipsed early on, first by Brazil and later by Angola.

Few Portuguese could be induced to settle in the islands, where they risked agricultural ruin and often went for years on end without being visited by a vessel from the metropole. The Cape Verde Islands became a haven for political exiles, banished criminals, smugglers, and adventurers. African slaves were part of the first contingent of colonists, who found the archipelago uninhabited, and the Africans soon came to predominate over the Portuguese and the other Europeans. The result was a mulatto, Creole-speaking population that today numbers 275,165 (1970 census figures), and whose variations in physical type reflect their cosmopolitan origins. Great differences in complexion, hair type and other features can be found, sometimes even within the same nuclear family.

This book focuses on the colonial experience of the Cape Verdes, both in the distant and in the more recent past, and places special emphasis on the system of racial relations it fostered. Colonialism is now part of history for Cape Verdeans, but that history will continue to bear directly upon their lives for the foreseeable future. Though many anthropologists have done research in colonial situations, colonialism itself -- the relations of power that comprise it and shape everyday social life -- was usually ignored or treated as natural and inevitable, rather than as a problem for study. That colonialism came to be the focal point of this study owes much to the benefit of hindsight gained through the critiques of anthropology and her imperial origins that began to be voiced in the late 1960s, as well as to the particular circumstances of my field research, as discussed in Chapter I.

The race relations and ideology of colonial Cape Verde are in certain respects unique, and thus of interest for the general understanding of racial systems. Race had a quite different meaning in the islands than, for example, in the United States, where a dichotomy exists between "black" and "white." Rather, the Cape Verdean racial system resembles the Brazilian in its lack of a history of legalized discrimination, along with informal patterns of racism, understood as the making of invidious social distinctions on the basis of certain visible physical traits (phenotypes) and/or ancestry. But unlike Brazil, which became independent in 1822, Cape Verde remained a Portuguese colony until quite recently. Chapters VI and VII are concerned with why and how the Cape Verdean pattern of race relations came to be as it is. Obviously, this is one area of behavior and attitudes that is likely to change in the post-independence political context.

For several other reasons, the Cape Verde Islands are of wider interest than their geographical isolation and historical obscurity might suggest. It would surprise most Americans to know that the history of this distant archipelago is intertwined with their own. Yet the peculiar type of colonialism and race relations that shaped Cape Verde forms the heritage of an estimated 200,000 Afro-Americans. For tens of thousands of Africans who eventually arrived in the New World as slaves, Cape Verde was the last place before the infamous Middle Passage. It was there that slaves were "seasoned," in the callous expression of the day; it was there that many captives underwent the devastating personal processes graphically depicted in Elkin's classic, *Slavery* (1959). Though little discussed in the present volume, it is worth noting that it was Cape Verdean immigrants who took over the New England whaling industry in its twilight phase. Like the Irish, Azorean Portuguese, French Canadians and many others, they provided the labor power for New England's industrial development in the late nineteenth and early twentieth centuries.

For reasons mentioned in Chapter I, many Cape Verdean-Americans do not define themselves as Afro-Americans. Strictly speaking, they are Afro-Portuguese-Americans, and for many, their Portuguese origins are a particularly valued aspect of social identity. But Cape Verdeans are hardly unique in this respect, if one considers the French heritage of Haitian-Americans and the Spanish background of Puerto Rican and Cuban "Blacks" in the United States. However, Cape Verdeans' relatively small numbers have added special complexity to their problem of social identity and search for recognition in the United States. Moreover, Cape Verde herself was something of a backwater in the Portuguese empire, little known to outsiders except for the mariners and slave traders for whom the archipelago was but a way station on a longer journey. Of conditions during the catastrophic famine in the colony, one Cape Verdean poet wrote:

> No one knows
> No one pays any notice
> The radio doesn't talk about it
> The newspapers don't report it
> No one telegrams.*

If nothing else, it is hoped that this book will contribute to lessening the "double invisibility" that marks the experience of Cape Verdean-Americans.

---

*Ninguém sabe
ninguém dá por isso
a rádio não fala
os jornais não dizem
ninguém telegrafa
(Barbosa 1961:32;
my translation).

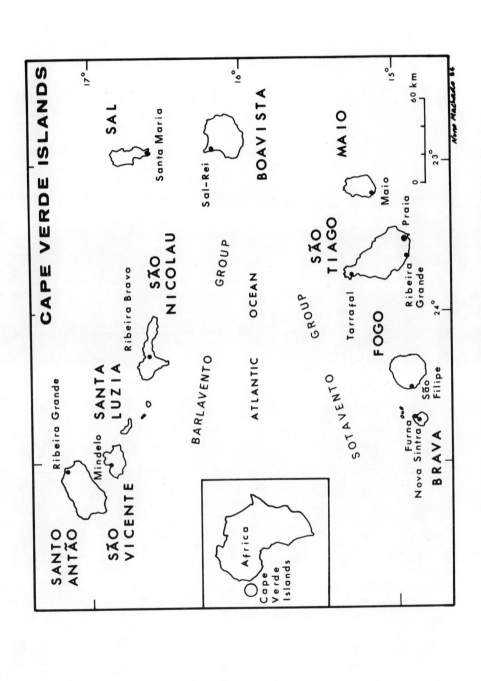

CAPE VERDE ISLANDS

SANTO ANTÃO

Ribeira Grande

SÃO VICENTE

Mindelo

SANTA LUZIA

Ribeira Brava

SÃO NICOLAU

SAL

Santa Maria

BOAVISTA

Sal-Rei

BARLAVENTO GROUP

ATLANTIC OCEAN

SOTAVENTO GROUP

FOGO

Tarrafal

São Filipe

BRAVA

Furna

Nova Sintra

Ribeira Grande

SÃO TIAGO

Praia

MAIO

Maio

17°

16°

15°

23°

24°

0   60 km

Africa

Cape Verde Islands

Nino Machado 84

I

THE FIELD WORK

Introduction

This study began as part of a Brown University doctoral
thesis project on the racial and ethnic identity of Cape
Verdean-Americans in the Providence, Rhode Island area, to
which they came from the Cape Verde Islands, some 2800 miles
across the Atlantic, off the western coast of Africa. Fox
Point, a neighborhood only a few minutes' walk from the university campus, was the traditional point of debarcation for
Cape Verdeans, as well as for Azorean and other "white Portuguese" immigrants arriving in Providence. Located near what
was once a busy waterfront, the three-story frame houses of
"the Point" gave shelter to several generations of "green-
horns," as the newcomers are called. By informal estimates,
about half of the Black population in the Providence area is,
in fact, Cape Verdean.[1]

The total Cape Verdean-American population is usually
estimated at some 200,000.[2] The accuracy of this figure is
difficult to judge, since many Cape Verdean immigrants have
claimed to be Portuguese, having in fact arrived in the states
as Portuguese citizens; still others became "lost," genealo-
gically speaking, in the American Black population.

The saga of the Cape Verdean immigration to the United
States began in the early nineteenth century, when American
whalers stopping for victuals and repairs in the Cape Verde
Islands took on occasional crewmen who eventually made their
way to New England's port cities, including Providence, Newport, New Bedford, Boston, and Nantucket.[3] In the latter
decades of the nineteenth century, Cape Verdeans took over
New Bedford's dying whaling industry, and eventually found
their way into a variety of maritime and shore occupations,
New England's own laborers having been lost to the burgeoning
textile industry. Most of these immigrants and their descendants became blue collar workers, with a small but highly
visible few moving into the liberal professions. (On the
history of the Cape Verdean immigration to the United States,
see Platzer and Machado 1978.)

The mother tongue of Cape Verdeans and of many Cape
Verdean-Americans is Crioulo, sometimes called Caboverdeano.
This is a Creole language greatly influenced by Portuguese in

its vocabulary; however, the two are quite different in structure and are not mutually intelligible. Cape Verdeans are commonly known as "black Portuguese" or, more exactly, as "black Portagees" in the Providence-New Bedford area; however, "white Portuguese" originating in Madeira, the Azores, or continental Portugal, tend not to mingle with Cape Verdeans, regarding them as "African." Cape Verdeans, for their part, vary in how they present themselves, whether as white or black, Portuguese, Afro-American, or some other designation. Investigation of these issues (treated more fully in Machado 1981) indicated that racial and ethnic identity were problematic for Cape Verdeans even before their arrival in the United States. This, along with the fact that no cultural anthropological research had been done in Cape Verde and that very little information of any kind was available, especially in English,[4] provided the impetus for the research on race relations and racial ideology in the islands presented in later chapters.

Field Work in Cape Verde

Before taking up the results of the study, certain issues pertaining to the process of the research itself warrant examination. If in the past neophyte anthropologists felt confronted by a "conspiracy of silence" on the realities of field work (Berreman 1962:4), a growing literature has begun to remedy the situation. A handful of authors has given extended first-hand accounts of particular research experiences (e.g., Powdermaker 1966, Wax 1971), and there are many briefer and more partial accounts found throughout the literature. Systematic discussion of typical phases and problems, such as entree to the field setting and role definition, is still the province of a few, notably Williams (1967), Edgerton and Langness (1974), and Agar (1980).

Yet another body of pertinent literature concerns the ways in which anthropological research and analysis have been shaped by the political context of colonialism. In this controversial area, anthropologists have been criticized variously as having participated in the colonial enterprise, ignoring its impact on the societies they studied, and having been blind to its influence on their own interpretations and theory. Here the critiques of roles played by British social anthropologists presented in Asad (1973) come to mind, as do the enlightening and sometimes vigorous rejoinders made by several of those who began their careers in territories under British colonial rule (e.g., Firth 1977).[5]

Entree

To be studying race relations in a Portuguese colony in 1972 was by no means an innocuous project. Portugal was then waging a war to keep possession of her African territories and at the same time, was engaged in a propaganda effort to convince her allies and the United Nations of the benevolent quality of her colonial rule. Though Cape Verde was not a scene of military conflict, she was particularly important as both a military base and a showcase of Luso-African racial harmony.

In such circumstances, entree to the field situation might certainly be difficult; witness Marvin Harris' somewhat earlier experiences in Mozambique, and his unsuccessful attempts to return there (1966). In fact, five months of efforts to obtain a visa through official channels failed. Fortunately, personal networks among Cape Verdean-Americans proved useful for dealing with the formal, bureaucratic aspects of entree as well as for the informal process of getting established in the islands. A Cape Verdean merchant who made frequent visits to relatives in Providence was able to obtain a visa for me in a matter of days. He and his family offered a home base for the research, in Brava, whence many of the immigrants to the United States have originated.

As a number of writers have pointed out, the social status of such an intermediary can have determining and often limiting effects on the field work (Williams 1967; Agar 1980; see also Berreman 1962 for a discussion of the effects of his interpreters' caste on his research in India). Living in the household of one of the archipelago's most successful merchants initially seemed likely to impede formation of a wide network of field relationships across class boundaries. However, it would have been unsuitable in local terms for a single woman to have set up an independent residence. In addition, my prospective host, in securing my visa, had taken on a certain responsibility for my welfare and conduct that he and his wife felt could only be properly met by providing me with a home for the duration of my stay.

Thus, the town of Nova Sintra, Brava, came to be the base of the field work for some eight months. Named for a town near Lisbon that once served as a resort for Portugal's nobility, Nova Sintra herself was something of a traditional retreat for Cape Verde's governors and bishops seeking to escape the heat and humidity of Praia, the capital city. With her stone and stucco cottages nestled in the arc of an ancient crater high above the shoreline, Nova Sintra's appearance is one of exceptional charm. At a time when the rest of the archipelago had been laid barren by drought, thick clouds floated through her cobbled streets, pierced by the scarlet

4

of *cardeal* flowers (a type of lobelia) and by the deep green
of vines that trailed along her low stone walls, giving the
town an air of enchantment.

As it happened, living in such a household offered a number of advantages for the research. Because of the local
prominence of my host and his wife, the household vibrated
from dawn to dusk with the comings and goings of a large
entourage, easily visible from the vantage point of my room,
which was located across the internal courtyard from the main
part of the house. Besides my hosts and their three children,
four women employed in various capacities lived there permanently, while dozens of others -- part-time employees,
"clients" and visitors -- appeared regularly. Though structured by hierarchy, relations between Cape Verdeans of differing social classes may be close, even intimate, such that
residence in this household provided a useful starting point
for developing relationships in the community. Living with a
family who belonged to the Church of the Nazarene, while being
of Catholic background myself, was also something of an advantage. In Brava, tensions between Catholics and Protestants
had produced violent conflict only a decade or so before, and
religious affiliation was still an important factor in shaping
an individual's social networks.

The Ethnographic Role

Discussions of field work method usually present the
ethnographer's role as something to be defined in the earliest
phase of the research. However, Edgerton and Langness suggest
that this role "undergoes continual revision" as the anthropologist "makes friends and enemies throughout his fieldwork"
(1974:22). It was my experience that the perceptions of
others may be many and varied not only because of changes over
time but also because of the heterogeneity of the study population. The better-educated members of the economic and
bureaucratic elites usually perceived the research as a folklorist study of certain "backward" elements of the population,
though some regarded it as a more "sociological" effort that
would validate Portuguese claims about the quality of Cape
Verdean race relations.

Agar confesses to being "something of a fatalist" regarding how much the ethnographer can control how her or his role
is perceived (1980:60). If such is the case when dealing with
the relatively well educated, it seems all the more true in a
setting such as Brava, where adult literacy is low. Like many
anthropologists working in diverse cultural environments, I
came to be known as "someone who is going to write a book
about us," and I had the typical ethnographer's experience of
being instructed to take notes or photographs on certain
occasions.

Nonetheless, perceptions of my role were structured to a large degree by non-professional criteria such as age, sex, and racial type. It is interesting to note that it is most often female ethnographers who have remarked the importance of these "biological," yet culturally defined attributes (e.g., Lacoste-Dujardin 1977; Powdermaker 1966; Wax 1971), possibly because female ethnographers must often negotiate some type of compromise between local norms of proper female behavior and the requirements of the ethnographer's role. Also, the spheres of behavior to which women usually have the easiest access have only recently been attriuted much importance by a large number of anthropologists, such that female ethnographers were more likely than males to experience their sex as a possible disadvantage. Cape Verdean women envied my physical and social mobility. Not only had I seen more of the archipelago than most Cape Verdeans ever would, but, as a shopkeeper's wife put it, "you have a nice *serviço* [job]; you can mix with people of all levels and no one criticizes you for it."

While as a woman I was probably allowed easier incorporation into a household than would have been possible for a male, being a single woman in my mid-twenties was sometimes a frustrating social handicap, in that it relegated me to a quasi-adolescent status in a number of contexts. For example, married women, even those of my own age, tended to discuss the intimate aspects of the conjugal relationship only elliptically, as local consideration of propriety dictated when in the presence of a young, unmarried woman. This is not everywhere the case; Melanesian women studied by Powdermaker manifested no such reticence (1966:108), nor did women in sectors of Cape Verdean society where Iberian gender norms were less influential than in Brava. For example, market women from Santiago's interior eagerly plied me with questions about birth control methods used in the United States.

If in some ways fieldworkers must create a new social status for themselves, at least where anthropologists are not already familiar figures, in other ways, group members often fit the researcher into pre-existing social categories. It is commonplace for anthropologists working in kin-based societies to be adopted into a lineage, thus giving them a meaningful status in relation to all members of the group. In Cape Verde, racial category and island of origin constitute important kinds of social designation. Habituated to think of myself as "white," I found that in the Cape Verdean racial schema I was less "white" than some others. Because of my dark hair and eyes, I was told several times, "you must have some African ancestry somewhere." Hortense Powdermaker, working in Mississippi in the mid-thirties, recalls that "I was mistaken for a Negro by colored and white people . . . one of my friends explained that everyone thought I was a Negro 'high yellow' . . ." She adds in a footnote that, at the

time, "any white person mixing with Negroes would be considered Negro by members of both races" (1966:135).

Many people outside Brava assumed that I was a returned
emigrant born in Brava; normally the term *americano/a* refers
to Cape Verdeans who have lived in the United States. This
was plausible, since many of Brava's families are of fair complexion and I spoke Crioulo with a Bravense accent. This
assumption about my identity was useful in that it allowed
direct experience of the negative stereotypes of *americanos*
current in some parts of Cape Verde. *Americanos* are widely
thought of as uncultivated bumpkins who, by brutish toil, have
managed to acquire some of the accoutrements of a plastic
civilization. Once a couple of street urchins in Praia asked
me the time. I began to explain that I was not wearing a
watch when one turned to the other and said with disdain,
"Oh, she's an *americana* -- she doesn't know how to tell time!"

Studying Race

Anthropologists frequently find that research projects
developed in advanced bear little relevance to contemporary
conditions in the field situation (Henry 1969:3; Moone 1973;
Gutkind 1969; and Wax 1960 give case examples of this problem).
Fortunately, the earlier research among Cape Verdean-Americans
made it possible to design a research plan that was, by and
large, a viable one. Still, I found myself making unexpected
forays into such areas as religion, sociolinguistics, and
music. This can be attributed in part to the holistic emphasis
in anthropological training that predisposes the fieldworker
to seek out hidden connections between apparently unrelated
cultural and social phenomena,[6] and partly to the naturalistic
tendency traditional to American anthropology which encourages
systematic description of cultural forms that might otherwise
pass unrecorded into disuse. As it turned out, race was so
pervasive a theme in Cape Verdean social life that these areas
proved quite germane to the focus of the research.

In yet another sense, the purview of the research became
wider than anticipated. Gutkind (1969) discovered that
research on the social organization of unemployed men in Lagos,
Nigeria, required a grasp of larger political and economic processes whose importance he had not anticipated. Similarly, it
became quickly apparent that Cape Verdean race relations could
not be understood from a narrowly local, ahistorical perspective, but rather required an understanding of the history and
contemporary policies of Portuguese colonial rule. This would
eventually take me beyond the confines of Brava to interview
urban bureaucratic intellectuals and professionals -- a development that would pose new problems of public and interpersonal
role definition.

Day-to-day observation provided a wealth of information about race, but I also wanted to use a projective test to elicit racial terms, of which there were many. The test comprised a series of full-faced drawings, and had been devised by Marvin Harris for studies done in various regions of Brazil. Edgerton and Langness (1974) and Agar (1980) have brought up some of the problems such techniques pose for anthropologists. First, there is the question of cross-cultural validity. On this score, Harris' work in constructing the test seems to exemplify what anthropologists should be doing; that is, developing research instruments suited to the population under study. I believe that my use of the same tool in Cape Verde is justifiable based on the similarity of culture and racial composition of her population to that of Brazil. It is true that such tests require people to perform a task that is new and strange, which may jeopardize the ethnographer's rapport with the community, not to mention the validity of the tests.

Because of the first question, it seemed advisable to introduce the drawings only in my last month of residence in Brava. The question of validity should encourage caution in interpreting results. In truth, respondents seemed to find the test both amusing and somewhat embarrassing. There appeared to be some incongruity in the situation that produced gales of laughter among the participants whom I knew well whenever I explained the procedure and began showing the pictures. (I presume that others were amused but did not wish to offend me by laughing.) Perhaps this was because the test made explicit an area of thought and behavior normally shrouded in ambiguity and an elaborate etiquette. Perhaps I seemed oddly naïve, or even a bit rude, in my attempt to reproduce through this mechanical process what is in everyday life a matter of some delicacy, touching as it does the core of persons' identities and valuations of self. In any event, the test was useful for enlarging my inventory of racial terms. It also brought to light the importance of context for understanding racial categories by providing a controlled environment for the use of racial terms that could be compared with the "natural" contexts of their use in everyday life.

Discrepancies between verbally expressed ideals and actual behavior are a familiar problem to social science researchers, and one that the methodology of extended participant observation seems particularly well suited to overcoming (Edgerton and Langness 1974:31-32). In the study of racial ideology, such contradictions proved often to be the result of initial deference to a stranger defined as a "respectable" person (*de respeito*). Customs such as women smoking pipes might be disparaged as "African" and "backward" by the very women who enjoyed a smoke on occasion, and who lit up without embarrassment in my presence later on in the fieldwork. To some degree, also, my own behavior and views were being tested; many remarked on the fact that I touched women while conversing with them (customary between social equals of the same sex), irrespective of their color or social position.

Not all discrepancies could be so easily explained. Some of the contradictions between different statements by the same individual, or between actions and behavior, had roots in a disjuncture that was real and profound to them, something that could be established only by asking what are loosely called "leading questions." Though verboten in the traditional canons of structured interviewing methods, such questions are, in practice, frequently asked by most anthropologists, since they are a useful way of falsifying the interviewer's emergent conclusions (Agar 1980:93). Leading questions about race sometimes provoked acute discomfort, manifested by nervous laughter or a rising tone of voice. Several volunteered at a later point that the conversation had left them feeling upset or depressed.

This presented an unexpected ethical problem. The individuals in question tended to be articulate civil servants or professionals who already walked a tightrope between their own convictions and the constraints inherent in maintaining their positions and livelihoods. For them, the interviews had set in relief what was usually ignored or repressed for the sake of survival, constituting a sort of uninvited consciousness raising that, if useful for me, offered little to them but increased frustration. Could such lines of questioning be justified? I came to believe they could not, since I could offer nothing to improve their circumstances. As Spradley remarks, "Personal gain becomes exploitative when the informant gains nothing or actually suffers harm in the research" (1979:38).

Research on the Colonial Context

To be doing field work in one of the last bastions of European colonialism seemed a somewhat anachronistic undertaking in 1972, given the critiques of anthropology as a "tool of imperialism" that had arisen out of the debate over ethnographers' roles in Southeast Asia before and during the Vietnam war. The works of Gough (1968) and others had led me, like many students of the time, to question the validity of the anthropological enterprise. I was thus surprised to discover that Cape Verdeans generally welcomed the study, a few expecting that it would validate Portuguese claims of racial harmony in her colonies, but many more hoping that it would publicize conditions in the islands and rescue their experience as a people from historial oblivion.

I discovered through my own experience the constraints to be endured if one hoped to do research at all in a colonial situation, as well as the limits of toleration of a colonial regime for the traditional anthropological method of participant observation, though I was far from being the first to do so.[7] Given that Portugal was at war against African liberation forces, and that Cape Verde was strategically as well as ideologically important in that struggle, it is perhaps not surprising that I encountered a Portuguese security agent among the Cape Verdean immigrants I interviewed prior to departure. In Cape Verde, sympathetic officials warned me from the first to exercise caution in my letters home, and in general, prudence seemed advisable, since my visa was subject to renewal every three months.

The examination of anthropology's ties to colonialism and other forms of imperialism which had begun in the late 1960s and early 1970s benefited the research since it led to the realization that not only the colonized but also colonialism itself ought to be the object of study. At the same time, and quite apart from this debate, developments in various subfields of the discipline were making it clear that many problems of interest to anthropologists could not be adequately handled exclusively by participant observation at the level of a small community. Indeed, as many studies of peasants suggest, processes at the regional and national levels are often important determinants of what goes on in a small village. Furthermore, the societies traditionally studied by anthropologists are themselves undergoing changes that have brought formerly remote outposts into the orbit of national and international trends and influences.

In this light, the officials and elites once considered somewhat marginal to the fieldworker's daily concerns (cf. Williams 1967:31-33; 57-58) became an integral part of the study population, something that Powdermaker was aware of even in the mid-1950s in her study of the Rhodesian copperbelt:

> . . . I did not see how Europeans could
> be omitted from the study of contemporary
> African life, but at that time I was
> apparently the only anthropologist in
> Northern Rhodesia with that view (1966:250).

She goes on to recount that an anthropologist working in a rural area boasted that he had engaged in a barroom fight with a European because of the latter's racist comments about Africans. Powdermaker told him, "But you should have been taking notes" (Ibid.). Raymond Firth, who was able to "virtually ignore" colonial authorities during his 1928-29 stay in Tikopia, then visited only by missionaries, found himself in direct and active contact with them in 1952, when famine threatened the island. In 1966, his study focused on a taxation dispute between the colonial government and local chiefs (1977:19-20).

The new dilemmas I encountered once the research took me away from Brava to the cities of Praia, the capital, and Mindelo, the hub of the archipelago's economic and intellectual life, seem not at all peculiar to the colonial context. Rather, they seem part and parcel of modern-day conditions of field work where the research touches upon politically sensitive topics (sometimes a wide range indeed) in a conflictual situation. A propos of this, I.M. Lewis remarks wryly that "I have certainly been more subject to pressures, often elusively subtle ones, in post- than in pre-independence Somalia" (1977:101).

One area that presents a challenge to the fieldworker involves dealing with research subjects who are of higher status than oneself, a difficulty elucidated by Henry in her account of work in Trinidad. "The interviewer must present himself and the research problem in far more detail . . . he will be called upon to provide information regarding his own personal attitudes" (1969:44). Or, as she puts it in another context, "In interviewing elites, a researcher cannot expect to merely ask questions and await replies -- he is called upon to participate and, in fact, be interviewed himself" (1969:44).

As a woman working in what she terms an "explosive" political situation, Henry found that taking a "feminine," naïve role with male subjects in positions of political power could result in obtaining more information than a male interviewer might have received (1966:53). (Barnes counters that the advantages of feigned naivete are not restricted to female researchers.[8]) I found displaying knowledgeability a more effective stance when dealing with those in powerful positions, for several reasons. Some of these men, who had been schooled in Lisbon and who had traveled in Europe, had acquired stereotypes of American women as exponents of what they termed *amor libre*, such that securing their professional respect was doubly important. (Henry mentions the problem of "vulnerability" inherent in the "naïve Female" role [1966:553]). Secondly, by investigating opposing points of view on the issues at hand, making my own observations and confronting such individuals with a request for "their side" of the story, I elicited less patronizing and superficial responses than when I seemed the ingenue. On the other hand, this approach probably fueled the suspicions of some that I did not fully support Portugal's position in her colonies.

Henry discovered, during a period of particularly acute struggle between labor unions and government in Trinidad, that neither feigned ignorance nor a guise of neutrality were possible: "Without some degree of commitment on my part, the person would not have divulged any further information and might have influenced others not to cooperate" (Ibid.). She felt "forced to indicate some degree of agreement or at least sympathy with a particular point of view" (1969:45).

In the political context of Cape Verde in 1972, this was not an option. Portugal had suffered setbacks in the wars on the continent, and even in Cape Verde, signs of restiveness were apparent by the summer of that year. The loyalties of Cape Verdeans were all the more suspect, yet more important than ever for Portugal's propaganda efforts. Only overt and enthusiastic support of colonial rule could provide sufficient reassurances that one was not in favor of the revolutionaries, and given Portugal's ever-increasing control of local institutions such as the press, secondary schools, and the police, conspicuous silence was often an eloquent form of protest.

The extremely repressive conditions in Cape Verde, along with the prolonged nature of the conflict -- Portugal having been at war in Africa since 1961 -- made this a rather different situation than that confronting Henry in Trinidad in 1965. Contacts with urban intellectuals and bureaucrats made for increased visibility during a particularly tense period. Suddenly, after some nine months of relative tranquility spent mostly in Brava and other rural areas, I became the subject of unpleasant rumors about my character and political interests; if I was not a spy for the CIA, then I must be working for the PAIGC [Partido Africano da Independencia de Cabo Verde, the revolutionary movement]. Eventually I was asked to leave, mainly to avoid the visit to São Nicolau that I had planned for the last two weeks of my stay. There, some fifteen years of drought had resulted in near-famine and visible symptoms of malnutrition in the population. Once the trip was canceled, I was offered whatever time I needed to wrap up my own affairs.

All of this suggests that "developing rapport" is not necessarily a linear process, contrary to what one might expect from most discussions of what Williams calls "false status-role assignment." Role definition is usually seen as constituting a problem in the initial phase of field work such that, over the long term, consistent and ethical behavior should give the lie to any false assumptions about the ethnographer's identity (Agar 1980:60; Barnes 1966; Williams 1967: 45). Patrick Morris reports a somewhat similar experience of false rumors and role difficulties occuring in the later phase of field work, when he was studying a stratified community in India.

It is likely that the experiences of others doing research under contemporary conditions, whether in the Third World or in their own societies, will eventually lead to the development of a new methodological vocabulary to describe the

field work process, since the present one seems best adapted
to situations of societal homogeneity and political tranquility
where the anthropologist is permitted to maintain the privileged position of an outsider. Here come to mind notions such
as "rapport" and "informant" (one who gives usually reliable
information on "the culture"), not to mention the "anthropolo-
gist-informant relationship," the dyadic interchange between
the researcher and such an individual. Such terms have a
curiously archaic ring to at least some of us who find our-
selves working in situations of conflict and social heterogeneity (e.g., class or ethnic differences) where the anthropologist's relations with institutions and collectivities* loom
large in the research process and where, willingly or not, the
anthropologist is perceived as an actor whose work is of political consequence.

Conclusion and Prologue

The foregoing discussion of methodological issues, along
with the historical and geographical survey presented in Chapters II, III, and IV, provide a context for the focused discussion of Cape Verdean slavery and race relations that occupy
the central chapters of the book. Chapter V points out the
resemblance of Cape Verdean slavery to the "Iberian" model that
characterized parts of the Western hemisphere, and Chapter VI
pursues the comparison on the level of contemporary race relations. The Cape Verdean data give evidence that racist ideology and racial discrimination are quite compatible with a
multicategory racial system of the Iberian sort, where legalized discrimination is absent. Chapter VII treats the wider
political context of Cape Verdean race relations, examining the
colony's unique role in the Portuguese empire. This chapter
examines the notions of "culture" as a key element in Portuguese racial policy and in the dominant folk ideology of race,
as well as in the popular forms of resistance to the colonial
regime that were evident in the last years of Portuguese rule.
The concluding chapter treats some of the implications of the
study for furthering understanding of racial systems elsewhere.
I suggest that Iberian-type racial systems, such as those in
Brazil and colonial Cape Verde, bear a closer resemblance to
"Anglo" models, such as that of the United States, than has
generally been understood to date.

---

*
E.g., in Canada, with band councils, the Department of
Indian Affairs, and the James Bay Development Corporation.

Notes

1. Cape Verdean-Americans are estimated at some 20,000 in the Providence-New Bedford area (Dujardin 1979).

2. This figure is the current estimate among Cape Verdean-American community leaders. Though a special category for Cape Verdean-Americans was introduced for the 1980 census, an accurate figure remains difficult to obtain. Many persons of Cape Verdean descent define themselves as American Black or as Portuguese-American, so that any census result will no doubt be considerably lower than the real number.

3. The American novelist Herman Melville, who made a number of whaling voyages, gives a colorful, but highly racist, account of stopping in the "Cape de Verdes" to pick up "gees" (Portuguese) as crewmen, in "The 'Gees," *Harper's New Monthly Magazine* XII:507-9 (1856).

4. This is still the case, though the recent translation into English of Carreira's *Migrações nas Ilhas de Cabo Verde* (1977) comprises a welcome and needed addition to the sparse literature on Cabo Verde.

5. See this and other responses to Asad (1973) in a special issue of *Anthropological Forum* 4 (1977).

6. This emphasis sometimes degenerates into what Agar calls the "holistic fallacy," whereby connections are established only because of the ethnographer's bias toward finding them (1980:75-76).

7. See, for example, Brown's well-documented account (1973) of the opposition to Godfrey Wilson's efforts to conduct participant observation among African miners in Northern Rhodesia during his tenure as first director of the Rhodes-Livingstone Institute (1938-41).

8. "Many times I have found it advantageous in the field to appear stupid, and have never found this difficult to achieve; it comes naturally. The point to watch is not to be really stupid or naïve" (Barnes 1966:554).

II

AFRICAN ISLANDS IN THE ATLANTIC:
THE PHYSICAL SETTING

Islands

Travelers who land at the international airport in Sal
hardly glimpse that island before proceeding on to Santiago
or São Vicente. Because of her seaport, Mindelo, São Vicente
is the center of the archipelago's shipping traffic and the
first stop for those traveling by sea to the outlying islands.
For those arriving as I did, in a period of drought, the
island presents a specter of almost unearthly desolation. Lack
of rain strips the land of all vegetation but the hardy sisals
and a few scrawny *purgueira* trees, their naked branches claw-
ing heavenward like witches' fingers. Inland, ancient
volcanic craters lay bare, more lunar than terrestrial. All
of this is cast in a mirage-like shimmer by the fierce brilliance of the equatorial sun.

The next few chapters introduce the reader to the geography, population and early history of the Cape Verdes, with
special emphasis on how the physical environment shaped their
role in the Portuguese empire. Of paramount importance are
the catastrophic droughts which have usually resulted in widespread starvation, the subject of a later chapter. Here we
are concerned with the more normal and constant physical conditions of the islands, the variations of climate and topogra-
phy within the archipelago, and the regular changes of the
seasons. First to be considered are two physical factors so
obvious that they might escape notice: Cape Verde's insular-
ity and her geographical location.

Ten islands comprise the archipelago, nine of them inhabited, as well as several uninhabited islets used by fishermen
for overnight encampments. Surface areas range from 24.7
square miles for the small island of Brava to 382 square miles
for Santiago. In *Atlantic Islands*, T. Bentley Duncan explains
in vivid terms the historical importance of islands, pointing
out that in the cartography of the sixteenth and seventeenth
centuries, the size of those in the Atlantic was grossly
exaggerated due to their value to mariners of the day (1972:
2-3). Before the advent of radio and radar, islands were crucial for orientation; in the Cape Verdes, flames issuing from
Fogo's volcano (the island's name means "fire") provided a
natural beacon for passing ships. Sailors depended on islands

as sources of supplies and as places of refuge from inclement weather, functions for which the Cape Verdes came to hold an important place in the annals of sailing navigation.

The series of volcanic eruptions that brought the Cape Verdes into existence remain much in evidence. Occasional earth tremors make Fogo's still-smoking peak seem all the more awesome, flanked as it is by grey lava deposits from the four eruptions of the last century and by darker lava from that of 1951. Once, while traveling by jeep across the desolate lava plain within the more ancient crater encircling today's cone, I witnessed a bizarre apparition: across that expanse of deadly silence, a solitary cow ran loose, romping across the moon, or so it seemed. Below Fogo's principal town, São Felipe, the waves beat against shores of basaltic black sand that color the ocean an extraordinarily deep blue, creating beaches of savage beauty. The volcanoes have also endowed the islands with jagged coastlines and surrounded them with irregular sea-floors, marked by rocks and shallows that make navigation difficult.

For most of their history, life in these islands has been truly insular. On a visit to Maio in 1699, the English Captain Dampier found people waiting to board his vessel for Santiago, only three miles away (Masefield 1906 II:307), an experience echoed in Roberts's account of a voyage in 1721 (1968:624 passim). Even at the end of Portuguese rule, some two and a half centuries later, islands of lesser importance such as Brava could go as long as six weeks without mail or supplies from the outside world. Apart from telegrams, the radio stations in Praia and Mindelo provided the most accessible form of communication throughout the archipelago.

The infrequency and expense of interisland transport has made the sea a barrier as well as a frontier. In more mountainous islands, few inhabitants even know how to swim. Peasant boys fleeing the rigors of service in the Portuguese army around the turn of the century had to learn to swim in order to ship out on American whalers that lay at anchor in Brava's secluded little harbors. Although Cape Verdeans were to gain fame as sailors and harpooners in the United States, as displays in New Bedford's Whaling Museum attest (Cohn and Platzer 1978:86-89), this was more the beginning than the climax of a seafaring "tradition." Even offshore fishing has occupied only a small proportion of the population: just one percent, according to a 1958 study (Gutterres, Oliveira and Costa 1961: 53).

Until 1975, most interisland transport was done by two-masted schooners, of the type that had brought many Cape Verdeans to America. The drama of interisland travel in these vessels suggests something of the ordeal that the transatlantic crossings must have been. Even with thirty or so passengers

and half a dozen crewmen, the schooners, now equipped with
diesel motors, seem crowded. Yet unscrupulous owners and captains often crammed as many as 150 passengers into such vessels making the Atlantic crossing (Tyak 1952:26).

Seasickness invariably prevented me from making a photo-
graphic record of the scenes on board, but the sounds and
images remain unforgettable. In rough seas, which are frequent in the narrow channels between the islands, men, women
and children huddled together supporting friend and stranger ,
alike against the rocking of the vessel. The squawking and
squealing of terrified goats, pigs, chickens, and the odd cow
mingled in eerie concert with the wails and retching of the
passengers, who invoked indiscriminately the mother of God
and their own mothers. *"Ai nha mae! Ave Maria!"*[1] Finally,
as the weather calmed, the passengers would become quieter,
only moaning now and again in their distress. Then, almost
miraculously, the entire ambience would be transformed as we
headed into port. Their tears all but forgotten, the women
and girls would calmly and meticulously arrange their hair and
change into their best clothes, emerging fresh as new butter-
flies from the drenched and foul-smelling hold.

Lack of contact between the islands has made for differences of dialect in Crioulo; each island has its pecularities
of pronunciation and vocabulary, which is true, to a lesser
degree, of each village and hamlet as well. The fact that
women tie their headkerchiefs differently on each island sym-
bolizes to Cape Verdeans themselves the cultural distinctiveness of each island. Distance and limited contact have also
made for stereotyping. To take the two islands with which I
am most familiar, Brava's inhabitants are widely supposed to
be mild-mannered (*manso*, literally "tame") and pious. People
from nearby Fogo, by contrast, are reputed to be haughty
(*soberbo*), proud (*orgulhuso*), volatile ("like their volcano").

It is little wonder that Cape Verdean immigrants in
America speak of their particular island as their homeland
(*nha terra*). For today's independent Cabo Verde, the problems
of communication and transportation between the islands are
critical ones, not only for economic development but also for
the political process of building a nation. The fact that the
population is spread over nine different islands also affects
the form in which health and educational services should be
provided; decentralization, now a social goal in many developed countries, is enforced by geography in Cabo Verde.

Location

Situated between 17°13' and 14°48' North latitude and
between 22°40' and 25°22' West longitude, the Cape Verdes lie
some 283 miles from the African coast at the nearest points.

The archipelago's proximity to Africa, and her favorable position with respect to winds and currents, made the Cape Verdes a maritime crossroads during the sixteenth century. Portuguese caravels, speeded by the Northeast trade winds, stopped on the out-voyage to Brazil and sometimes on the return from São Tomé, a Portuguese island colony to the south, and from the East Indies (Blake 1937:13; Duncan 1972:167). Though the Cape Verdes had lost their commercial importance by the seventeenth century, when Portugal was being outstripped by her competitors in the slave trade on the Guinea coast, the islands continued to play the humbler, yet essential role of a "victualling" and repair stop for slavers and whalers for another 300 years.[2]

Meanwhile, the archipelago's location suited her to yet other maritime functions. Pirates made her small harbors and inlets their lair, as they lay in wait for the odd Portuguese caravel struggling behind the rest of the fleet (Blake 1937:103). Slavers and other traders found the Cape Verdes useful for fixing their position and for picking up advance knowledge of their competitors' activities on the coast. A letter of 1811 from the Massachusetts shipowner Samuel Swan advises one of his captains that "vessels bound down the coast should at all times make Cape Verde to correct and be certain of their situation." This layover would mean no loss of time, for goods could be sold "to advantage" in the islands, and "much serviceable information may be obtained of the general state of the coast to the leeward" (Bennett and Brooks 1965:48).[3]

The Cape Verdes' geographical importance as a potential springboard to Africa has been no less important in modern times. Portugal used them as a base of operations during her wars in the colonies on the continent from 1961 to 1974. Even today, the interest of major world powers in the nation's future is tied to her strategic importance.

Climate and Regional Variations

The Cape Verdes enjoy relatively even temperatures the year round, ranging, on the average, from 20° to 24° Celsius, and varying more with altitude than with the seasons. Annual average rainfall is quite low, only 250 to 300 mm, a level characteristic of arid to semi-arid climates. This average says little, though, about actual precipitation, as this may vary a great deal from one year to the next. Drought has posed severe problems for the islands from the earliest days of colonization, but her drier and milder climate made her an attractive retreat for the Portuguese from the sultry, humid conditions of Guinea and Angola. Matthew Perry, as the next chapter relates, chose the Cape Verdes as the base for American anti-slaving operations, beginning in 1842, since

their climate was far less dangerous for his men than that of
the coast, where infectious diseases flourished (Brooks 1970:
118).

Geographically, the islands are divided into the Barlavento (Leeward) and Sotavento (Windward) groups, the names
referring to their respective positions in respect to the
northeast wind. This division was reflected in the governmental structures of Portuguese rule, such as the two districts within the judicial system. Longstanding patterns of
interisland contact have also tended to demarcate the two
groups' distinctiveness. Rural-to-urban migration stimulated
by the famines has centered around Mindelo for the peasants of
Barlavento, and around the city of Praia, Santiago, for those
of Sotavento. Contacts have tended to be more frequent and
regular within each group than between the two, such that the
dialects of Crioulo spoken in Barlavento are distinct from
those of Sotavento (Silva 1957; Almada 1961).

The 'Flat' Islands

The most economically significant environmental contrast
within the archipelago is that between the low, flat islands
(*ilhas rasas*) and the mountainous ones (*ilhas montanhosas*).
Maio, Sal and Boa Vista, which belong to the first category,
are so dry and sandy that agriculture has never been an important means of livelihood; rather, animal husbandry (pigs,
donkeys, mules, cows and the ubiquitous goat) is the primary
occupation of the population. Apart from various palm species,
including tamarind and coconut, few food-bearing plants are
grown, and in time of drought, these islands are veritable
deserts. Without an agricultural base, population in the flat
islands is sparse, as figures in the Appendix show.

Yet some of the most striking natural splendors of the
archipelago are to be found in the low-lying islands. The
pristine dunes and scattered groves of palms of Boa Vista con-
jure up the pirates' island of childhood imagination and, in
fact, ancient lookout towers attest to that erstwhile danger.
Marauders were a menace in all of the islands (see Chapter
III), but must have been especially terrifying in these flat
islands where nature offered little in the way of refuge.

One of the perils of the salt and hide trade of Boa Vista
and Maio that is discussed in the following chapter was the
treacherous waters around them, full of reefs and shallows,
that made approach difficult. (See Captain Dampier's account,
in Masefield 1906:358-60; also Lima 1844, Part 2: 46-47). In
Boa Vista, the danger was compounded by the fact that the
island was incorrectly placed on navigation maps during the
sailing era. Also, metallic deposits in the island's interior
are believed to cause compass needles to malfunction. For the

islanders this was something of a boon, since they could salvage for themselves whatever was washed ashore, an economic activity of no small importance, given that there were more than a hundred shipwrecks in the nineteenth century.[4] The most recent casualty of Boa Vista's geography was a Spanish freighter run aground sometime in the late 1960s. She remains to this day on the otherwise desolate shore where she met her end, bunches of garlic awash in the waves that lap against her sides. The other major items of cargo appear to have been wooden panels destined for a church in Brazil, and thousands of copies of a single issue of a Spanish pornographic magazine, stacks of which could be found in homes all over the island.

Boa Vista's remarkable beaches, all the more stunning in their utter silence when the sea is calm, have been viewed as having touristic potential, but the scarcity of essentials such as food, water and electrical power makes this unlikely for the foreseeable future. During my short visit in 1972, there was no meat or fish to be had, since all of the livestock save a few pigs had perished in the drought and it happened to be an "unlucky" time for the fishermen. Perforce I developed a taste for the inevitable *lagosta* (a species of lobster resembling North American crayfish) that formed the basis of every meal for ten consecutive days.

The Mountainous Islands

These comprise all of the other inhabited islands: Brava, Fogo, Santiago, São Nicolau, Santo Antão and São Vicente. The last-mentioned is atypical, in that she lacks fresh water. Until a desalinization plant was built in the 1960s, water for Mindelo's approximately 25,000 inhabitants was brought daily by schooner from nearby Santo Antão. Commerce, rather than agriculture, has always been the island's main source of livelihood.

Unlike the flat islands with their relatively uniform temperatures and terrains, the densely populated mountainous islands are veritable mosaics of microclimates. Besides the changes of temperature and humidity associated with differences of altitude, differential exposure to wind is caused by irregularities of relief. Thus, soil and vegetation may vary considerably within a small area, allowing for a fairly wide range of cultigens. In the hotter lowlands, one finds papaya, mango, coconut, and orange trees, along with bananas and sugar cane; higher up, maize is planted along with certain robust varieties of beans, squash and gourds in such a way that the vines of the smaller plants grow entwined around the maize stalks. Still higher, in the moist, cool zones of Brava and Fogo, very fine coffee is produced. Although grown in very small quantities today, this coffee was formerly used to

upgrade the lesser varieties that came from Angola. Wine
grapes are sometimes cultivated in the highlands. One of the
Cape Verdes' exports to Brazil in the seventeenth century
(Ribeiro 1960:126), they are now grown for home consumption,
and this only in rare cases.

In Brava, mineral springs provide slightly gaseous,
pleasant-tasting water. There is usually enough fresh water
available for some irrigation in the lower altitudes, but this
is made difficult by soil composition and irregular terrain.
With irrigation, a winter crop of maize and other vegetables
such as manioc and Irish potatoes can be grown. Households
able to afford the necessary water and seed often make gardens
of lettuce, tomatoes and carrots in their *quintal*, the
enclosed courtyard behind the main part of the house. There,
a pig, and perhaps a few chickens and a goat or two may be
kept, depending on the family's means. Pigs, especially, constitute live savings accounts for the peasant household, which
is likely to have little else in the way of capital. Probably for this reason, great care, pride and affection are
vested in these animals.

Exactly when Brava was first settled is a matter of dispute,[5] but a number of families impoverished by a volcanic
eruption and earthquake in Fogo arrived in 1680. They probably
did not find the island completely uninhabited, for it had
long served as a pasture for goats and probably also as a
refuge for freed or escaped slaves in need of land. Early
settlement took place in the vicinity of Nova Sintra,
described in Chapter I. Furna, now the main port, was probably settled much later; only in 1843 was a small dock constructed there (Barcelos 1905 III:13). Several other, more
sheltered, harbors located on the other side of the island
were in use until about the turn of the century.

Many newcomers before me were similarly impressed by
Brava's verdance and relatively temperate climate. During the
nineteenth century, the island was something of a resort and
summer residence for bishops and governors seeking relief from
the heat and malaria epidemics of Santiago. Colonial officials
returning home often spent a few months there in order to
smooth the transition from the climate of the African continent to that of Portugal. Since Brava was often spared the
devastation and loss of life suffered in drier islands during
the major droughts, she often served as a refuge for those
fleeing famine.

The Portuguese colonial administrators, who considered
Cape Verde something of a bureaucratic exile, were charmed by
Brava's resemblance to northern Portugal, a likeness no doubt
exaggerated by nostalgia and by the contrast between Brava and
other parts of the archipelago. The island's name, meaning
"wild," now seems ill-inspired, for her air of well-tended

domestication is unique in the archipelago. All but the most hopeless and remote areas of land are under cultivation, with stone terraces ringing the steeper slopes. As far back as 1720, Brava was the most densely populated of all the islands, and this remained the case until the 1970s, despite high out-migration (see figures in Duncan 1972:256).

The Seasons

While the Cape Verdes enjoy fairly even temperatures the year round, there are marked seasonal variations, especially noticeable in the mountainous islands. November sees the arrival of the so-called "windy season" that lasts until March. Winds from the northeast prevail, mostly dry, but sometimes carrying precipitation in the higher altitudes where the cooler air has a lower saturation point. This rain benefits the cultivator very little, since the growing season for maize, the staple crop, falls between late July and early January. In the first two months of the year, these winds bring masses of very dry tropical air called harmattans. Then the sun shines with a clear brilliance while hot winds cover everything with a yellowish dust. Dryness of the nose and throat caused by the low humidity gives one the sensation of perpetual, unsla-keable thirst. The harmattans were more than a nuisance for the Yankee merchants of an earlier day who traded in the Cape Verdes. Not only did they occasion discomfort for the crew, but the extreme dryness they brought damaged cargoes and the vessels themselves, shrinking and cracking the timbers of the hulls (Brooks 1970:81).

Relative calm prevails from April through June, punctuated rarely by cold, humid winds from the North Atlantic, again bringing precipitation that does not directly benefit the crops. In Brava and other mountainous islands, cool, heavy fog wafts over the ground at the higher altitudes, so thick that villagers accustomed to living in full view of their neighbors enjoy temporary, though intermittent, invisibility. Children exploit this natural shield for minor escapades while, if one is to believe the rumors, some of their elders welcome its protective cover for dalliances of their own. After the tho-roughly disagreeable wind of the preceeding months, this sharp, humid air gives the sensation that one is breathing for the first time.

The end of June brings suspense and anxiety, because in the so-called "good" years, the intertropical pluvogenic front moves north bringing the rain needed for crops as well as for the scrub vegetation foraged by animals. Unfortunately, the Cape Verdes are situated at the northern limit of this front; since the archipelago is so small in surface area (1,556.4 sq. mi.), even small changes in global weather patterns portend potential disaster.

For the next few months every cloud is studied, specu-
lated upon, wagered against. Past rains are remembered and
recreated in the conversations that never stray for long from
this pressing topic. Not only is there the question of whether it will rain, but also of when. If the cultivator sows
too early, rain may come too late for the seeds to germinate;
delaying, on the other hand, means risking loss of the benefits of what may prove to be the only heavy rains of the season.

The Population

From the very beginnings of colonization in 1462, Cabo
Verde has hosted a population of cosmopolitan origins. The
first group of settlers included not only Portuguese and
Africans but Castilians and Genoese as well (Blake 1942:27).
Later came French and English traders, as well as occasional
pirates and other seamen who married into the local population
and settled in the islands.[6] Some of Brava's families have
non-Portuguese surnames such as Spencer, Burgo and Gibeau; the
temperate climate of the interior highlands of Brava, São
Nicolau, and Santo Antão attracted European political exiles
and fortune-seekers.

The African contribution to the Cape Verdean population
was by far the most important one. Carreira presents evidence
for the presence of demographic influences from at least
twenty-seven different African groups, from the area of
present-day Senegal to Sierra Leone (1972:316-34). Nineteen
of these groups are represented in a census taken in 1856
(Ibid., pp. 510-11). A 1956 physical anthropological study
found significant or very significant correspondence in blood
type distribution between Cape Verdeans and six different
African groups: Wolof, Bambara, Lebu, Tucoro, Fula and
Mandinka (Lessa 1959:122-26). As early as 1565, Wolof and
Fula slaves were engaged as interpreters for slaving expedi-
tions based in Santiago,[7] and Wolof women were prized as
slaves because they were considered "handsome and noble" as
well as fine weavers (Carreira 1972:13).

A few cultural traits can be traced to specific African
cultural origins, such as the numerous words of Mandinka etymology that occur in Crioulo (Meintel 1975:242-43); Carreira
has traced certain personal and place names to Fula and
Mandinka origins (1972:446). It is intriguing and puzzling
that no vestige of Islam remains, for this religion had
reached the West African coast by the early sixteenth century
(Rodney 1970:229), and no doubt some of the slaves were
Muslim. Carreira suggests that these were probably recent
converts, unlikely to continue practicing the faith without
social support (personal communication). As later chapters

show, conversion to Catholicism held certain practical advantages for the slaves.

Most of the African cultural elements to be observed in
Cabo Verde today are those that were common to many of the
African groups represented in the slave population, such as
modes of food preparation, use of the mortar and pestle (as
well as the Iberian stone handmill) to grind corn, weaving
techniques, and so on. No doubt the conditions of slavery
prevented the continuation of many cultural practices that
were embedded in a specific type of social organization; other
customs must have been modified and transformed in the new
environment. However, it must be added that no one familiar
with the various cultures of West Africa has yet undertaken a
systematic cultural survey in Cabo Verde.

Of greatest importance, aside from the African component,
was the Portuguese contribution to the Cape Verdean demographic base. Most of the metropolitan settlers came from the
south, especially the provinces of Algarve and Alentejo, and
from Madeira. A few were probably of aristocratic background,
as Lima claims (1844, Part 2: 8). One observer of 1784 heard
of a one-time nobility in Santiago who scrutinized newcomers
carefully before admitting them into their midst (Carreira
1972:290). The genealogy of the Medina family in Fogo, formerly of the Azores, reveals a number of noble antecedents.
But for the most part, any local aristocracy seems to have
become such in Cabo Verde. For the few Portuguese migrants of
means and name, the empire held more attractive possibilities,
such as Brazil, and Portuguese settlers who were able to do so
were fleeing back to the continent from Cape Verde as early as
the famine of 1580 (Ibid., p. 190; Lima 1844, Part 2: 9).

Pre-twentieth century census materials, which admittedly
leave much to be desired, converge in showing a relatively
small white population. In 1582, a Portuguese missionary
reported "perhaps a hundred" whites in Santiago and Fogo, the
first islands to be heavily settled, at a time when slaves
were said to number some 13,700 (Carreira 1972:289). An 1807
count found 1,752 whites in a total population of 59,400
(Chelmiki and Varnhagen 1841:321). By 1869, there were 919,
only 1.2 percent of the population.[8]

The criminals and political "undesirables" sent from
Portugal, called *degredados*, must once have comprised a considerable proportion of the white element. Between 1802 and
1882, there were 2,433 such involuntary immigrants. More than
half of these were sentenced to terms of five years or less
(Carreira 1972:496), but some remained permanently to become
prosperous and even respectable (Chelmiki and Varnhagen 1841:
241). Since most were males arriving without wives or children, they no doubt contributed to the process of mesticiza-
tion, or African and European mixture, that formed today's
population.

The practice of using Cape Verde as a place of banishment began as early as 1500 (Carreira 1972:290) and continued
until the end of Portuguese rule. Although many *degredados*
were common criminals, some were quite respectable citizens
who had fallen from political grace. Mario Soares, the
socialist leader, spent one of his many terms of exile on the
island of São Nicolau. Bravenses still remember with affection the Portuguese army officer António Casmiro, who spent
several years of exile there in the 1930s. Arriving shortly
after the death of the beloved poet Eugenio Tavares, whom he
was fortunate to resemble, Casmiro learned enough Crioulo to
compose several *mornas* (a traditional musical form) that are
still sung today, and in 1940 published a charming literary
portrait of the island.[9]

Besides the political and criminal exiles, there came
refugees from political and religious persecution in Europe.
Some of the first Cape Verdean traders on the Guinea coast
were Jews, or so-called "New Christians," Jews converted to
Christianity under the pressures of the Inquisition (Ibid.,
p. 48). Although formally forbidden to live in the colony
without special royal permission, they were usually able to
bribe local officials for protection. Theirs must have been
an unenviable lot, because it was common to blame smuggling
on the Jews, often without evidence (Barcelos 1899 I: 83).
Socially they were despised. Considered to be of "impure
blood" in Santiago's genealogy-conscious white society of the
late sixteenth century, the Jews were isolated in a sort of
ghetto in the city of Praia (Anonymous 1784:19-20).

Another influx arrived after the Liberal Wars of the
1820s when some of the Jewish Miguelistas fled to the mountains of Santo Antão. Several became important traders, and
their descendants today include an impressive number of doc-
tors, lawyers and other professionals. In the mid-nineteenth
century, when wars between France and Britain threatened to
involve Morocco, Jews left Rabat for the Cape Verdes. Some
went to Boa Vista, where they prospered in the trade in pelts
and hides.

While no Jewish congregation can be found today, many
traces of the Jewish presence remain. Santo Antão has two
Jewish cemeteries, now in disuse, and another is believed to
have existed in Brava in a place called *Cova do Judeu* [Jew's
Grave]. The cemeteries of Praia and Mindelo have sections
once reserved for Jews (George Brooks: personal communication).
In Ribeira Grande, Santo Antão, a man in his nineties recounted
that although the Jews of that island had no rabbi, the eldest
male, one David Cohen, used to lead them in prayer in the
village now known as Sinagoga.

The great variety of physical types in today's population reflects all of these diverse origins as well as a long

history of miscegenation between Africans and Europeans, a
process discussed more fully in Chapter V. One can read much
of each island's particular history in the faces of her inhabitants. São Vicente, for example, is a veritable genetic
melting pot, because her port of Mindelo attracted migrants
from the other islands of Barlavento seeking employment. Prostitution with foreign seamen thrived and has left its traces
in the city's population. In the early 1960s, one could see
many street urchins born of Nordic fathers; later, when fishing rights in the offshore waters were leased by Portugal to
the Japanese, oriental paternity became more evident among
these youngsters. In the hills of Brava, where slaves were
few, most settlers came from the Azores or Madeira, along with
a few from other parts of Europe. Today's inhabitants range
from fair to dark brown in complexion, and blue and green eyes
are common. Brava's port of Furna, however, was a haven for
the destitute from other islands in times of famine, and that
town's population is noticeably darker than that of the rest
of this small island. Fogo's population reflects the African
origins of the slaves who once worked her plantations, except
for the lighter-complexioned descendants of the one-time landlords, concentrated in the town of São Felipe. In Maio, one
finds considerably less phenotypical variety, since most of
the inhabitants are descended from slave herders and fishermen,
except for the Evora family who once virtually owned the
island.

African Islands of the New World

While geography, culture and demographic origins tie Cabo
Verde to Africa, these islands are in a certain sense part of
the New World constituted by European mercantile expansion in
the fifteenth and sixteenth centuries. The discovery of the
archipelago, related in the next chapter, came only thirty-
seven years before Columbus's arrival in the West Indies. Both
voyages were part of the European quest for a maritime route
to the Orient. The history of Cabo Verde, so far as it is
known, came into being with that of the European colonies in
the Americas. Thereafter, the two were bound first by the
slave trade, then by other commercial links, and most recently
by patterns of migration.

In her physical geography, culture and history, Cabo
Verde has much in common with the islands of the "Caribbean
region" as described by Mintz (1971a). Her volcanic origins,
climate and Creole language and culture make for a close
resemblance, one that is heightened by certain points of con-
vergence in social history. Patterns of widespread miscegenation and manumissions are found in Cabo Verde's history as
well as in many parts of the Caribbean, along with the presence of a universalistic religion (Catholicism in both cases),
this last being a factor that Mintz considers essential for

the development of a Creole culture. The ambiguous colonial role of Cabo Verde, described in later chapters, seems to parallel somewhat those of Martinique and Guadeloupe as discussed in the writings of Aime Cesaire and Frantz Fanon.

Nonetheless, Cabo Verde's future lies with Africa. Historical ties with Guinea-Bissau, along with their geographical proximity, bound the two nations closely together in a common struggle for liberation from Portuguese colonialism. This bond, along with others now being forged with African nations sharing common ecological and economic problems, gives new meaning and political significance to Cabo Verde's traditional role as a "springboard to Africa."

Notes

1. Terms and phrases given in the vernacular are provided in Portuguese in cases where the Crioulo version is nearly the same. Where the Crioulo version is markedly different from the Portuguese equivalent, the notation "Cr." appears, and the word or phrase is given in Crioulo, using Portuguese orthography.

2. Duncan describes these functions in detail, with extensive documentation, in his highly readable and informative study (1972: Chapters 1, 8, and 9).

3. See also the account of Enoch Ware's voyage, provided by the same authors, p. 285. Brooks writes that in 1803, during a period of intermittent hostilities between Britain and France, some British based in Goree paid the Cape Verdes a visit in order to inform themselves of political conditions in Europe and thus gain advantage over their enemies once hostilities were renewed (1970:42).

4. This information was provided by Sr. Felix Monteiro, at the time director of the Customs House (*Fazenda*) in Praia, and by avocation an accomplished historian and folklorist.

5. Duncan favors the account that holds that Brava was settled "sometime before 1545" (1972:182-83). For other discussions of Brava's settlement and early history, see Barcelos (1899 I: 24, 37, and 122), Lima (1844, Part 2: 24, and Ribeiro (1960:230).

6. According to Barcelos, the governor of the colony complained in 1700 to the bishop that marriages had been celebrated between Cape Verdean women and foreign pirates in the islands of São Nicolau and Santo Antão, despite the fact that "His Majesty does not want foreigners, much less pirates" in the colony (1900 I: 163).

7. See the record of Diego Carreira's slaving expedition, provided by Teixeira da Mota (1970:10).

8. This figure may or may not include the 234 permanent exiles from Portugal then living in the islands.

9. I first learned of Casmiro's period of exile in Brava in a rather interesting manner: an old man of my acquaintance there described at some length a Portuguese who had visited the island "some days ago," a man "who knew everybody and went to all the saints' feasts and wrote everything down in his notebook just like you do." He was referring to Casmiro.

III

A SOCIETY BUILT ON THE SLAVE TRADE:
AN HISTORICAL OUTLINE

Discovery[1]

It is probable that the first human beings to set foot in
these islands were Africans, though no archaeological records
of such a presence have been found. Santiago may have served
the Wolofs of coastal West Africa as a refuge from their enemies. Arabs or islamicized Africans may also have visited the
island of Sal to procure the salt for which it is named
(Carreira 1972:294-95; Marques 1972 I: 199). When Antonio da
Noli, a Genoese navigator in the service of Portugal, came
upon Santiago and four other islands in 1455, he met no sign
of human life. Nor did Diogo Afonso, squire to Prince Henry
the Navigator, who sighted the other islands of the archipelago some five or six years later.[2] Because the islands were
located a few degrees to the north of a promontory (today's
Cap Vert) claimed for Portugal eleven years earlier, they came
to be called the Islands of Cabo Verde (*Ilhas de Cabo Verde*),
usually shortened to Cabo Verde, meaning "Green Point." Thus
the drought-ridden archipelago came to bear its singularly
inappropriate name.

The Cape Verdes would prove a disappointing acquisition
for Portugal, compared to her earlier Atlantic discoveries,
Madeira and the Azores. At first it seemed that Madeira, settled c. 1425, would be the model for the colonization of the
Cape Verdes. Profitable sugar cane plantations were already
thriving in that semi-tropical island, with the backing of
Genoese capital (Duncan 1972:19). Like Madeira, Santiago,
considered the "largest and least infertile" of the Cape
Verdes, was divided into two captaincies, under da Noli and
Afonso respectively. When settlement began in 1462, da Noli
brought slaves from the Guinea coast with the aim of setting
up sugar plantations.

Expectations of duplicating the success of Madeira were
soon disappointed. The arid and unpredictable climate, along
with the difficulty of irrigation caused by irregular terrain
and porous soil composition, all but precluded monocrop agriculture. Gifted with no edible native plants but the fruit of
the tamarind tree, the islands proved inhospitable to wheat
and other cereals of the metropole. The food-bearing plants
most important in the Cape Verdean diet would come from Latin

America (maize, sweet potatoes, manioc, certain beans and fruits), Asia (certain yams, fava beans, bananas, coconuts), and Africa (coffee, other types of yams and beans, nuts). Portugal's contribution was mostly limited to those vegetables grown in household gardens, water supply permitting, and fruits (apples, quince, figs, pomegranates)(Ribeiro 1960:112-17; also, George Brooks, personal communication).

Brazil became an important source for nonfood crops, notably tobacco and the *purgeira*, a hardy, tree-like plant of her northeast. *Purgeira* oil was burned in lamps and used for making soap, while the trunk and branches went for fuel in stoves and fireplaces. Cotton, the only plant ever to hold real commercial importance, came by way of Portugal (Ribeiro 1960:114).

Early Settlement

Drought, fire, epidemics, and an attack by Castilian raiders who returned to Europe with da Noli and some of his followers as prisoners, all made the early days of the colony precarious ones (Blake 1942:27-28; Duncan 1972:19-20). Not only did the Cape Verdes lack the potential the Azores and Madeira had shown for generating wealth in the form of export crops, but they were also much further from Lisbon, about 1,734 miles. Dom Afonso V of Portugal concluded that it would be difficult to attract settlers "without very great liberties and exemptions." To this end, he granted Santiago's residents exclusive rights over the slave trade in the part of the Guinea coast nearest the Cape Verdes, in a decree of 1466. But only six years later, the same monarch forbade the resale of slaves for transport elsewhere, thus closing off (at least in theory) this commercial opportunity to Santiago's colonists (Carreira 1972:22-23).

In 1469, a Lisbon merchant named Fernando Gomes[3] had been granted exclusive rights over the trade in slaves, gold and other valuables of the Guinea coast on condition that he "discover" 100 leagues of the coast and pay a fixed sum to the Crown for each of the five years of his contract. The area of the coast facing the Cape Verdes was exempted from his domain, along with that near the fortress at Arguim, the first having been alotted to Santiago traders. The latter, attracted by the increasing gains to be had in the slave trade, began to trespass on Gomes's zone of control. Seeing the threat to his interest, Gomes was able to use his considerable influence at court to have restrictions placed on the Cape Verdeans. Thus, beginning in 1472, their area of access was reduced, the items they could trade in limited to Cape Verde's products, partnerships with foreigners forbidden, and, as already mentioned, slaves taken only for personal use. Penalties included confiscation of both trade goods and vessels. This system of individual contracts continued with little intermission until the mid-seventeenth century (Blake 1937:26-30; Carreira 1972: 24-27).

The strictures imposed on the Santiago slave traders are historically important not only in and of themselves, but also for a more general understanding of Portuguese colonial policy in Cape Verde. These regulations were the beginning of a pattern of exploitation of the few resources and economic advantages these islands had to offer, a pattern that would continue in its general form until independence. That is, the exploitation of commercial opportunities was confined to external parties, whether individual or corporate, but usually based in Lisbon, while stringent controls were imposed on the entrepreneurial activities of Cape Verdeans. Typically, the degree of detail and rigor of the formal regulations was matched only by Portugal's ineffectiveness in enforcing them. The result was that smuggling became commonplace, even a necessity, fostering corruption on a prodigious scale. A Protestant clergyman put it thus: "To get rich here, one must cheat the government, the people or both."

The *Lançados*

Cast in a rhetoric of concern for avoiding the violence that had marked the beginnings of the Guinea trade, the establishment of the system of individual contracts was clearly aimed at controlling the Santiago traders, whose number and distance from Lisbon made them all but unmanageable. As Carreira observes, if the Crown's desire to settle the Cape Verdes was great, its desire to monopolize the exploitation of the riches of the West African coast was even greater (1972: 24-25). The railing against foreign competitors, the harsh penalties stipulated for the Portuguese subjects who collaborated with them, and the great detail of the prescriptions and prohibitions related to trading procedures (as typical of certain periods of the nineteenth century as they were of the fifteenth) must be understood in this light. It was, in other words, no mindless xenophobia that informed the many bans made on commercial dealings with foreigners; rather, it was very practical material interest.

If they had been followed, the policies laid out in 1472 would have eliminated the lucrative middlemen's roles that Santiago's colonists were already controlling, only ten years after da Noli's settlement was founded. By then they were sending their trusted agents, called *lançados* [from the Portuguese *lançar*, "to send out"], to the Guinea coast. At first these were Portuguese whites, often Jews, but their functions were soon taken over by freed blacks and mulattoes, some no doubt working for their former owners (Ibid., p. 48).

In some cases, the mulattoes were probably the illegitimate sons of their employers (Rodney 1967:17).

The *lançados* were an adventurous lot. Traveling up the rivers of the Guinea coastal regions, they made contacts with local African groups, often adopting their modes of dress, language, and customs. Some even underwent initiation rites, participated in religious cults, and married into chiefs' lineages. As Rodney describes it, "the Africans were obviously extending to the Portuguese at the outset the norms of hospitality they were accustomed to apply among themselves" (1970: 94). The *lançado* might be offered shelter, protection, and even a wife, but in return he was expected to give the appropriate gifts to the chief who was his host, along with other forms of deference, and to fulfill his marital obligations, including fidelity. The closer relationship that obtained between Africans and the *lançados*, as compared with other Europeans, was epitomized linguistically, by terms that designated the *lançados* as "guests" and other traders as "foreigners" (Ibid., pp. 74-94; see also Blake 1942:29-30 and Carreira 1972:47-49).

When the 1472 order did not succeed in intimidating Santiago's merchants or reducing the threat of foreign competition, further rulings were issued to undercut the bases of the forbidden trade. In 1497, Portuguese subjects were not to sell iron to "Negro infidels"; next, in 1514, certain valuable shells and necklaces, also necessary trade items, became *mercadorias defesas* [forbidden merchandise]. The same year, textiles from India and Flanders, along with various other goods, were prohibited from entering Cape Verde at all. Also, in 1512, slaving vessels were ordered to detour to Lisbon before proceeding to the Americas, as a control measure (Carreira 1972:34-38).

The *lançados* themselves became the subject of a whole series of royal pronouncements, each more strident and threatening than the last. In 1519, the Santiago merchants were forbidden to send any more agents to the mainland and in 1520, the *lançados* already there were ordered to "return to the kingdom" on pain of loss of property, excommunication, and death. One Bernadim Gomes was commissioned to captain a special expedition to the coast to round up all "Christians" found in Guinea; failing that, he was instructed to bribe the African chiefs to deliver or execute any *lançados* remaining (Barcelos 1899 I: 87-88; Carreira 1972: 63-65).

All of these measures seem to have done little to hinder the *lançados*. Instead, they only accomplished the estrangement of these "marginal men" from Portugal and eventually, from their base in Santiago. Disowned by the metropole, they were left free of the onerous regulations that hampered even the recognized contractors. The latter, forbidden to trade

with foreigners, were obliged to obtain all trade goods from
another Crown monopoly, the House of Guiné and Mina, with the
result that they were less well equipped than their rivals
(Carreira 1972:136). The *lançados*, on the other hand, nego-
tiated with whom they chose, often enough with English, French
and Dutch slavers, becoming more and more a commercial power
in their own right.

While the Crown usually blamed them for Portugal's loss
of pre-eminence in the coastal trade, the *lançados* in fact
represented the most effective Portuguese penetration of the
African continent of their day. Hostilities between these
middlemen and Africans on the upper Guinea coast in the late
sixteen century, from which the latter emerged victorious,
marked a turning point in the relations between the two. But
the *lançados* who stayed, and their descendants, came to form a
mulatto trading class allied with the chiefly lineages. As
early as 1600, mulatto Portuguese settlements were established
along the Gambia River and in the area that is now Sierra
Leone (Blake 1942:29-30). Over the seventeenth century, they
increased in size and number, partly through the arrival of
refugees fleeing famine in Santiago (Carreira 1972:169).

For European traders seeking slaves, ivory and amber, the
lançados and their descendants became indispensable intermediaries. They also became useful in purely internal African
commerce, "carrying rice, millet, palm wine . . . from regions
of abundance to regions of scarcity" (Duncan 1972:215). The
lançados had acclimatized themselves to an environment that
most Portuguese deemed intolerable, returning to Cape Verde as
soon as the rainy season set in. In the process of accommoda-
tion to the customs of the African groups they dealt with,
these "cultural brokers" made Portuguese, or more correctly,
Cape Verdean Crioulo, a lingua franca on the Guinea coast.
Their descendants regarded themselves as Portuguese and jealously maintained certain cultural traits that signified their
distinctiveness from the Africans around them. Despite their
disdain for these "sons of the land" (*filhos da terra*), as
they were called, the Portuguese came to use them for lower-
level administrative positions in Guinea, thus taking advantage of their ties with the local African elites (Rodney 1970:
203-4).

A 'Maritime Crossroads'

The half-century of Portugal's subjugation to Castilian
rule[4] saw redoubled efforts by the Crown to gain control of
the Guinea trade. Owing to "the harm caused by foreign and
native merchants," foreigners were forbidden entry in
Portuguese-controlled African ports, including those of the
Cape Verdes, in 1591. Use of foreign ships, crew members and
interpreters was outlawed (Carreira 1972:141). A policy change

in 1619 allowed slavers to pay duty at Cacheu rather than
Santiago, further prejudicing that island's commerce (Ibid.,
p. 159).

Apparently, these regulations were enforced neither
effectively nor consistently. For their part, the Cape
Verdean merchants raised protest after protest, all the while
continuing to trade in contraband and avoid taxes (cf. Duncan
1972:207). Despite all the legal constraints, the Cape Verdes
were a veritable maritime crossroads in the sixteenth and
seventeenth centuries, for, as Blake puts it, "they stood at
the confluence of several of the highways of the sea" (1942:
103). Portuguese caravels going to Brazil or coming from East
India found the islands a convenient stopping point, as would
American slavers somewhat later.

During the sixteenth century, a marvelous variety of
goods from Europe, India and Spanish America were funneled
through Santiago to the Guinea coast: metals, textiles, beads,
spices, silver coins used in making jewelry, bracelets and
other trinkets, as well as wine, brandy and European manufactures (Duncan 1972:215). From Africa came ivory, beeswax,
and, most importantly, slaves.

Unfortunately, pirates as well as traders found the archipelago conveniently situated, and her thriving commerce constituted a further attraction. The marauders represented many
nationalities: French, English, Dutch and Castilians all
attacked the poorly fortified and defended islands, taking
advantage of their concealed inlets and harbors to lie in wait
for Portuguese fishing and trading caravels, and sometimes
invading the islands themselves.

One of the most massive attacks was led by Francis Drake
in 1585. Arriving in Santiago with a force of 25 ships, Drake
and his 2,300 men proceeded to sack and burn the then-capital,
Ribeira Grande (Barcelos 1899 I: 158; Duncan 1972:176). Even
more destructive, in terms of loss of human lives, was a 1712
attack by a French squadron of 12 warships. Again Ribeira
Grande was destroyed; according to Barcelos, nothing bronze
escaped the hands of the invaders, nor did the gold and silver
liturgical vessels they found in the churches. Women and
children were taken hostage to avoid reprisals, and when the
French left, they took 110 captured slaves with them (1900 II:
225). Assaults of this type, occasioned by hostilities between
Portugal and other European nations, continued through the
eighteenth century. Many inhabitants of Santiago and Fogo
were impelled to flee the coast, giving rise to new permanent
settlements in the interior. Occasionally, slaves joined the
exodus and took advantage of the occasion to escape their masters (Carreira 1972:354).

Santiago's Slave Trade

Nineteenth century estimates of the number of slaves
transshipped via the Cape Verdes to the Americas range from
650 to 800 per year between 1501 and 1600 (Ibid., p. 125).
The numbers diminished progressively over the next century;
Duncan calculates that about 28,000 slaves passed through
Santiago en route to the New World between 1601 and 1700.
Most were headed for the Spanish West Indies, and the rest for
Brazil and other parts of Latin America (1972:210).

Most of these slaves originated from the area of coastal
West Africa that lies between present-day Senegal and Sierra
Leone. Some were criminals being sold as punishment, but
more often they were the victims of kidnappings or raids by
hostile groups encouraged by the *lançados* and other Europeans.
(See Rodney 1970:103-4.) Captives were taken to Santiago by
small craft, and resold in Santiago, usually after only a
short time. Their value, however, increased with the length
of their stay, since during this period they became "ladino-
ized"; that is, they learned Crioulo, acquired habits of
docility and, sometimes, were baptized.

Since slaves went for higher prices in Santiago than on
the coast, what might have induced the foreigners to make
their purchases in Cape Verde? Duncan offers several possible
reasons. First, the pattern of winds and currents made it
likely that vessels coming from the Americas or from Europe
would pass near the Cape Verdes on their way to the coast;
any need for repairs or supplies would necessitate a stop
there. Second, the Guinea trade required the disposition of a
variety of items, such as "iron bars, cloth, haberdashery,
brandy, guns, gunpowder, . . ."; traders had to be "well-
assorted," in the expression of the time (Duncan 1972:211).
Cape Verdean merchants could offer a range of goods that a
European or American slaver might find difficult to assemble
in home port. Third, the textiles woven in Cape Verde were
themselves an important trade item. Finally, once on the
coast, a slaver would in all probability have to deal with
Portuguese mulatto intermediaries anyway -- i.e., the *lançados*
of Cape Verde and their descendants.

By purchasing the higher-priced slaves of Santiago, the
trader avoided the health and navigation hazards of the humid
coast, as well as the often lengthy and frustrating process of
barter. He also avoided the sometimes heavy competition from
other slavers. Also, the slaves to be had in Santiago were
considered to be of higher quality than those on the continent, their ranks having been thinned of the most sickly,
depressed and rebellious. Those left were probably habituated,
if not resigned, to their status as "chattels."[6]

The Triangular Commerce

Cape Verde's role as a slave entrêpot brought her into
what came to be known as the "triangular" trade between the
New England colonies and the West Indies, whose midpoint was
the "wine islands" (the Azores and Madeira) and/or the West
African coast. The stimulus for this commerce lay in New
England's need for English manufactures in the seventeenth and
early eighteenth centuries. Unlike tobacco-growing Virginia,
New England produced no commodity easily marketable in England;
neither her pipestaves nor her timber constituted "first class"
exports, owing to their low retail value in relation to size
and weight (Duncan 1972:70).

In the triangular commerce New England traders became
slavers, though the primary importance of the slaves was as a
middle term in the obtaining of other goods. Small vessels of
40 to 70 tons carried slaves from the Guinea coast or Cape
Verde, then sold the human cargo in the West Indies for bills
of lading that could be used in London or Bristol, and for
molasses used to make rum. That product, of course, could be
bartered along with other goods in the slave trade (Dow 1927:
255; Pares 1956:57).

The earliest contact between the Yankee traders and Cape
Verde occurred, so far as is known, in the first triangular
voyage (1643), described in *Winthrop's Journal* (Jamieson 1908
II:227). On this occasion, a New England trading ship obtained
tobacco in Barbados "in exchange for Africoes, which she carried from the Isle of Maio" (Bailyn 1955:84). It is probable
that the Yankee traders brought the first Cape Verdean "immigrants," albeit involuntary ones, to New England. There, supposed educability for skilled or semi-skilled labor was preferred to physical strength, and already "domesticated"
slaves were preferred (McManus 1973:20). In at least one
recorded case, Cape Verdeans from Maio were kidnapped and
brought to the United States, but a Maryland court decision of
1749 forced the ship's captain to return them home.[7] As the
next chapter relates, famine often occasioned the sale of Cape
Verdean-born slaves to foreigners.

Secondary Forms of Trade

The traffic in slaves tended to stimulate other kinds of
trade that would not, by themselves, have attracted foreign
vessels. Live animals, for example, figured in the triangular
commerce. These included a local breed of mule much sought
after by the Americans for trade in the Antilles. A ban of
1721 on the selling of live animals was less effective than
the very volume of the trade in bringing it to an end. With
time, the Americans managed to acquire enough female animals
to carry on breeding in the New World (Carreira 1972:231-32).

The salt mentioned in Winthrop's description of the first triangular voyage probably came from Maio along with the slaves obtained there. In that island there was "enough salt to fill a thousand ships," in the words of an astonished Portuguese sailor visiting in 1670 (Blake 1942:147). The natural salt beds of the "flat islands" interested foreign traders because salt was not merely a seasoning but also a food preservative, and its weight made it useful as ballast. It could also be traded on the African continent, and it was frequently exchanged for lime in the Gambia (Brooks 1970:150).

Britain's codfish fleet made yearly stops in the Cape Verdes on its way to the fisheries of Newfoundland and New England.[8] Over the seventeenth century, some 80 vessels a year, mostly English, picked up salt in the islands (Duncan 1972:189). At Maio, the salt was carried half a mile from the beds to the water's edge, and then transported through the swells and shoals in special small boats of very tight construction called "frapes," to the trading vessels anchored some distance offshore (Masefield 1906:358-60). The approach to Maio came to be known as the "English road," and today her main settlement is known as Porto Inglês. By 1686, salt from Maio was being sold in Boston;[9] a century later, American ships were coming to Cape Verde with great frequency, many of them stopping to take on salt. During the nineteenth century, the Americans outstripped even the British, running second only to the Portuguese (Carreira 1972:235).[10]

Barter rather than cash payment was the norm in the salt trade, due at least in part to the constant shortage of Portuguese currency in the colony and to the confusion that reigned as to the value of foreign coins. Visitors to Maio marveled at the islanders' readiness to accept old clothing as payment for the salt and the work of loading it (cf. Dampier's memoirs of a 1683 voyage, recounted in Masefield 1906:101). Evidently, sufficient clothing for protection from the sun and from the evening's cool breezes was then a luxury, as it still was for many people nearly three hundred years later. Numerous complaints, dating as early as 1624, were made by the colonial government about the behavior of foreigners in the salt trade, some of them specifically naming the Americans (cf. Barcelos 1900 II: 111).

For the most part, the foreigners proceeded with insouciance, landing without permission and ignoring regulations concerning the terms of the barter.[11] The seriousness of the government's attempts at control can be questioned; Maio's Porto Inglês lies in full view of Santiago and there, at least, the salt traffic could easily have been monitored. The only important local attempt to capitalize on the salt was made by the entrepreneur Manuel Antonio Martins, who set up a fairly sophisticated apparatus for the extraction and conveyance of the product on the island of Sal in the early

nineteenth century, by which time Brazil had become the most
important outlet. For the most part, any real gains from the
shipping trade were indirect ones in that it helped increase
shipping traffic in the Cape Verdes and, thus, the demand for
victuals, repairs, and other products of the islands.

Controls and Contraband

Even before the end of the sixteenth century, Portugal's
control of the Guinea coast was far more limited than she
liked to claim.[12] A half-century of Castilian rule (1580-
1640), the war to recover the throne, followed by a period of
maritime struggle with England (1650-54), her longtime ally
against Spain, further weakened Portugal's hold on the Guinea
commerce. The fortress at Arguim fell to the Dutch in 1638,
so that soon the latter controlled not only the Gold Coast and
its tremendous revenues, but even the supply of slaves to
Pernambuco (Brazil), the latter under the aegis of the Dutch
West India Company. By 1640, Portugal's sphere of influence
on the coast had shrunk to little more than what is now Guinea-
Bissau. Even Cacheu, long an important trading center,
remained in Portuguese hands "more miraculously than naturally," so poorly fortified and supplied was the town (Overseas Council Report of 1670, quoted in Carreira 1972:171).

The Crown contractors could no longer profit in the spectacular fashion of Fernando Gomes. Unrealistic expectations
of gain bound them to heavy payments that in two cases were
not met, resulting in the arrest of the contract holders
(Duncan 1972:225-26). These legitimate traders were at a competitive disadvantage with the Cape Verdean smugglers, a disadvantage they attempted to reduce through illegal maneuvers
of their own, such as bribing port officials to ignore violation of regulations concerning port taxes, the number of
slaves allowed on board, vessel size, and so on, while charg-
ing Cape Verdeans exorbitant prices for imported goods
(Carreira 1972:226). However, the onerous strictures built
into the contracts, along with the risks of the trade (such as
shipwreck and slave mortality), and ever-increasing foreign
competition, all made the contracts less and less desirable.
Contractors began to sublet their rights, a situation which
further facilitated the already rampant smuggling.

Typically, civil and military officials of the colony, as
well as the clergy, tried to capitalize on their positions by
engaging in contraband slaving. The very governors exploited
their powers of office to ruin their competitors.[13] One of
the most infamous cases of miscreant governors was Castelo
Branco, in office 1651-52. Not only did he trade with
foreigners, an illegal but common enough activity, but he also
seized foreign vessels whenever it suited his purpose. His
misdeeds, such as the treacherous murder of the crew of the

English ship *Walsingham* at Maio, finally resulted in his
arrest and removal from office (Duncan 1972:217). Though this
was a particularly flagrant case, the avarice of governors was
the subject of repeated complaints to Lisbon. A 1623 letter
from the *Câmara* [Town Council] of Ribeira Grande, Santiago,
laments the "miserable" state of the island, blaming it on
"the governors' taking for themselves the commerce of Guiné .
. . becoming absolute lords of land and sea" (Barcelos 1899
I: 226).

As Duncan observes, protests were not raised against smuggling itself, even that undertaken by the governors, except
when the latter presumed to appropriate too large a share for
themselves (1972:217). Commercial opportunities constituted
one of the few advantages of what was otherwise a hardship
post, given the food shortages, epidemics, and distance from
Lisbon. (Over the seventeenth and eighteenth centuries,
fourteen governors died in office.) In sum, the most important
result of all the Crown restrictions on Cape Verdean trade
arose from their very ineffectiveness. Given that ineffectiveness, the Crown's own avarice was repaid by that of its own
appointed governors and agents, such that corruption became a
constant feature of the colony's administration, one that
became all the more evident under the monopoly companies
established later.

Monopoly Companies

After 1640, the system of individual leases fell into disuse, but Crown monopolies were revived in a new form with the
founding of the Company of Cacheu (1675-90) and later, that of
Cacheu and Cabo Verde (1690-1700). Under the contract of the
first company, Cape Verdeans were allowed to trade only their
own products in Guinea (textiles, salt, etc.), while the Company, responsible for the fortification of Cacheu, received
control of imports to both territories -- then administered as
one colony -- and of most of the slave trade (Carreira 1969:
31-44; Duncan 1972:226-28). Predictably, the merchants of
Santiago and the governor of Cape Verde disliked the new policies. The latter took the head of the new company prisoner for
a year, amidst accusations and counter-accusations of fraud and
illegal trade with foreigners -- probably with reason on both
sides, as Duncan remarks (1972:227-28; see also Barcelos 1900
II: 84).

Any such opposition from the governor was forestalled by
the charter of the second company, whereby the governor could
not engage in trade, while his salary was to be raised and to
be paid by the Company. The legalized control of the colony's
administration by monopoly interests would take even more
extreme form after the mid-eighteenth century. Meanwhile,
from 1700 to 1755, the colony enjoyed a period of liberalized

trade laws, largely through the influence of an unusually com-
petent governor, Antonio Salgado (Barcelos 1900 II: 151-52;
233-34). By then, however, the islands were in a state of
decay, the "ruin of the towns and plantations" all but complete
(Carreira 1972:190). Most of the better-off had fled to the
metropole, and those who remained were in such dire need that
foreigners could usually obtain not only salt, but also textiles, hides and other goods in exchange for cloth or used
clothing.[13] The relatively benign economic policies of this
period were in any case only temporary, to be succeeded by an
era of mercantile exploitation unprecedented in its ruthless-
ness.

In 1757, Portugal's powerful Secretary of State, the
Marquês de Pombal, sponsored the charter of the Company of
Grao Pará and Maranhão. In exchange for providing a dependable
supply of slaves to the Brazilian states for which it was
named, the Company received exclusive rights to the commerce of
Cape Verde and Guinea, as well as complete control over the
civil and military government of the colony, "in the greatest
secrecy so long as there exist political motives requiring it
to be such," as the charter stated (Carreira 1969:345; the
document is reproduced in the same work, pp. 344-46.) The
last phrase is certainly a telling one, because the document
was virtually inaccessible until the fall of Caetano in 1974.[14]
For twenty years, the Company virtually owned Cape Verde, its
interests untrammeled by the slightest humanitarian concern.
Drought provided occasion to raise the price of foodstuffs and
to lower those of Cape Verdean products, with tragic consequences for the population (see Chapter IV). The Company's
hegemony ended with the fall from power of the Marquês de
Pombal in 1777, shortly after the death of the monarch Dom
José I.

The two most important Cape Verdean products traded by
the Company were textiles woven by the slaves, and orchil
(*urzela*), a dye-bearing lichen native to the rocky precipices
overlooking the sea of the mountainous islands. The plant was
much sought after in Europe because, with certain additives,
it could be made to yield scarlet, purple, and blue dyes. Other
than sea salt, orchil was the only readily extracted form of
natural wealth in the archipelago. Since 1469, it had been
the practice for the Crown to lease rights to the orchil,
usually to foreigners, though by way of exception, the Cape
Verdean merchant Manuel Antonio Martins was an *urzeleiro*. The
contractors had to contend with contraband sales of the lichen
to foreigners, but otherwise little is known of this trade
until the era of the Company, which realized considerable
income from this source -- approximately 240 *contos* -- between

---

[*] 1 *conto* equaled 1000 *escudos*; see Duncan 1972, Appendix
IV, for contemporary rates of exchange.

1760 and 1781 (Carreira 1969:215-16).

The monopolists used a variety of tactics to maximize profits from the orchil while ensuring a continuous supply from the gatherers. These were usually boys or young men who scaled the cliffs of the narrow gorges along the coast, a risky endeavor that sometimes ended in loss of life or limb. The collectors purchased the ropes, sacks and scrapers they needed from local merchants. The latter, dependent as they were upon the Company for their stock, had perforce become its agents, exchanging overvalued foodstuffs for the orchil and then selling it cheaply at prices set by the Company. The latter insisted that the orchil be dried, thus lowering its weight, before purchasing it; they then re-moistened it for sale in Lisbon. The collectors sometimes retaliated by adding sand to the orchil, or by refusing to gather it while the Company ships lay waiting in port (Ibid., pp. 197-99).

Understandably, the collectors preferred to sell to foreigners whenever possible, so that the growth of the legal commerce was always closely shadowed by that of the contraband. The commerce in orchil passed into the hands of another Portuguese company after 1777, and only in 1838 was the lichen allowed to be traded freely by the Cape Verdeans. By then, seventy years of intensive exploitation had diminished the quality as well as the quantity available, and the huge supplies of the lichen available in Mozambique and Angola had greatly reduced demand for what Cape Verde could supply (Duncan 1972:192).

Cotton Textiles

The most important Cape Verdean product the Company traded in was cotton textiles, sales of which yielded a gross profit of more than 630 *contos* over the period 1757-70 (Carreira 1969: 237). For some 250 years, these weavings of indigo blue or black designs on a white background were prized on the African mainland and so by slavers as well. Certain types of cloths [*panos*] were valued at over 13 *milreis* apiece (about £4 sterling at the time) on the Guinea coast, when the average price being paid there for a slave was a bit over 48 *milreis* (Ibid., p. 284). A cloth of the standard variety was known as a *barafula*, a basic unit of exchange on the coast, two *barafulas* being worth one standard iron bar in the 1680s. In the dearth of metal coinage, they served as currency in the Cape Verdes. The textiles, while never formally recognized as legal tender by Portugal, were accepted on occasion in payment of fines, and were used to pay the wages of civil employees in the seventeenth century (Carreira 1968:21, 85; Duncan 1972:218).[15]

Raw cotton, the only really successful cash crop in Cape Verde, had been successfully introduced from Portugal and was being exported not only to the metropole but also to Flanders, Spain and West Africa in the early decades of the sixteenth century. The plant can still be found growing wild in parts of Santiago. With the importation of slaves skilled in the arts of spinning, weaving and dye-making, Cape Verdean cotton went into the production of textiles, using techniques brought by Mandinka, Wolof and other West African slaves. Like those on the mainland, each Cape Verdean weaving consisted of six strips of cloth about two yards long, each strip a *palmo* wide [a "palm" being 8.62 inches], so that when stitched together, the total width was about one yard. Indigo brought from the Rio Nuno region of Guinea was cultivated locally and treated by relatively simple processes to yield black and blue dyes, the dyeing usually being done by the spinners and weavers themselves (Carreira 1969:19).

Production of the textiles was done on a household basis; the slave retinue of the more important landowners typically included a group of spinners, usually female, and weavers, usually male (Duncan 1972:219). Even in the early nineteenth century, when the textiles had lost some of their commercial importance, certain households numbered as many as thirty weavers and spinners among their slaves (Carreira 1968:78). Slaves sometimes bought their freedom by weaving on Sundays and saints' feast days (Ibid., p. 53). Households of free peasants and sharecroppers also produced textiles, because besides comprising an export commodity and medium of exchange, these cloths were part of the dress of all but the local *fidalgos* [aristocrats].

As the Cape Verdean *panos* began to surpass those of the mainland in both variety and workmanship, they came to be considered a necessity in the slave barter, particularly in the period from about 1550 to 1825 (Carreira 1969:232).[16] The greatest number and best quality of weavings came from Fogo, where cotton flourished as nowhere else in the archipelago. Carreira lists some twenty-four different designs in use during the period 1757-82, each commanding its own price (Ibid., p. 237). Among the most sought-after were the *panos de bicho* [*bicho*: animal], so named because of the resemblance of the designs to the markings of certain animal hides. The designs were apparently eclectic in their inspiration; one was patterned after the square, blunt cross emblazoned on Portuguese sails of the time.

A series of laws dating from 1721 prohibited the sale of Cape Verdean textiles to foreigners on pain of death. Such severity can only be understood in light of the great demand for them and the paranoia of metropolitan interests regarding foreign competition. To a certain degree, these much sought-after weavings compensated for Portugal's lack of iron, another essential item in the slave commerce. Local authorities repeatedly protested the controls, but to no avail; removal of the prohibitions came only in 1804, when the industry had almost disappeared (Carreira 1968:45-48; Barros 1936:58).

Meanwhile, port officials, civil authorities and the very agents of the Company engaged in contraband. Higher selling prices and avoidance of export duties provided ample motivation even for the monopolists, while the scarcity of Portuguese trading vessels during the years preceding and following the existence of the Company made contraband a virtual necessity for the Cape Verdeans. During the period of the Company's hegemony, low prices were paid for the *panos* in relation to their resale value, on the specious grounds that this was "the custom of the land" (Carreira 1969:234). Small landowners were especially vulnerable to exploitation, since they depended on the Company for supplies of cotton (Carreira 1968:118).

For their part, foreigners looked upon the Portuguese regulations with nonchalance, when indeed they were even aware of them. One English captain unwittingly outraged the governor of Cape Verde in 1726 by inquiring why he could not buy textiles in Santiago, since in Fogo the port official who had sold him cloth goods had personally brought the merchandise aboard the trading vessel (Barcelos 1905 III: 65). The Americans were particularly provocative. Refusing to pay port duty, their vessels sailed for Guinea laden with the forbidden goods, which injury was compounded by "insulting the officials of the customs and the inhabitants" (Ibid., p. 111).[17]

Cotton cultivation and weaving began to decline sometime in the mid-eighteenth century, so that by the first decade of the next century, textiles accounted for only about seven percent of Cape Verdean exports. Earlier writers have blamed this on a lack of slaves to cultivate cotton, as these had become much more expensive under the Company's rule, but Carreira calls attention to a number of other factors, such as drought, plant disease, and the loss of trade with foreigners (1968:48-49). This last was probably the result of Portugal's overall loss of prominence in the Guinea trade, but certainly cannot have been helped by the plethora of regulations surrounding Cape Verdean commerce.

Woven textiles of the sort that came to be fabricated in Cape Verde figured in the internal market system of the Guinea coastal region well before the appearance of the Europeans. They served not only as clothing but also as status markers, and this for the dead as well as the living. The elaborate mortuary rituals of such groups as the Papels, for example, called for exhibition of the corpse shrouded in the finest weavings owned by the deceased, their number varying with the individual's rank (Ibid., pp. 10-11). In Cabo Verde, they hold both practical and ceremonial importance even today. Women of peasant origin wear them over their skirts, knotted at the waist. Children spend most of their first years of

life in these cloths, carried on the hips of mothers or elder
sisters. Loose change is knotted securely in their folds and
heavier burdens are borne on the back with their support. The
chants and dances of *bataque*, a traditional musical form of
West African origin, are accompanied by only one instrument,
the *pano*, wadded into a tight ball and beaten by the hands,
like a drum. In one part of the annual festivities in honor
of Fogo's patron, Saint Philip, men, women and children from
the poorer classes parade down to the beach early in the morning, led by five horsemen invited as honored guests. In former times, these roles were taken by slaves and aristocrats,
respectively, and when I observed the feast, the class difference between the two types of participants was still evident.
At the climax of the ritual, the women take the cloths from
around their waists and form a canopy for the horsemen, now
dismounted. Whatever its true significance, this gesture
neatly epitomizes the protection once afforded the landed
classes by the *pano* industry. In Fogo especially, the crafts-
manship and artisanry of the slave weavers and spinners under-
wrote to a large extent the privileged position of the
landlord-merchants, providing them with a margin of security
that agriculture alone would never have afforded.

But while they superficially resemble the hand- woven and
spun cloths of old, the *panos* worn today are mass-produced
and, ironically, imported from Guinea-Bissau. In 1964, there
were 61 weavers in the Tarrafal district of Santiago
(Carreira 1968:51), only a few of whom were still alive at
the end of colonial rule. Since independence, efforts have
been made to preserve and transmit to younger artists this
valuable part of the national heritage.

British and American Ties

Early in the nineteenth century, British and American
commercial influence came to predominate over that of the
Portuguese. Britain, long a favored trading partner of
Portugal, enjoyed particularly great influence in São Vicente.
This most barren of the islands is blessed with a wide, shal-
low bay, well protected from the wind for most of the year.
In 1838, an Englishman set up the first coal deposit in
Mindelo to supply tradeships going to and from the East Indies
(Lyall 1938:26, 78; Duncan 1972:161). The Royal Mail Steam
Packet Company built a coaling station to service its ships
en route to and from Brazil in 1850 and also made some
improvements in the harbor. A British telegraph company
founded in 1890, and shipping houses established by British
concerns, stimulated the growth of Mindelo from a mere hamlet[18] to a city of some 25,000 (1970 figure, Agência Geral
do Ultramar).

Portugal tried to profit indirectly from these enterprises through the various fees (for docking, water, etc.) it levied on vessels putting in at Mindelo. These port charges were always considered unreasonably high by shippers and at the end of colonial rule, Mindelo was still a notoriously expensive port (Duncan 1972:169). Still, the city's efflourescence drew impoverished fortune seekers from all of Barlavento, hoping for crumbs of the city's affluence. Opportunities for legitimate employment, as well as for contraband and prostitution, made Mindelo a haven from famine, and the city still continues to grow in an ever-widening arc around the natural one shaped by her harbor.

If British traders were more welcome than the Portuguese, the most appreciated of all seem to have been the Americans, whose products were "generally good and her prices very reasonable" (Barros 1936:60). American trade must have been thriving for some time before the War of 1812, because when the British prevented American vessels from entering the islands' ports during that period, Cape Verdeans missed their supplies of American tobacco, as well as that outlet for the hides and salt they had to sell. After the war ended and especially after 1820, when Portugal became embroiled in civil strife, the Cape Verdean trade with the Yankees resumed with even greater vigor than before.

Cattle and goat skins and hides from Boa Vista and Maio were important Cape Verdean exports in the nineteenth century, and the United States was their principal market. It was a profitable trade for the buyers, who could sell goatskins in Boston for at least double what they had paid in Cape Verde.[19] Drought, of course, meant a windfall for the Yankee traders, since thousands of animals would be slaughtered prematurely. In one such two-year period (1792-93), some 30,000 hides went to North America (Carreira 1972:240), and Cape Verdean goat skins were still being imported to the United States in the early decades of the twentieth century (Duncan 1972:171).

Some of the Americans procuring salt, hides and supplies in Cape Verde were slavers, but often they were legitimate traders doing business on the West African coast. The relationship between the two types of trade was, in any case, a close one -- "symbiotic," according to Brooks (1970:4). Whalers came as well; in the eighteenth century they fished the waters off the islands and sometimes cleaned their catches on Cape Verdean shores (Reyes 1797). Once the practice of picking up supplies and the odd hand in the Cape Verdes had become well established, probably early in the nineteenth century, the whalers came weighted with New England manufactures (useful as ballast on the outward journey) to be sold during their stops in the islands. Sometimes the Yankees formed partnerships with Cape Verdean agents, who sold the goods during the year that passed between visits from the Americans. Before mid-century,

48

the United States was supplying the Cape Verdes with wood, household furnishings, clothing, foodstuffs, and a host of other goods. Emigration to the United States from Brava and Fogo was well underway, and a Portuguese observer of the time speaks of "anxiously awaiting the day when these islands will return to being Portuguese colonies" (Lima 1844:100).

Slave Smugglers and Abolitionists

Though Cape Verde never regained her early pre-eminence in the slave trade, she became something of a center for both slave smuggling and anti-slavery operations in the nineteenth century. The slave traffic was outlawed by the United States in 1809, but Americans continued to engage in slaving with the help of ruses such as disguising the function of their vessels and taking the flag of nations less opposed to the commerce.[20] At certain periods, notably the 1820s and 1830s (DuBois 1969: 143), the Portuguese flag was a useful one to sail under and Cape Verde a convenient place for foreigners to change their ships' names and nationalities (Brooks 1970:312-13).

The Webster-Ashburton Treaty, concluded in 1842, provided for the establishment of British and American naval forces to enforce the anti-slaving laws of their nations. Under pressure from Britain, Portugal had reluctantly forbidden the slave traffic in her territories north of the equator in 1815; this was extended to the rest of her empire in 1836. When Matthew Perry, later celebrated for his entry into Japan, brought the first American Africa Squadron to make its base in Cape Verde, slaves were still being sold "by the pound" there (Thomas 1968:335). This may have been legal, for the internal slave market of Cape Verde continued to function until the abolition process began in the colony in 1856. Perry was much criticized for basing the squadron in the Cape Verdes, since the islands lay about two thousand miles north of the area they were to patrol in the Gulf of Guinea; this area shifted even further south in the 1850s, to the coast of Angola (Brooks 1970:118). For Perry, however, the Cape Verdes offered the important advantage of a relatively dry climate, promising less exposure to the tropical fevers to which the Americans had little resistance than the areas closer to the squadron's operations. Even so, a number of men returned from their forays south to die in Cape Verde, and special cemeteries were prepared for them in the cities of Praia and Mindelo (Thomas 1968: 332).

Cape Verde at Mid-nineteenth Century

Thomas' account of conditions in Cape Verde during his stint of duty as chaplain is acerbic, even racist, but he manages to convey the desolation wrought by the many years of drought and neglect. Boa Vista he found "almost a desert," with her four thousand or so inhabitants "always hungry." There, in his picturesque description, "cattle with sad faces and tears in their eyes walk solemnly in cudless rumination over grassless fields" (1968:330). The 1850s saw an almost unbroken series of droughts. In Thomas's uncharitable estimation, "a few more as such as that which has just passed will leave the islands without inhabitants, and when they are gone, the world will be just as good and quite as intelligent as it was with them" (Ibid., p. 329).

Whalers were still coming for provisions and hands, and salt was still being traded at Maio, Sal and Boa Vista, but otherwise commerce was severely restricted. Importation of many scarce but essential goods, such as cloth and shoes, was prohibited and exorbitantly high import duty was levied on other foriegn goods. Despite the rarity of maritime contact with Lisbon,[21] all imports were supposed to be introduced by Portuguese vessels. To exacerbate the situation, high taxes were set on Cape Verdean exports to the metropole, with preference given the products of Brazil, thus reducing sales of Cape Verdean coffee, *aguardente* [sugar cane rum], and hides (Barros 1936:61-62).

By the time that trade controls were eased in 1871, the Civil War in America had dealt a heavy blow to her trade with Cape Verde. American goods would continue to find their way to the archipelago, but not through traders. Rather, they would be sent by the emigrants who were, by then, going to America in ever-increasing numbers, for reasons explored in the next chapter.

Conclusion

As the subtitle of Carreira's history, *Cabo Verde: Uma Sociedade Escravocrata* (1972) proposes, this was a society based on the institution of slavery and the traffic in slaves. The present chapter has focused on the latter aspect, showing how Cabo Verde's economic history was shaped by the slave trade and the secondary commercial activities that it engendered, such as victualling and the trade in salt, hides, and textiles. Portugal tried to appropriate the fruits of the Guinea trade by instituting Crown monopolies, surrounded by rigid and copiously detailed regulations that she was incapable of enforcing. The result was protracted struggle among different factions of Cape Verde's ruling class for control of the colony's commerce. Cape Verdean landlord-merchants vied with government administrators and the clergy for the profits to be had in contraband trade, while both competed against the "legitimate traders," the Crown monopolists.

Portuguese economic policy in Cape Verde remained remarkably constant, in broad outline, throughout the colonial period. The monopolies and protectionist regulations -- as well as the flourishing contraband commerce -- of the slavery era had their modern counterparts. In the early 1970s a metropolitan company, the *Sociedade Geral*, held a monopoly on the shipment of goods imported from Portugal. This, combined with the profiteering of the shopkeepers, put the prices of goods from Portugal at two or three times their sale value in the marketplace; yet those sold in Cape Verde were often of markedly poorer quality. Higher tariffs were applied to goods from elsewhere, e.g., the Netherlands, Japan and the United States, though more competitive shipping operations tended to bring the prices of those imports as low or lower than their Portuguese equivalents.

Smuggling was so rampant as to be, from what I could observe, institutionalized. Portuguese military personnel were regular participants, in collusion with employees of the customs houses and Cape Verdean merchants, in the business of circumventing tariff regulations. For example, Portuguese officers told of such incongruous items as motorcycles and refrigerators being "sold" to the navy; tax-free, such goods would be dispatched aboard a warship and then "sold" again to local merchants. Whole shipments of smaller items, such as cassette tape recorders, would disappear mysteriously from the customs house, only to find their way to shop windows. Thus, appliances came relatively cheap, whereas electrical power was scarce, and city shops lined their shelves with fine whiskey and Perrier water, while fresh vegetables were often not to be had.

Notes

1. In this chapter, I have relied heavily on the works of
   Antonio Carreira, especially *Cabo Verde* (1972), which
   includes reproductions of or extensive quotations from
   numerous documents and texts difficult to obtain outside
   of Portugal. Besides Carreira's works and Barcelos's
   earlier history of Cabo Verde and Guinea, there are
   several sources in English worthy of note for the interested reader. These include Duncan's study of the
   Portuguese islands in the Atlantic (the Azores, Madeira
   and the Cape Verdes) in the seventeenth century (1972),
   and George Brooks's well-documented *Yankee Traders, Old
   Coasters and African Middlemen* (1970). The latter con-
   tains many helpful references to materials available in
   the United States. Also, Bennett and Brooks's *New
   England Merchants in Africa* (1965) makes available a number of documents pertinent to the study of Cape Verdean
   history.

2. Several different dates have been posited for the arrival
   of Europeans in Cabo Verde. Here I follow Duncan's
   assessment of available evidence (1972:18-19).

3. In 1508, for example, Santiago produced only 4,000
   arrobas of sugar, one *arroba* being the equivalent of
   about 32 pounds, and this in a year when the Azores produced 20,000 *arrobas* and Madeira 70,000 (Duncan 1972:21).

4. The island of Fogo distinguished itself as the only
   Portuguese territory that never flew the Castilian flag.
   As a reward, her principal settlement, São Felipe, was
   given the administrative status of *cidade* [city] after
   Portugal regained the throne in 1640.

5. Blake writes that ships normally stopped at the Cape
   Verdes on the outward voyage to India (1942:105), while
   Duncan holds that they did so more often on the return
   trip (1972:167).

6. Slaves sold on the Santiago market were categorized in
   three types. In order of ascending sale value, these
   were *boçais* [from *boçal*: ignorant], slaves recently
   imported who spoke only their native languages; *ladinos*,
   slaves of longer residence in Santiago who had learned
   Crioulo, had been baptized and "taught to work"; and
   naturais [*natural*: native-born], those born in Cabo
   Verde (Carreira 1972:267).

7. One of the six was believed to be a freeman; better
   clothed than the others, "he could sound a trumpet, play
   on the fiddle and was a weaver" (Donnan 1930 IV: 30).

8. By an act of 1660, all salt used for England's fishing
   industry, most of which came from Maio or the Tortugas,
   was relieved of import duty (Innes 1940:96).

9. Duncan mentions the 1686 arrival of two ships at the port
   of Boston, Massachusetts, laden with Cape Verdean salt;
   another carrying 70 tons of it is recorded in 1688.

10. Between 1826 and 1880, 338 American vessels are recorded
    as having put in to Maio for salt (Carreira 1971:71).

11. A 1753 list of items that were supposed to serve in the
    salt barter allows a glimpse of the scarcity of certain
    goods at the time. In order of descending value, they
    were silk, paper, cotton cloth, gunpowder, wine, and wool
    cloth (Carreira 1972:247).

12. Cf. England's refusal during the reign of Elizabeth I to
    recognize claims by Portugal's envoys that their country
    controlled the Guinea coast (Rose et al. 1929:45-46).

13. A letter written by Messrs. William and Samuel Vernon,
    Rhode Island shipowners, c. 1764, complains that one of
    their captains was given $100 to purchase "high cloths"
    (weavings) in the Cape Verdes, but instead obtained them
    by barter and kept the money for himself (Donnan 1930
    IV: 201-2).

14. Carreira notes mischievously that he obtained the docu-
    ment "by happenstance" (1969:40).

15. After the terrible famine of 1772-75, the debt-ridden
    population received the Queen's permission to pay what it
    owed the Company in textiles over a period of ten years
    (Carreira 1969:239-40).

16. The report of the Royal African Company to the Committee
    of Trade in London, 1729, makes it clear that Cape
    Verdean textiles were an essential item in their trading
    inventory (Donnan 1930 II: 259).

17. Boston shipowner Samuel Waldo, writing to one of his
    captains in 1734, instructs him to arrange to have one of
    his schooners pick up salt in Maio and "Cape de Verde
    cloths" in "St. Jago" (Santiago), noting that there may
    be "some hazard" in taking the textiles aboard (Donnan
    1930 III: 43).

18. Bridge saw only "eighty or ninety miserable hovels" in
    1842 (1968:9).

19. A single goat skin selling for between 160 and 300 *reis* in the Cape Verdes could be marketed in Boston for the equivalent of 600 *reis* (Duncan 1972:171).

20. Curtin estimates that approximately one million slaves were illicitly imported to the United States between 1809 and 1861 (1961:13).

21. This was a perennial complaint; in 1753, a civil servant wrote to Lisbon that he hoped that an English vessel might stop at Santiago so that he might visit several of the islands he had not yet visited due to lack of transport. He added that connections with Lisbon were also difficult, because the Portuguese vessels that did put in at the Cape Verdes were usually on their way to Guinea and Brazil (Carreira 1972:221). Earlier, in 1712, a report on a French pirate invasion in Santiago mentions the near-absence of maritime contact with Portugal for a period of eight years preceeding the French attack (Ibid., p. 234).

IV

THE *CRISES*:
DROUGHT AND ITS SOCIAL CONSEQUENCES

Introduction

The recurrent droughts and famines Cabo Verde has known
since the colony's earliest days of settlement have had profound effects on her history. This chapter supplements the preceding geographical and historical overview with an examination
of the nature and causes of these ecological disasters, as well
as some of their social consequences. Besides causing high
mortality and social upheaval, the famines that usually followed droughts have stimulated heavy outmigration since the
mid-nineteenth century, sometimes under lamentable conditions.
Today drought is the major problem facing the young Republic of
Cabo Verde, for lack of sufficient rainfall from 1968 to the
present has forced the nation to depend almost exclusively on
foreign aid to feed her population of some 302,000 (1978 estimate).

Drought and *Crises*

Drought (*seca*) has its own subvocabulary in Cabo Verde.
"Good years" refer to those with enough rainfall for an abundant harvest, while "bad years" are those in which little rain
falls from July to September, when it is needed for the crops.
One hears of "partial drought" when only some of the islands
are affected; "total drought" means disaster for the whole
archipelago. The first type has generated interisland migrations to less afflicted areas; Brava's port village of Furna is
a living artifact of the partial droughts of the past. Total
drought has brought peasants to the towns and cities for alms
and public relief, giving rise to squatters' settlements.
There, all manner of materials go into the construction of
makeshift dwellings, with flattened oil drums one of the most
popular in recent years. Thus has arisen the name "tin can
houses" (*casas de lata*) for the squatters' areas.

There is the *seca suave*, drought of short duration and
mild intensity, that stands in contrast to the *seca extrema*,
such as the one of recent years described near the end of this
chapter, when drought afflicts the whole archipelago for a number of years in succession. Though the term *crise* [crisis] is
often used interchangeably with *seca*, each refers to a different

manifestation of these catastrophes. *Seca* denotes the specifically climatic event of drought, *crise*, the social and economic upheaval that has so often followed.

In the preceding chapter, we saw that Cabo Verde's development as a colony was in large part conditioned by the fact
that her climate was too arid to permit plantation agriculture.
The present chapter is concerned with the periodic droughts
insofar as they jeopardize even the subsistence of the local
population. Though drought is a factor of climate, its consequences for this society have been shaped to a large degree by
the colonial context. It is in this light that the migration
of Cape Verdean laborers, men and women, to the cacao plantations of São Tome and Príncipe are examined later in the chapter. For under Portuguese rule, this "modern slavery," as
one writer called it, constituted an obvious "solution" to the
problem of starvation in Cape Verde.

The Causes of Drought

Cabo Verde depends for rain on clouds borne by the intertropical pluvogenic front formed by the meeting of dry harmattans coming from the northeast over the African continent,
with hot, humid air masses from the South Atlantic. Exactly
what determines the movement of this front is the subject of
much debate. From 1969 to 1976, it did not move far enough
north to reach a large area of West Africa known as the Sahel.[1]
Any drought affecting that region is usually felt with even
greater severity and for longer duration in the Cape Verdes,
because the archipelago lies at the northernmost extremity of
the intertropical pluvogenic front. Often it reaches only as
far as the Sotavento islands, leaving Barlavento dry. When
the front arrives, precipitation is caused by convection: the
high relief of the mountainous islands forces the air to rise
so that it becomes colder, and condensation results (Ribeiro
1960:61-69; Albouy and Boulenger 1975:41-55).

Given the Cape Verdes' position in relation to the movements of this rain-bearing front, annual rainfall is not only
low, but also highly variable from one year to another. One
study of a twenty-five year period found annual totals ranging from 37 mm in seven days of rain, to 1,050 mm in forty-
seven days, while in eighteen of the years studied, rainfall
was less than 200 mm (Ribeiro 1960:64-66).

One explanation frequently offered for drought in West
Africa posits a link between changes in the level of precipitation and cycles of solar activity, as indicated by the
occurrence of sunspots, but so far no conclusive findings have
been established (Winstanley 1976:205). Using such an
approach, a Cape Verdean scientist, Humberto Fonseca, has

hypothesized that major ("total") drought lasting for two to
three years would occur in the Cape Verdes every twenty-three
years (1961:19). While this seems to correspond with data
from the past, it does not accord as well with the events of
recent decades: since 1940, major droughts have occurred in
1940-43, 1946-48, and 1967-76.[2] Part of the difficulty of such
studies lies in the problem of determining exactly when a
drought begins (Albouy and Boulenger 1975:58). In Cabo Verde,
for example, a partial or less acute drought may precede one
that is more generalized and severe; areas of São Nicolau and
Fogo had been suffering drought for years before other parts
of the archipelago were affected in the late 1960s.

For the Sahel region as a whole, there is some evidence
for variable precipitation and for the process of desertifica-
tion (and also the reverse) as far back as the Middle Ages.
The question now is whether the rate of climatic change -- a
crucial factor for the survival of biological populations --
is presently accelerating (Winstanley 1976:192). Some ecolo-
gists believe that factors exterior to the Sahel have played
havoc with its climate. Industrial pollution coming from the
north has increased the levels of dust particles in the atmosphere, which is thought to have affected temperatures and
wind patterns in West Africa (Bryson 1973; Winstanley 1976:
207-13).

Drought in Cabo Verde. Drought is more than a matter of
the level of precipitation in these islands, for the effects
of both low and erratic rainfall are exacerbated by a number
of other factors, both natural and man-made. Volcanic basalts
in the soil make it extremely porous, so that groundwater is
not retained well. The one exception is Maio, a nearly tree-
less, desert-like island, where limestone in the soil permits
more retention of water. This was made evident in the 1960s
when a remarkable administrator, transferred to this insigni-
ficant post following a dispute with his superiors, had hundreds of shallow wells dug, bringing easily accessible water
to many settlements for the first time.

The original plant cover, not lush to begin with, was
devoured by goats, whose hardiness still makes them a mainstay
of the poor cultivators' domestic economy (Ribeiro 1960:83).
For centuries, the landlords of Santiago and Fogo allowed
their animals to graze practically untended on smaller islands
such as Brava and Maio. In dry periods, both humans and animals have foraged wherever they could, both consuming plants
normally left untouched. One of the famines of the 1940s is
called the "tree-stump hunger" because then even the tough
bases of banana trees were eaten. These unusual patterns of
plant consumption have left their mark on the local ecology,
in the form of proliferation of inedible weeds (Teixeira and
Barbosa 1958:3).

Experiments in reforestation were carried out successfully in the 1960s; the planted zones attracted rain while the surrounding areas remained dry. However, this was not followed up by a serious program of reforestation until after independence. As a result of the lack of sufficient green cover, frustrated peasants have often had to watch the long-awaited rain fall into the sea. Another consequence has been the aggravation of erosion once rain does fall on the land.

Besides causing the loss of topsoil and with it, the newly planted crops, heavy rains bring the danger of rock-falls, since large rocks are frequently wrested from the mountainsides during the storms, "cascading with a deafening roar down toward the sea, levelling crops and stone walls in their paths" (Ribeiro 1960:63-64). Occasional floods have caused drownings and destruction of property; some two decades ago, a whole village in Fogo was washed away in a rainstorm.

Before independence, there were few public cisterns to take advantage of the rains when they came, leaving most of the population to depend on springs for all their water needs. The springs are often located several hours away from the villages; every dawn sees a procession of slender women and children, balancing jugs of up to five gallons' capacity on their heads as they nimbly maneuver, barefoot, over the rocky mountain paths. With thorough washing and bathing impossible in many areas, infectious diseases, including leprosy, have spread all the more easily.

The Specter of Famine

In the past, drought nearly always meant catastrophe: tens of thousands of deaths by starvation and incalculable suffering from the effects of malnutrition, along with other sorts of material privation that must be endured when the need for food becomes paramount above all others. Homes were sold, clothing worn to tatters, schooling foregone, and all manner of deprivations suffered, along with the overwhelming one of hunger. Famine has usually brought epidemics in its wake, contagions that spread easily among the already weakened population via the insects and rats feeding on the rotting corpses. Physical suffering was immeasurably compounded by the degradation of social order during the *crises*, manifested in cruelty, violence, and the breakdown of normal rules of sociability. One of the most striking aspects of the historical acconts of *crises* discussed here is their lack of temporal specificity. Apart from certain details, the description that follows of a famine of 1609-11 could be that of one that occurred in the 1940s.

Balthazar Barreira, a Portuguese missionary to Santiago, recounts the famine of 1609-11 in a report to his superiors.

He tells of villages standing in ghostly abandon, the corpses
of the inhabitants lying in their houses, while a few survi-
vors scavenge for edible weeds. More bodies line the road-
ways, remains of the desperate flight to larger settlements
where aid might be sought. Former slaveowners have taken
poison to avoid the humiliation of death by starvation, and
once-respectable women have submitted to rape to feed themselves or their children. Famished marauders attack man and
beast alike. In the fields, rotting cattle carcasses are
sucked dry by the flies that multiply in pestilential numbers.
Horrified, Barreira describes a young girl whose body has been
found on the road, life drained from it by the bloodsucking
insects. Still clasped in the child's hand is the stick she
used to beat the flies away with, until exhaustion overcame
her. An epidemic of smallpox has made pariahs of its victims,
many of whom succumb. Meanwhile, aid expected from the metropole does not materialize, and the price of food in the towns
rises drastically. For lack of tax revenues, the salaries of
public employees go unpaid (Brásio 1968; Series 2, Vol. IV,
Document No. 111).

The horrors of famine catalogued by Barreira remain typical of the *crises* in Cabo Verde even today. Almost three-and-
a-half centuries later, Luis Romano's thinly fictionalized
roman à clef, *Famintos* (1975) depicts the same miseries in a
famine of the 1940s: widespread mortality, especially in the
outlying hamlets, rapes and assaults, epidemics, insect
plagues, speculation in foodstuffs, and lack of aid from
Lisbon.

Barcelos remarks that mortality during a famine of 1689
in Santiago did not exceed 4,000 because the populace was able
to sustain itself on horse and dog meat (1900 II: 100). Cats
and animal hides were also consumed in times of *crise*.
Records from the eighteenth and nineteenth centuries give
reports of consumption of human flesh; parents are said to
have eaten the corpses of their children during the famine of
1738-40 on the island of São Nicolau (Carreira 1972:193-95;
Barcelos 1900 II: 304, and 1905 III: 398).

One of the most devastating famines occurred in 1773-75,
during the hegemony of the Company of Grao Pará and Maranhão.
Estimates of mortality range between 22,000 and 32,500
(Barcelos 1905 III: 68; Carreira 1972:195). The Company and
local merchants colluded in setting exorbitant prices for foodstuffs, and foreigners profiteered as well. English and French
traders took many free persons as slaves, sometimes by force,
sometimes merely by enticing them with promises of food
(Barcelos 1905 III: 69).

In light of all this, the near-veneration for the United
States provoked by American relief efforts during the famine
of 1830-33 becomes understandable. As usual, Portugal had

sent no aid, nor had the English, despite their long history
of trading contacts with Cape Verde and their favored status
in all of Portugal's colonies. In consequence, over 30,000
lives were lost (Barcelos 1905 III: 395; Carreira 1972:200).

The American aid was based simply on moral and humanistic
grounds, perhaps influenced by the fact that the United States
had no colonial interests in Africa. The consul at Praia,
Samuel Hodges,[3] took the risk of distributing his own stores
of food and appealed to his countrymen for help. Fundraising
campaigns were conducted throughout New England with great
success, and a sea captain who regularly traded in Cape Verde
convinced Congress to send eleven ships laden with provisions.
Ten years later when Horatio Bridge,[4] a New England Yankee and
a friend of Nathaniel Hawthorne, arrived with the Africa
Squadron, he was moved to find that "men still speak of it
with quivering lips and faltering voice . . . women, with
streaming eyes, invoke blessings on that foreign land that fed
their children" (Bridge 1968:22-23; see also Barcelos 1905
III: 400-2 and Ribeiro 1960:207).

Bridge's story holds a tragically contemporary ring,
because since his time, Portugal's neglect of Cabo Verde during the famines has been the rule save for rare exceptions, as
when the Governor, Serpa Pinto (famous for his explorations in
Africa), took measures to allay famine during the drought of
1896-97. Aid, when it came, usually came from Cape Verdean
immigrants in the United States. A Cape Verdean physician and
writer of the late nineteenth century remarks bitterly that
"for the majority of those who call themselves 'civilized,'
the death of a black is but something more than the death of a
dog, yet much less than the death of a man" (Martins 1891:77).

Famine in Modern Times

The famines of 1941-43 and 1947-48 resulted in a combined
loss of some 45,000 lives (Carreira 1977:238). Scenes from
these catastrophes are still alive in popular memory. What
follows are the recollections of a few individuals who sur-
vived these times in different ways, depending on locale and
class of origin.

Dona Teresa* is the wife of a government office employee,
about forty-five years of age. As the child of a family of
civil servants and lesser landlords, she had a comfortable

*Dona is a term of respect applied to women on the basis
of age and/or social position.

61

childhood. Nevertheless, she says of the famine, "It was
dreadful." Eating was done in secret, with doors and windows
closed, so as to avoid the stares and pleas of the less fortunate. On her way to school each morning, she would find as
many as a dozen new corpses lying along the road leading into
the town of São Felipe, Fogo. Starving and often fatally
weakened, peasants from the outlying hamlets poured into the
town, where they would usually have to wait a day or two
before receiving a half-liter of raw maize from the scant
stores of the municipal government. Sometimes, she says, the
desperately hungry tried to eat the grain without cooking it,
only to die and have the half-chewed kernels wrested from
their mouths by other unfortunates.

Nhô Chiquinho* recalls the same era from the perspective
of a landless laborer. A small, wiry man in his mid-sixties,
he lives in a one-room stucco dwelling in one of the squatters'
settlements on the outskirts of São Felipe. At the time of
the interviews, Nhô Chiquinho was mourning the death of his
wife a few months earlier. He himself was not in the best of
health, and was often unable to complete a day's work "on the
road," the popular term of reference for state work projects.
The one source of pleasure in his life seemed to be the ten-
year-old niece living with him, whom he spoiled to the limit
of his slender means. Chiquinho is a well-known local person-
age, famous for his musical talents, his feisty temper and his
cunning. His recollections are those of an expert survivor.

"In a *crise*," he says, "one must go to the city. To stay
out in the countryside is death. In town, there are three
places to 'hit': Nhô Padre (the priest), Nhô Dimistrador (the
official), and Nhô Doutor (the physician). You can't go to
the same one every day." He continues, "Once the administrator accused me of selling the potatoes he had given me. 'Of
course I did,' I told him. 'You can't expect me to live on
just potatoes!'" "*Atrevido!*" [roughly translated, "What
cheek!"] people exclaim at hearing this, admiration in their
voices. What would bring another severe reprisals, Chiquinho
has always carried off with such panache as to earn the grudg-
ing respect of even the most authoritarian administrators.

In one of the famines, he convinced the administrator to
give him a job carting away corpses from the street and trans-
porting them to a common grave, in exchange for food.
Chiquinho is known for his lively vendettas with the high as
well as the low, but his archenemy was a woman almost as poor
as he, Nha Juliana. According to popular lore, Chiquinho discovered her lying faint with hunger and exhaustion as he plied

---

*Nhô: Senhor; nha: senhora.

the streets with his wheelbarrow. "On you go!" he chortled, hoisting her up, while the poor woman began to scream frantically that she was very much alive, until a crowd came to her rescue.

The worst of the famines was felt, as Nhô Chiquinho relates, in the rural areas where relief supplies were non-existent in the 1940s. Nha Louise was a small girl in the remote hamlet of Tantum, Brava during this period. Now in her forties, she looks about the same age as her mother, who is about twenty years her elder. Both are very thin and wizened, of light brown complexion, and bereft of nearly all their teeth due to malnutrition. Their dwelling is a two-room stone cottage, its packed-dirt floor free of any debris. The only adornment to be seen is a transistor radio and a can of Del Monte peaches. (I wonder if, and for what occasion, it will ever be opened.) Nha Louise sits on the narrow bed and offers me the only chair. As we talk, her mother sits on the doorstep chopping a long wad of golden-brown tobacco into pieces; a friend has sent this from Praia. Some she will smoke herself, in a pipe, and some she will sell to her neighbors. She refuses a proferred cigarette, but Nha Louisa accepts one and begins to talk. When asked about her experiences in the famine of the early 1940s (it is called the famine of 1942, for this was the most terrible year of the three), tears well up in her eyes. She remembers how her sister, close to death, was taken to a shelter for the terminally ill in the town of Nova Sintra, the island's administrative center. There the very ill were given food, but nearly all who entered the shelter died shortly thereafter, and many believe that they were thrown into common graves even before they had breathed their last. Nha Louisa's sister was taken to the shelter and was never seen again.

"Mostly we ate *kandē* (a sugar and water confection)[5] . . . we ate green papayas, anything. . . . One day I walked to Furna (a day's journey) and waited a day there for a half-liter of corn. Along the road you could see lots of bodies, with insects crawling into their mouths and noses. I was only eleven years old." But more than these macabre sights, what seems to have impressed the child most -- for Nha Louisa returns to the point several times -- was the absence of customary greetings on the road. In normal times, passers-by wish each other good day and inquire as to the other's health. (This last is expressed by a Crioulo phrase that means, literally, "Your body?") If the travelers know each other, similar concern is expressed for their families. Finally, before each goes on, they bid farewell: "God be with you." "And with you." During times of famine, these traditional courtesies are ignored and no words are spoken, except to ask whether food has arrived.

The *crise* of 1941-43 was especially calamitous for Brava because the war prevented Cape Verdeans in the United States from sending food supplies. Some *americanos*, Cape Verdeans who had worked for decades in the United States, were visiting the island and were trapped there when war broke out. In certain cases, the *americanos* sold even their gold fillings to survive. In one particularly tragic episode, fifty-one persons, *americanos* and their close relatives, set sail in 1943 in a schooner called the *Mathilde*. The vessel was not in good condition, and to make matters worse, the sailing coincided with the season of tropical storms. The *Mathilde* and all aboard her were lost shortly thereafter.

As is always the case, the famines of the 1940s had their profiteers. A certain merchant-landowner in Brava, once a servant and porter, arrived from America in 1941 with abundant supplies of food that he was able to exchange for parcels of land. Families sold the very roofs over their heads, tile by tile, to unscrupulous entrepreneurs such as this. In the queues of the hungry waiting for food at the *Câmara* (town hall), and among the pitiful road crews of emaciated construction workers, the rule of the whip prevailed. Overseers on public works projects sometimes became petty tyrants, raping and beating at will. In Brava, the frustrated populace gathered in the central plaza and nearly stormed the *Câmara*. The administrator resigned and was replaced by a physician from one of the island's landlord families. Like several administrators of his time, this man was quick to use his riding whip when piqued. Even importunate patients were likely to be slapped about. For the hungry and destitute populace, a *crise* meant much more than hunger; it amounted to a virtual reign of terror.

'Solutions' to the Problem of Famine

The devastating famine of 1862-65, which took some 30,000 lives, about a third of the colony's population (Carreira 1972: 202), saw the first systematic efforts at famine relief by Portugal. Most important among these were state-sponsored public works projects on the one hand, and directed labor migration on the other. Both would remain the pillars of famine relief policy for the duration of Portuguese rule.

The earliest reference to the creation of state construction projects as a means of using the labor power of peasants idled by drought and of providing them with cash with which to purchase food appears in 1864 (Barcelos 1912 VI: 241). Then, as in later *crises*, most of the funds allocated for this purpose went into road construction. With only picks, hammers, and other simple tools, the mostly unskilled workers produced great stone jigsaws of brown, beige, red and ochre. Decorative as well as functional, these roads wind like multicolored ribbons around island contours, incongruously beautiful memorials of famines past. The labor was often dangerous, given the lax enforcement of measures to protect workers from rockfalls and dynamite blasts. The workers' low salaries (discussed more fully in a later chapter) could only have been imposed in a time of famine. The sight of roads leading apparently to nowhere, left unfinished at the end of the *crise* that begot them, lends some credence to Martins's accusation that Portugal was taking advantage of the famines to get public construction done more cheaply (1891).

The weight of calculations extraneous to the problem of hunger in Cape Verde is clearer in regard to state-directed emigration. The first statement of policy on the question, appearing in a royal order of 1864 to the governor of Cape Verde, proposes exporting laborers from Santiago to São Tomé as "an efficient means of giving help to the inhabitants of Cabo Verde most affected by the famine, with great utility for another Portuguese possession." Accordingly, the governor is commanded to "facilitate the emigration of free labourers in conditions favorable to their utilization by the landowners." Less than six months later, he is further instructed "to have transported up to 1,000 individuals of both sexes to the islands of São Tomé and Príncipe, *employing to this end all possible means of persuasion*" (emphasis added).[6] Other measures propounded in the same order include halting the migration to Praia from outlying areas, prompt burial of corpses, and procedures to ensure equitable food distribution in the various districts of the island of Santiago.

Migration to the 'Cacao Islands.' São Tomé and Príncipe, islands in the Gulf of Guinea administered as one colony by Portugal, had seen the introduction of coffee as a cash crop around the beginning of the nineteenth century, and that of cacao in 1822. Both crops prospered in the hot and humid climate of the two islands, but their success brought with it the decline of their traditional creole elite landlords, bought out (or their land expropriated outright) by metropolitans over the course of the nineteenth century, as well as the problem of securing an adequate labor supply for the plantations. This was problematical even before 1858, when slavery was abolished in these islands, since their dense, mountainous jungles offered a tempting refuge to would-be runaways. After that date, however, it became a crucial issue. The newly freed slaves (*libertos*) refused to remain indentured to their former masters, as the decree of abolition stipulated they do for a period of nine years. Instead, in what Tenreiro terms "an authentic revolution" (1961:80), the *libertos* deserted in large numbers, leaving the harvest to rot on the trees.

Until abolition, Angolan slaves were imported to the plantations, though clandestinely after 1842, when Portugal was obliged by Great Britain to end her slave traffic. Later, "vagrancy" laws subjected subsistence farmers in Angola and Mozambique to conscription for labor in São Tomé and Príncipe. These were first enacted in 1875, a year when labor shortages in São Tomé threatened the planters with ruin. Vagrancy laws were later to form part of Salazar's policies on "indigenous" peoples, the *Indigenato*, discussed in a later chapter. Cape Verdeans, though not subjected to the same rulings, were often compelled to "go south," as the Crioulo euphemism put it, when famine threatened. Over the fifty-two years of the twentieth century for which statistics are available, 79,392 departures of Cape Verdean workers to the cacao islands are recorded (Carreira 1977:248). (See Appendix 2.) The number of Cape Verdean laborers was much lower than the number of workers from Angola and Mozambique, but it represented a much higher proportion of the sending population.[7]

Just how coercive were the means of labor recruitment in Cabo Verde is unclear, though the wording of the 1863 order ("by all possible means of persuasion") is certainly suggestive. A policy statement from Lisbon in the following year announces that "it has become necessary to avoid the departure and transport of Cape Verdean emigrants to foreign countries" (Ibid., p. 152). By this time, the United States was attracting many Cape Verdeans. The intent to channel emigration to the cacao islands is clear in Governor Paula Cid's order that passports or travel permits not be given to the indigent, except to those with contracts to work in São Tomé, so as to avoid emigration to Dakar (where wages were higher than in the Portuguese colonies) or to other foreign destinations (Barcelos 1904:84). For this, Paula Cid, reputed to have financial interests of his own in the cacao plantations, received fulsome thanks from one of São Tomé's planters for his "patriotic assistance"! A fee of 4,800 *reis*, a sum beyond the means of most prospective emigrants, was imposed on those leaving for the United States (Carreira 1977:181-82). Whether this last measure succeeded or not is questionable; it may have served only to increase the volume of clandestine emigration to America, at least in the case of Brava, which provided very few of the laborers going to São Tomé.

In 1903, Portugal allowed the establishment of "emigration agencies" so that private citizens could recruit laborers (Ibid., pp. 167-68). This system, whereby recruiters earned so much "per head," tied the interests of Cape Verde's merchant-landlords to those of the planters of São Tomé. Of course the merchants, or their agents who did the recruiting, exaggerated the benefits to be gained. The distrust of the popular classes found expression in a well-known song from Fogo:

>Burros and beasts of burden[8]
>They go to São Tomé
>While Sobido (a merchant) sits in his office
>'Eating' (getting rich from) cacao.

This system of labor recruitment continued into the
1950s. It was prohibited in the Barlavento islands (Ibid.,
p. 190). Instead, recruitment was concentrated in Santiago
and Fogo, where the archipelago's most rigid class/color hierarchies prevailed. It was the *badius* of Santiago's interior,
peasants descended for the most part from runaway slaves, who
provided the backbone of the emigration to São Tomé and
Príncipe. The very designation *badiu* is a corruption of the
Portuguese *vadio* [vagrant] -- a loaded term indeed under colonial rule.

The labor migrations to the cacao islands comprise a particularly sordid chapter of Portuguese colonialism, and one
that has been the subject of a voluminous literature, beginning with Nevinson's scathing attack on what he called *A Modern Slavery*.[9] Carreira's copious documentation of the realities of life on the plantations (1977:148-235) leaves no doubt
that it amounted to a prolongation of slavery in many respects.
An 1844 account by a former governor of São Tomé reveals tor-
tures equal to the worst excesses of that institution, including beatings, use of chains to confine workers, beatings on
the soles of the feet, and in the case of alleged misdeeds,
the use of scourges and of red hot wires driven through the
hands and feet to extract confessions (quoted in Carreira
1977:159).

Joachim Paiva de Carvalho was removed from his post as
Curador [Curator] of contract laborers in Príncipe for reasons that can be guessed from reading his account of abuses he
witnessed, including the rape of black women in front of their
men, and the atrocious reprisals accorded recaptured runaways.[11] Carvalho found the workers afflicted with sleeping
sickness, malaria, tuberculosis, leprosy, syphilis, and other
diseases -- which would be brought back to Cabo Verde by the
returning migrants, posing serious dangers to the public
health. Also, by Carvalho's account, the workers were tricked
or intimidated into signing new contracts.[*]

Tenreiro's study (1961) provides a more recent account of
conditions on the plantations. These are described in
reserved, almost euphemistic fashion, as might be expected in
a work published under the auspices of Salazar's government.

---

[*] Carvalho's 1912 report is quoted at length in Carreira
1977:175-80.

Tenreiro mentions "the powerful organization of the plantations" that kept workers "isolated" from the world outside
(p. 143). The strongest tie among them, apart from kinship,
was that obtaining between persons who had come in the same
ship. Individuals were designated as being "of my ship" (*do
meu navio*), an expression Tenreiro finds "archaic and apparently related to earlier days of the traffic in blacks" (p.
191). The Cape Verdean contingent was unique in having an
equal proportion of women to men, with sometimes whole nuclear
families present. "Often I saw women weeding, a scythe in the
right hand, an infant on the back and another hanging on her
skirts" (pp. 192-93).

Tenreiro's account indicates that planters continued to
enjoy something close to absolute rule and that workers were
kept on the plantation by force. While oral accounts collected
in Fogo suggest that atrocities still occurred, we may surmise,
without undue optimism, that these were less frequent than earlier in the century, if only because of their potential for
discrediting Portugal in the later decades of colonial rule.
Wages were still pitiful at the time of Tenreiro's research; in
1957, the median sum taken home by workers after three years of
labor was two to three *contos*, or several hundred dollars
(Carreira 1977:216).

Wages more than tripled between 1963 and 1970 (Ibid., pp.
212-13). Workers returning to Cape Verde told of drastic
improvements in living conditions and medical care. These
changes were in part a response to the shortage of labor
affecting the plantations, a shortage traceable to the revolu-
tions in Portugal's African colonies and the migration of Cape
Verdean workers to Portugal that gathered momentum in the '60s
and continues today. But they were also part of the general
reformist tendency in colonial policy whose effects were being
felt in Cabo Verde herself.

Reformist Policies of Famine Relief. 1972 was the fifth
consecutive year of total drought in Cape Verde. Partial
drought had gone on much longer; São Nicolau, for example, had
not had sufficient rainfall for fourteen years. That island's
springs had mostly dried up and, according to a physician who
knew the situation well, signs of starvation were evident,
especially among the children. By the end of the same year,
Santo Antão's water supply was very low and water was being
strictly rationed in Boa Vista. Drought was a constant preoccupation that invaded almost every sphere of human relationships. Personal ambitions of any sort -- buying a pig, putting up a new roof, sending a child to secondary school -- were
predicated on the eventuality of rain. Seed, representing a
considerable expense for the small cultivator, was sown once
again that year, pitting hope against the experience of the
previous half-decade.

Despite the severity of this drought, its consequences for the population were mild, compared to earlier *crises*. This was not by chance. While Portugal's concerns for her public image at this crucial period meant that international relief agencies were not allowed to function in Cape Verde, it also stimulated her to much greater efforts than previously to avoid loss of life. Beans and maize were distributed to the needy, and milk and vitamins were made available to children as well as to pregnant and nursing mothers. The elderly received food allotments and a stipend equivalent to about $2.50 U.S. per month. During 1971, some 300 *contos*, approximately $12 million U.S., were spent on public construction projects, including roads, public buildings and, in Boa Vista, the collection of sea salt. Working conditions on state projects were far more humane than in the past, and safety procedures had been instituted to minimize the dangers of dynamite blasts to the workers (though helmets were still not provided as protection against rockfalls). Wages were low, at 12 *escudos* a day (about $0.50 U.S. at the time) for women and 15 *escudos* a day (about $0.50 U.S.) for men; skilled male workers such as stonemasons made about double the usual male wage. The value of these sums is better understood when compared to the prices of food staples at the time, as follows:

maize	6 *escudos*/liter
groundnuts	5 *escudos*/liter
fava beans	25 *edcudos*/liter
potatoes	20 *escudos*/liter

Olive oil from Portugal and other imported foodstuffs, such as sugar, sold at higher prices than in Europe.

Survival was possible on such low wages only because of remittances from relatives living abroad. In cases of severe need among those receiving no assistance from other sources, the state provided food allotments. Another factor allowing peasants to manage with very little cash was the fact that few paid rent for housing, most either owning their dwelling or having been given it in usufruct. Land rents were, however, a matter for dispute in Santiago. Though the state could annul the tenants' rental obligations in a "bad" year, landlords were wont to pressure the authorities to enforce payment as usual.

While no corpses were to be found on the roadside during this famine, every day saw tiny coffins borne in funeral processions through the streets of São Vicente. Physicians confirmed what no statistics were then available to demonstrate: namely, that malnutrition was claiming lives, especially those of infants. At the time of independence, infant mortality was 120/1,000 (Decraene 1977). São Nicolau, Maio and Boa Vista had no resident physicians; Santo Antão had only one for a population of 34,000 scattered over mountainous terrain.

Medical personnel worked to the point of mental and physical
breakdown, sometimes going for years without a vacation and
forced to function without such basic equipment as x-ray appa-
rati. Nurses constantly had to compensate for inadequate formal preparation with experience and fortitude. The sheer volume of demand for curative services made much-needed preventive
care and education nearly impossible to provide.

Vitamin and mineral deficiencies were readily apparent in
the scaly and discolored skin of both adults and children
(pellagra), and in the skeletal malformations of some youngsters whose bow-legged appearance was attributable to rickets.
Teeth were already missing from the smiles of many adolescents.
The unhealthy, faded-looking hair and patches of peeled skin
symptomatic of kwashkiorkor, a protein-deficiency disease, were
also in evidence. One could see, from time to time, the peculiar flush of the leprous, and occasionally laborers on the
road gangs would hide their hands from strangers' eyes. Victims of leprosy were not supposed to be employed on state projects, but instead were encouraged to seek treatment at Fogo's
small leprosarium. Still, those stricken with the disease
often continued to work as long as they could conceal their
condition, fearing the loss of income and the separation from
their loved ones that treatment entailed.[11] The lack of energy
experienced by almost everyone was attributed to "low blood
pressure" (tensão baixa) among the more sophisticated, and simply to "weakness" (fraqueza) by others. In fact, the terms
"hunger" and "weakness" are used synonymously in Crioulo, so
that the inquiry, "Do you feel weak?" really means, "Are you
hungry?"

Treating the Symptoms

One senior colonial official, when queried whether emigration really provided a solution to the economic problems posed
by Cabo Verde's problem, responded, "Better than the Malthusian
one." But neither emigration and the remittances it brought,
nor the state work projects, did more than "cure only the symptoms and not the causes" of famine, to use the phrase of a Cape
Verdean observer of some eighty years earlier (Martins 1891:
67-68). Only after independence were concerted efforts made to
deal with the long-range causes of drought and famine (see
Chapter VII).

The history of labor migrations from Cabo Verde, and their
effect on economic and social life in the archipelago, merit a
volume of their own.* Elsewhere, I have argued that it is
oversimplifying the issue to regard drought as the sole cause

*The interested reader is referred to Carreira 1977.

of Cape Verdean migration (Meintel, forthcoming). It is worth noting that the large-scale out-migrations, both to São Tomé and to the United States, began at roughly the same period.

In the late 1860s, post-Civil War industrialization in the northeastern United States was depleting the labor supply of other sectors, such as whaling and farming, and it was niches such as these that Cape Verdeans were able to occupy. Yankee whalers had long made the Cape Verdes a victualling stop and now they began to count on the crew members they could pick up there, as well as in the Azores. At about the same time, São Tomé's plantations faced a labor shortage due, as we have seen, to the desertion of former slaves.

How Cabo Verde became such a ready source of migrant labor, supplying the needs of capitalist development elsewhere, becomes clearer in the next chapter. One of the important effects of abolition in 1858, and before that, the frequent manumissions of slaves, was to create a land-poor, largely destitute peasantry. Even when famine did not pose an immediate danger, this rural workforce would serve as a pool of potential migrants, first to the United States, and later, to Portugal and other parts of Europe.

Conditions in São Tomé, by contrast, were so undesirable that this migration tended to fluctuate in volume according to the climatic conditions of any given year in Cabo Verde. This migration is of particular interest for understanding Portuguese racial policy as it applied to Cabo Verde, a point taken up again in Chapter VII.

Notes

1. The Sahel includes the former French colonies of sub-Saharan West Africa: Upper Volta, Mali, Senegal, Chad, Niger, and Mauritania.

2. There is some historical precedent for the extended drought of recent years. 1738 to 1750 were years of "almost continuous" drought, and similarly, the decade from 1850-60 (Carreira 1972:194, 201).

3. Samuel Hodges, Jr., originally of Stoughton, Massachusetts, was the American consul in Cape Verde from 1818 until his death in 1827. As Brooks explains, consular representatives in West Africa were not paid salaries; usually they were the commercial agents of firms trading in the area, and one of the main rewards of the consular post was the useful contacts with local government authorities and information on other traders that it afforded (1970:130). Hodges was very active in trade between Cape Verde and the Gambia, operating in partnership with the powerful merchant, Manuel António Martins (Ibid., pp. 149-50). His papers are kept in the Peabody Museum at Salem, Massachusetts.

4. Bridges' articulate, if occasionally cantankerous, account of his visit to Cape Verde in 1842 provides a useful portrait of the archipelago (1968:10-27). One of the chaplains with Perry's Africa Squadron, Charles W. Thomas, published an account of his stay (1855-57), cited in the previous chapter.

5. This is one of the many derivatives from English terms to be found in the dialect of Crioulo spoken in Brava, a result of the island's long history of emigration to the United States. The Portuguese name for this sweet is *repousada*.

6. These two documents are to be found in the *Boletim de Cabo Verde* 1864, Nos. 3 and 150, respectively. Copies of these were kindly provided by António Carreira, who brought them to my notice.

7. Using the years for which figures are available between 1904 and 1922 for Cape Verde, Mozambique, and Angola, respectively, Carreira derives average figures of 997 migrants per year from Cape Verde, 2,228 from Mozambique, and 1,560 from Angola.

8. In Crioulo, *burro e besta*. This phrase has a double meaning, the second being "idiots and blockheads."

9. Other important accounts that document the conditions of forced labor in Portuguese Africa are Galvão's explosive report after his tenure as a colonial administrator (1950) and works by Marvin Harris that showed the continuation of the practice despite "reforms" (1958, 1966). Galvão later became known for his participation in the seizure of a Portuguese vessel, an event that focused world attention on Portugal and her colonies (Minter 1972:58; Marques 1972 II:370-71).

10. To give but one example, Carvalho relates a typical punishment, which consisted of forcing the captive to carry a wooden tub full of dirt and weighing some 65 pounds to some distant point and back again, normally over hilly terrain, for days on end without rest, all the while under the lash of two fellow laborers forced to perform this role (quoted in Carreira 1977:176).

11. Such a case is portrayed in Teixeira de Sousa's ethnographically rich novel, *Ilheu da Contenda* (1974), set in his native Fogo.

V

SLAVERY: THE LIVING PAST

A Racial System

From the viewpoint of physical anthropology, racial dif-
rerences appear to be of dubious scientific value (Brace 1967),
and the fact that racial differences are conceived of differently from one society to another lends further weight to such
skepticism. Here, however, we are concerned with race as a
social and cultural reality rather than as scientific fact.
One of the most complex aspects of Cabo Verde's colonial
legacy is the system of race relations that developed under
Portuguese rule: the definition of certain physical differences as significant criteria of social differentiation, the
categories of racial classification, how such categories
structure interaction and are themselves reconstituted in
everyday social life. Also part of any racial system is racial
ideology: images (e.g., stereotypes), beliefs and values about
race that guide and legitimize social behavior.

A colonialist ideology of race was actively promoted under
the regimes of Salazar and Caetano in the official press, the
eudcational system, and in public discourse. The explicit for-
mulation of this racial ideology became especially important
after World War II, when other European powers began to relinquish (or were forced to relinquish) their territorial claims
in Africa and Asia, in the effort to justify Portugal's continuing rule in her colonies. One of its central propositions was
that Portugal's colonial expansion had been singularly free of
racism and commercial motivation, and instead had been inspired
by the aim of "civilizing" and "Christianizing" the populations
of her conquests. As a consequence, Portugal's colonies were
said to be characterized not by a racial hierarchy but rather
by different gradations of assimilation to the "national"
(that is, Portuguese) culture.

Lusotropicalism

Colonial ideologues found support for their claims in the
work of the eminent Brazilian scholar, Gilberto Freyre.
Freyre's observations of his own society led him to affirm
that, however imperfect, Brazil's race relations were "probably
the nearest approach to paradise anywhere in the world" (1959:
19). This he saw as a consequence of Lusotropicalism; that is,

the unique and relatively benign character of Portuguese colonialism and slavery, a notion he first proposed in a 1940 work
suggestively entitled *The World the Portuguese Created*. In
Freyre's view, Lusotropicalism was the result, on the one hand,
of the Catholic religion that united slave and master, and on
the other hand, of the Moorish influence that predisposed the
Portuguese to intimate contact, including sexual relations,
with dark-skinned peoples.

Not surprisingly, Salazar's government greeted Freyre's
work with enthusiasm. In 1952, Freyre toured the African colonies as the guest of the Portuguese government, making a brief
stop in Cape Verde,[1] and later his essays on Portuguese colonialism were published in a special volume commemorating the
five hundredth anniversary of the death of Henry the Navigator
(1961). Here Freyre extended the notion of Lusotropicalism,
applying it not only to Brazil but to Portugal's modern empire
as well. Portuguese colonialism was described as "Christo-
centric" rather than "ethnocentric"; that is, as "transmitting
a set of values to non-Christian peoples, quite independently
of the national civilisation of the transmitter" (1961:13),
allowing the Portuguese to integrate colonized peoples on a
basis of equality. "Troubles" in Portuguese Africa were
ascribed to English, Belgian and South African influences on
Portuguese policy that had detracted from the integrative possibilities of "Luso-Christianity" (Ibid., p. 208).

Freyre's most influential work comprises a detailed examination of Brazilian slavery (1933). Under his influence, a
number of scholars, notably Tannenbaum (1947), Elkins (1959),
Hoetink (1967), and Degler (1971) have contrasted Iberian (or
Latin) slavery and modern-day racial systems with those of the
former English colonies in the Americas. Tannenbaum, Elkins,
and Degler, in particular, focus on the contrast between slavery in Brazil and in the United States.

Here, by way of prelude to the discussion of contemporary
race relations in Cabo Verde, we examine certain features of
the slavery system wherein lie their historical roots, paying
special attention to certain aspects of slavery emphasized by
Freyre and his successors in studies of race in the New World,
such as miscegenation, manumission, and the role of the
Catholic Church.

In brief, we find that Cape Verdean slavery closely fits
the Iberian model proposed by these scholars in a number of
respects: the tenor of the master-slave relationship, the
frequent incidence of manumission, the presence of a universalistic religion embraced (on the formal level, at least) by
both master and slave, the tolerance for miscegenation, and
the development of a large and socially significant mulatto
category. At the same time, the role of the Catholic Church
is shown to have been an ambiguous one, for if Church doctrine

emphasized the slaves' common humanity with their owners, in actual practice, religious ritual offered an occasion for reaffirmation of the prerogatives of the slave-owning class. Missionaries were often at odds with their local confreres, usually slaveowners themselves.

Abolition, we find, was a relatively peaceful process that in itself posed little immediate threat to the economic and social order. Here again, we note the parallel with Brazil's northeast, a comparison that will be pursued further in later chapters.

Land Tenure and Slavery in Cape Verde

Though none of the islands was really satisfactory for profitable plantation agriculture, Santiago and Fogo might be characterized as less unsuitable than the others on the basis of climate and terrain. There patterns of latifundia developed, beginning with royal land grants in the early sixteenth century,[2] and so these two islands came to monopolize the slave labor of the archipelago. When abolition was completed in 1869, their combined holdings accounted for 3,175, or 78.9 percent, of the 4,020 slaves in the archipelago (1868 figures, from Carreira 1972:420). The land grants were inherited, in theory on the basis of primogeniture, though there were apparently many divergences from this norm in Santiago.[3] Their association with particular families continued in Fogo even after primogeniture was abolished in 1864, as a result of that island's great isolation and tradition of marriage between close relatives.[4] (In Fogo, the preference for marriages between first cousins in the landlord class could still be observed in 1972.)

The landlord class that emerged in the less than propitious conditions of Cape Verde seems to have been little more than a parody of its own aspirations. Unlike Freyre's Frenchman, who marveled at the cuisine and the *politesse* of Bahia's landed families (1966:xxv), newcomers to Cape Verde were appalled at the shabby decadence of her elite: "indolent and haughty," according to one observer (Chelmiki 1841:153); "living in unsocialability, promiscuity and pride" in the words of another (Ribeiro 1956:616). The portrait that emerges is one of a pretentious would-be aristocracy, lazy and largely unschooled,[5] corrupted still further by the considerable numbers of deported criminals in their midst.

Furthermore, they usually fell far short of their seigneurial obligations to administer their properties and to provide for their slaves. A Portuguese missionary to Santiago in 1605 found owners of hundreds of slaves "who do not give them clothing and rarely food" (Carreira 1972:384). His account is echoed by Lima's nearly 250 years later: "The owners do not clothe or feed their slaves, but rather let them work one day a week for this" (1844:112). Another writer of the period considers the landlords "infatuated with the title of *morgado*[6] . . . they cede the administration of their holdings as soon as possible to some poorer relative . . . who does nothing but oppress the miserable slaves . . . " (Carreira 1972:375).

Master and Slave

Compared to the huge plantations of Brazil, the holdings of the Cape Verdean landlords were small indeed. Unlike the absentee owners of the British Caribbean and Dutch Surinam, their economic risks were concentrated in the colony, in what could be wrung from the land or culled from part-time trading. Both owners and slaves were subject to the same pirate raids, droughts and epidemics. Moreover, did they not inhabit the same moral universe? Unlike his sophisticated counterparts in many parts of the Caribbean and in Brazil, the Cape Verdean *senhor* was often ill at ease in the metropole; though he admired it from a distance, and might seek to ape what he knew of its ways, he was often little better educated than his slaves. More at home (like them) in Crioulo than in Portuguese, he circumvented as much as possible the metropolitan laws and institutions that so often favored outsiders at his expense. From the slave he acquired many elements of folklore, including belief in cures, spells and witchcraft; he added these, along with many of the staple dishes of the islands' cuisine, to his Portuguese heritage. With his slaves, he shared religion, celebrating the same saints' feasts (which he -- or his wife -- was expected to finance); he was often joined to them by the fictive kinship of godparenthood as well as by actual blood ties.

In the mountainous islands of Brava, Santo Antão, and São Nicolau, the slave supply was undependable; landholdings were generally small and the number of slaves per owner was usually quite low, usually only one or two by the end of the slavery period (Carreira 1972:512-48). In these islands, the master-slave relationship was characterized by constant face-to-face interaction and proximity, for it was common for slaves to live under the same roof as their owners. Perhaps it was too much to presume the quasi-familial relationships that some claim were the case between their forebears and the slaves they owned; still, any mistreatment must have been tempered by the fact that slaves were least expendable in these outlying islands.

Even in Fogo and Santiago, sadism did not take on the institutionalized quality it did in Brazil's northeast, with its profusion of specialized instruments and conventionalized methods of tortured, described by Ramos (1951:34-35).[7] Barbarities were not unknown, however. Dona Isabel de Barros,

wife of the governor Oliveira de Fonseca (in office during
1707), and her family, were notorious for cruelty toward their
slaves; some of the unfortunates were driven to suicide by
years of being held in chains and enduring daily whippings.
One, a pregnant woman, was tortured to death by burning embers
being placed on her belly (Barcelos 1900 II: 230). The rural
estates of Fogo had slave dungeons and whipping posts; in
Brava, one particularly brutal owner is reputed to have cut
off the hands of offending slaves and to have had others
thrown from cliffs into the sea. Harris's description of the
"friendly master" as a "myth" seems to apply as well to Cape
Verdean master-slave relationships as it does to those of
Brazil.

Less spectacular, but perhaps just as important, are the
drudgery and privation that, however taken for granted they
might have been, made up the slaves' daily lives. Besides
household and agricultural labor, they worked at weaving, carpentry, blacksmithing, construction, and in Maio and Boa
Vista, herding. The small sugar mills (*trapiches*) that are
now powered by oxen were once driven by men, whose mournful
work songs could be heard well into the night. In the face of
so many accounts that Cape Verdean slaves were ill-clothed and
poorly fed, it is no wonder that they were particularly vulnerable to the contagious diseases that usually followed famines and the fevers of the rainy season. While epidemics were
no respecters of class, they nonetheless exacted greater tolls
from the slave sector of the population. For example, those
of smallpox and cholera in 1855 took four times more slaves'
lives, in proportion to their numbers, than they did from the
rest of the population (from figures in Carreira 1972:201).
In times of famine, the slaves were the first to suffer and
the most likely to perish;[8] frequently, they were summarily
"freed" with no means of subsistence.

Except for the freedom to marry and to work for themselves on days of rest, the slaves had few human or civil
rights. Until 1842, they could, by law, be sold at will to an
owner on another island; in fact, slaves were sold illegally
to foreigners in some cases (Carreira 1972:412). Typical pun-
ishments included the stocks, beatings, and deprivation of
food and water (Ibid., pp. 361-62). The female slave, besides
being prey to the sexual whims of her owner, was sometimes
treated as a mere breeder, judging by a governor's report of
1856 that alludes to the "scandalous scenes of prostitution
that many *senhores* execute and exhibit in order to possess a
greater number of miserable slaves" (quoted in Carreira 1972:
414).

The Role of the Church

Catholic tradition, as Genovese puts it, "recognized slavery but declared it to be unnatural" (1971:100). By Portuguese law, all slaves transshipped through the ports of the
empire were to be baptized, although by papal consent this
could be done en masse; such baptisms often took place in the
ship's hold, the slaves having received no prior instruction
whatever in the faith (Carreira 1972:215; Duncan 1972:233).
Missionaries, at first Jesuits (expelled from the realm in
1647) and later Capuchins, often did try to improve the slaves'
conditions and to have them married in the Church. One bishop
felt strongly enough against slavery to communicate his "scru-
ple" to the king in 1731 (Barcelos 1900 II: 261). But, while
a few of the clery were ready to risk the landlords' displea-
sure, many others tolerated and even thrived upon the institution of slavery. Seven priest-slaveowners are listed in the
1856 census, including one with twenty slaves, at a time when
the average number of slaves per owner was 3.8 (from figures
in Carreira 1972:512-18). Priests were known to traffic in
slaves and to keep slave concubines as well.

Still, the implicit contradiction, however theoretical it
remained, between the concern for saving souls that was the
official justification for the Portuguese slave trade, and the
nature of slavery itself, seems not to have been lost on the
owners. A governor's report of 1718 speaks of owners trying
to undo the work of the missionaries by telling the slaves
that the Gospel was a lie (Barcelos 1900 II: 232). By admitting slaves to the fold, the Church undoubtedly fostered practices that bespoke recognition of the slaves' humanity: legal
marriages, ties of godparenthood between slaves and whites,
and manumission.

But religion also gave occasion for the reaffirmation of
distinctions and social distance between slaves and owners.
A sardonic little essay by one Lucas de Sena in 1818 portrays
the grand entrance of a wealthy *senhora* into church, attended
by her retinue of female slaves: "One carries a cloth upon
which the lady will kneel; this done, another arranges her
dress to cover her feet. A third attends to milady's head-
dress and yet a fourth scurries about greeting her mistress'
friends . . . " (quoted in Carreira 1972:292).

While masters and slaves venerated the saints in the same
religious feasts, they did so via ceremonial roles that
reflected their respective status. The landlords provided
food and drink, rode their mounts in procession (one bearing
the saint's banner), competed in displays of horsemanship,
and stood near the altar during Mass. Until the early twentieth century, the standard bearer rode up to the altar to
deliver the banner, a symbolically powerful gesture given the
status connotations of riding horses. It was as if, on feast

days, this privilege of the elite might be flaunted in the divine presence. Slaves, for their part, provided music, prepared the food, and followed the horsemen, on foot, in the procession. Role segregation was so complete that in Fogo, only a few descendants of the slaves know all the details of the parts of the rituals performed by their forbears. (See Chapter VI.)

Freyre, Tannenbaum and Elkins have all attributed to the Catholic Church a humanizing influence on the institution of slavery in Brazil, but in this case at least, her role was an ambiguous one. (See also Degler on the Church in Brazil, 1971:33-37.) The Church's apparently contradictory effects on the practice of slavery may be in part the reflection of contradictory tendencies in the ethos of Catholicism itself, such as the authoritarianism and respect for social hierarchy noted by Genovese (1971:192) that stand in contrast to a certain moral egalitarianism, whereby the proverbial rich man may have a more difficult time entering the kingdom of heaven than a poor one.

Differences between missionaries and local clergy also seem to have been at issue in the Cape Verdes, for it was only among the missionaries that we find the occasional zealot determined to baptize and catechize the slaves and to ensure that their owners would provide them with conditions allowing the observance of Catholic practice. Even in recent times, peasants tended to distinguish "foreign" (i.e., missionary) priests, whether from Portugal or elsewhere, from the *padres de terra*, or local clergy. If the former were not always exempt from charges of moral turpitude, they were usually much more insistent than the latter on the conventions of Catholic ritual. The Cape Verdean clergy tended to be a poorly educated lot, living more or less as petty *senhores* and interfering little with local ritual practices. Their personal lives, as we shall see, were often less than conducive to the clergy's assuming a role of moral and spiritual leadership.

Miscegenation

The tolerance of miscegenation in Portugal's colonies has often been viewed as a determining factor for the type of race relations that developed in such societies as Brazil. In Freyre's view, miscegenation was a fortunate consequence of Moorish cultural influences on pre-imperial Portugal, notably the practice of polygyny and the idealization of the "Moorish enchantress" (*a moura encantada*). Given this, the enervating heat of the tropics was sufficient to melt any scruples and kindle passions for slave women (1959:53-56; 1966:4-5). Hoetink's notion of "somatic norm image" is a testimony to the allure and persistence of Freyre's explanation. Hoetink proposes that the Iberians' concept of the appropriate or ideal

phenotype as considerably darker than that of northern Europeans, which thus allowed the former more acceptance of intimacy and equality, as well as sexual contact, with Africans
(1967).[9]

In fact, official tolerance of "race mixture" varied considerably in the Portuguese colonies. It was promoted as a
matter of Crown policy in humid, disease-ridden São Tomé,
where "all the unmarried men were provided with a Negress,
avowedly for breeding purposes, and a marriage seems to have
been optional" (Boxer 1963:15). But in Brazil, the Jesuit
Nobrega wrote to the king asking him to send unattached women,
"be they orphans or prostitutes," to Pernambuco, so that settlers would not have to marry Indian women (Mörner 1967:49).
Despite the Marquês de Pombal's 1755 policy of encouraging
white-Indian intermarriage, a viceroy of that time lowered an
officer's rank for "blemishing his blood" by marrying a Negro
woman (Ibid., p. 50).

Cape Verde was subject to at least one attempt by Lisbon
to curtail miscegenation. In 1620, the king ordered that the
women of ill fame who had customarily been exiled to Brazil be
thenceforth sent to Cape Verde instead, "with the objective of
having the race of mulattoes extinguished, insofar as possible" (Barcelos 1899 I: 210). Such measures amounted to too
little, too late; by 1807, mulattoes comprised 43.2 percent of
the population (from statistics in Chelmiki and Varnhagen
1841:321). Today, virtually no one in the islands can claim
unmixed lineage.

The factors cited by Freyre, among others, as causes of
miscegenation -- a shortage of white women, and the vulnerability of slave women -- were certainly present in Cape Verde.
The predominance of male over female immigrants from the
metropole must have continued well past the initial phase of
colonization, given that slave running and smuggling, rather
than agriculture, were the most lucrative activities in the
archipelago. In any case, as Degler points out, not even the
presence of a legitimate spouse was necessarily a deterrent to
the Portuguese male's promiscuity, given the machismo ethos
built into the Portuguese civil code as well as popular tradition (1971:234). A husband's infidelities were (and still
are) likely to be tolerated as long as he continued to provide
adequate support for his family. Unfortunately, such tolerance did not extend to the female slave; Carreira recounts a
case of a jealous wife gouging out the eyes of an attractive
slave girl with a fork (1972:459).

The clergy, far from condemning the *senhores*' behavior,
were wont to follow suit. Pope Gregory II complained to the
Bishop of Lisbon in 1581 that the Bishop of Santiago "lives
dishonestly in the filth of prostitution" (Barcelos 1899 I:
154). Laxity remained more the norm than the exception,[10]

save for rare individuals such as Vitoriano do Porto, Bishop
of Santiago from 1688 to 1705. This redoubtable prelate
earned the dislike of many priests and wealthy laymen by
descending upon them after nightfall and ejecting the concubines from their very beds (Barcelos 1900 II: 173).

In the normally permissive atmosphere that males in colonial Cape Verde enjoyed, sexual relationships between white
men and slave women were often matters of public knowledge.
Several governors lived openly with their mistresses; the aged
Zuzarte de Santa Maria (in office from 1741 to 1752) kept a
slave woman by whom he had two sons, and treated the children
as though legitimate (Mariano 1959:35). The fact that illegitimate filiation was public knowledge probably reinforced
stirrings of paternal conscience about the welfare of these
offspring. This seems to have been the case in several modern
instances observed during the fieldwork, where the children
were brought to live in the paternal household alongside their
lighter-complexioned half-siblings, though generally not on
completely equal footing.

That the matter was indeed one of conscience seems evident in an 1871 letter from one Cristiano of Santiago to his
brother-in-law, Julio of Fogo, whom Cristiano reprimanded for
"spreading progeny about . . . . Later on you will have to see
them badly off in this world and it will give you pain." In
what seems at first glance a rather curious sequitur, Cristiano
advises his brother-in-law to "enjoy" such women for a week
and then leave them, because "living with them is unbecoming
and people criticise it" (quoted in Carreira 1972:459). Such
brief liaisons would be less likely to result in illegitimate
offspring whose paternity could be established.

Duffy has termed the miscegenation that occurred in
Portuguese Africa a matter of "erotic expediency" that became
colonial policy only after the fact (1963:71). And, as Harris
observes, miscegenation occurred wherever slavery was practiced, in the United States and South Africa as well as in the
Portuguese colonies (1974:68-69). Attitudes toward miscegenation may have been less important in the development of racial
systems such as Cape Verde's, than the social constitution of
the "mixed-race" category. That is, what was the social fate
of the mulatto offspring of miscegenous unions?

The Mulatto in Cape Verdean Society

Treatment of mulattoes varied among Portugal's colonies
as much as did policies on miscegenation, as Boxer's *Race
Relations in the Portuguese Empire* amply demonstrates (1963).
A royal letter of 1528 declares mulattoes eligible for seats
in São Tomé's town council, "as long as they are married men
of substance" (Ibid., p. 32). But the same privilege was not

accorded them in eighteenth century Brazil, and mulattoes
there faced numerous other legal and social restrictions,
often being grouped with blacks in the wording of the law
(Ibid., p. 116). In Angola, as well, mulattoes were the
object of prejudice and discriminatory practice (Boxer 1961:
121-22).

By comparison, treatment of mulattoes in Cape Verde was
unusually benign. Legal discrimination was conspicuously
absent, and Padre Antonio Vieira's account of 1652 makes it
clear that the Church raised no color bar against black or
mulatto candidates for the priesthood. Vieira reports priests
and canons "black as jet, but so well-bred, so authoritative,
so learned . . . that they may be envied by those in our own
cathedrals at home" (quoted in Boxer 1963:14). Whatever educational institutions existed tended to be religious and
apparently nondiscriminatory on the basis of race.

The extent to which mulattoes were able to enter the
landlord class varied with the locale. This was more difficult in Santiago and Fogo because of the royal land grants,
though the missionary Barros mentions "black" (perhaps, in
fact, mulatto) slaveowners in Santiago (Carreira 1972:384).
The 1753 magistrate's report on irregularities in the inheri-
tance of land in Santiago gives the impression that in some
cases, illegitimate mulatto sons were made heirs (cf. note 3).

Census figures for 1959 show 69.6 percent of the Cape
Verdean population categorized as mulatto, the rest being
characterized as black or white. This high proportion is not
a simple reflection of the frequency of miscegenation; rather,
following Harris's discussion of mulattoes in Brazil, it is a
result of the fact that in Cape Verde, certain "interstitial"
positions were open to individuals of racially mixed background. That is, mulattoes took social and economic roles
that slaves could not perform, and eventually became a distinct, self-perpetuating category (cf. Harris 1974:84-89).
Commercial activities, especially the illegal ones that were
so important in Cape Verde, offered many such opportunities.
The *lançados* described earlier exemplify a pattern that continued throughout the colonial period, whereby a landlord-
merchant would set up an illegitimate son as a trader, to
their mutual profit. (Several such cases were noted during
the field work.) Fogo's and Brava's port records for the
nineteenth century show many traders moving between Cape Verde
and the Guinea coast who bear the surnames of leading families. According to present-day descendants, these traders
were often *filhos de fora* ["outside sons"; i.e., illegiti-
mate], as well as younger, legitimate sons of landlords.
Undoubtedly, they frequently dealt in contraband and had occasion to make use of their patrilineal kin networks that
usually included a few members of the colonial administration.
The society of Fogo, where blacks, whites and mulattoes formed

fairly distinct categories, has been portrayed by one of her
writers as having been divided into three classes until about
1930, typified by: the white in his *sobrado*, a large two-
story house with an enclosed courtyard and a verandah, analogous to the "big house" of Freyre's Brazil; the black in his
funco, a round dwelling made of stones and topped with a palm-
thatched roof; and the mulatto clerking in the shop located on
the ground floor of the *sobrado* (Sousa 1958).

Besides the existence of interstitial roles, and the
normative factors cited by Degler that made them available to
some mulatto sons of the landlords, norms of marital choice
may also have been important for the constitution of mulattoes
as a social category distinct from blacks. In contemporary
Cabo Verde, it is generally agreed that "like should marry
like," that marital partners should be roughly similar in
class, educational level and racial type (see Chapter VI). On
the premise that these norms prevailed in the past, mulattoes
probably took spouses of similarly mixed background.

Nonetheless, the nature of the local economy appears to
have been of greatest causal importance, if one compares Cape
Verde with São Tomé, another Portuguese island colony located
in the Gulf of Guinea. São Tomé's economic and social history
was generally similar to Cape Verde's until the early nineteenth century, when cacao and coffee cultivation for export
was successfully developed. This was soon followed by expropriation of the best lands from the local creole elite by
metropolitans, who began to import laborers from Angola and
Cape Verde on a contract basis. Between 1850 and 1950, the
mulatto or "mixed" population declined dramatically, while the
"black" category increased five times over (not including the
imported laborers, who were segregated from the local population). Tenreiro concludes that this increase can only be
explained by the inclusion of most of the local population,
among them many of "mixed" origin in the "black" category
(1961:110).

São Tomé might be said to have undergone the reverse of
the process Harris finds in Brazil, and that appears to have
occurred in Cape Verde; that is, in São Tomé, economic niches
for mulattoes disappeared and the category itself became much
reduced in social significance and numbers. The old elite
emigrated or was submerged in the "black" category, except for
a few who entered the governmental bureaucracy. The 6,000
"civilized natives" reported in 1900, when the total population was 10,100, included small landholders, public employees,
skilled workers and probably some household servants, and can
safely be assumed to have been mulattoes.[11] Fifty years
later, *mestiços* [i.e., mulattoes] comprised only 7.1 percent
of the population and included only 21 considered "civilized"
by the colonial regime (see chapter VII). Significantly, all
natives of São Tomé had come to be called *forros*, a term that,

in the nineteenth century, denoted freed slaves and their descendants, as distinct from the larger "mixed" sector of the population at that time.

It should not be assumed that miscegenation became less frequent; Tenreiro asserts that unions between metropolitans and local women were still common in 1950 (1961:200-1). Rather, the decline of São Tomé's mulatto category reflects profound social and economic changes. In Cape Verde, as Chapter VII shows, the last century or so of colonial rule brought new interstitial roles, i.e., new opportunities for Cape Verdeans to serve as Portugal's middlemen on the African continent, in roles somewhat analogous to those of the *lançados* of an earlier day.

Manumission

An important feature of Cape Verde's slavery regime that set the stage for abolition and race relations in the post-slavery period was the practice, apparently frequent, of manumission. In 1582, the slave population of Santiago and Fogo, the only islands fully colonized at the time, was estimated at 13,700, compared with some 400 "free married blacks" and 1,508 "neighbors and residents," probably both white and mulatto (Brásio 1964, ser. II, vol. III: 99).[12] By 1827, slaves comprised only 6.9 percent of the population, and in 1856, only 5.8 percent.

One contributing factor was the decrease in slave importations after Santiago's importance as a trading center began to decline early in the seventeenth century, and as prices and competition for slaves increased on the Guinea coast. During the era of the Company of Grão Pará and Maranhão, the cost of slaves became prohibitive, and net legal imports for the years 1756-88 totaled only 16 (Carreira 1972:388). But the dramatic reversal of the slave/free ratio over the slavery period cannot be explained by reduced importations alone. The available evidence makes it difficult to assess the relative weight of factors such as escapes and the higher mortality of slaves during famines and epidemics, but much of it suggests that manumissions were of singular importance.

The 400 "free married blacks" (*pretos forros casados*) reported in 1582 may well have been manumitted slaves; one implication of missionaries' efforts to baptize slaves was that the converts could be married in the Church. In that case, when one of the spouses was free, he or she could purchase the freedom of the other. Owners were supposed to facilitate this, but in fact they often obstructed such marriages by refusing to sell or by setting exorbitantly high prices.[13] In theory, it was possible for slaves to purchase their own freedom, though this must have been extremely difficult if the

owner refused to cooperate. As we saw earlier, any earnings
of slaves were usually absorbed by their own subsistence needs.
Those most capable of earning their freedom because of special
skills such as cooking, weaving or carpentry, had to pay higher
prices than other slaves; for example, the 1856 slave census
gives the price of a 21-to-40-year-old carpenter at 200 *milreis*. A cook of the same age category was valued at 130 *milreis*, while a male or female slave of that age group who had
no special skill was valued at 115 *milreis* (Carreira 1972:
481-82).

Probably much more common were manumissions instigated by
the owner. Freeing slaves on a holy day was an act of piety,
different only in degree from the present-day custom of showing gratitude to the saints by feeding the poor on their feast
days. *Compadrio*[godparenthood] relationships also resulted in
manumissions, and death provided yet another occasion for this
"meritorious act," as Governor Pusitch refers to it in his
1810 memoir (Ibid., p. 377). Testaments often provided for the
freeing of favorite slaves, sometimes out of gratitude for
services rendered, sometimes motivated by a sense of paternal
responsibility toward illegitimate mulatto children (whose
mothers were occasionally free as well). During the mid-
nineteenth century, one landlord of Brava's leading family,
the Martins, is said to have regularly freed slaves after they
had provided a decade of service, and to have paid for their
passage to America.

If the practice of freeing slaves promised heavenly
rewards, these only reinforced its earthly advantages for the
slaveowner. In fact, practicality was often the primary motivation, as with the slaves-turned-*lançados* or, under more com-
pelling circumstances, those freed during famines. If selling
"superfluous" slaves brought a greater immediate gain, manumission carried a certain prestige as a form of status valida-
tion for the owner. Moreover, the conditions under which manumission usually took place meant that the practice held long-
range benefits for the landlords as a class.

Slaves were usually granted their freedom with nothing
else to show for their years or service, and so they were
forced to become sharecroppers, often on the land of the former owner. If manumission was the result of the owner's testa-
ment, the new freemen sometimes emigrated to other islands to
avoid being tenants of the families they once served (Carreira
1972:377; Ribeiro 1956). Sharecroppers paid one-third to one-
half of their harvest in rent, besides providing the seeds for
sowing, an arrangement practiced until the end of the colonial
period. Freed of the slaveowner's moral obligations to provide
food, clothing and medical care, the landlord could expel
sharecroppers and raise tenants' rents at will. Contracts
were only verbal agreements, and usually for periods of only
one to three years (Carreira 1972:387). The economic risks of

agriculture, already considerable given the Cape Verdean climate, seem to have been considerably lessened for the pro-
prietors who rented to tenants or, more commonly, leased to
sharecroppers, as compared to having the land worked by slaves.
One may surmise that the two or three slaves held by most
owners at the end of the slavery period were probably house
slaves rather than agricultural laborers.

The escaped slave was a marginal, an outcast from respectable society; from the many accounts of the fugitives' van-
dalism and thievery, they appear to have been beyond the control of the law.[*]   In contrast, the manumitted sharecroppers
remained a prop of traditional owner-slave patterns of interaction. With their livelihood subject to the landlord's
caprice, it is little wonder that freed blacks continued to
show slavish deference to their former masters, of the sort
described in the following passage:

> The whites were very respected and vene-
> rated by the blacks, who remained their
> tenants; . . . a black, upon sighting a
> white a stone's throw away, dismounted
> if he were on horseback and waited for
> the white to pass . . . no black entered
> the city on horseback (Anonymous 1784:
> 19-20).[14]

Slave Resistance and Rebellion

The geography of the archipelago hardly favored slave
escapes or rebellions; most of the islands were too small or
too flat to offer safe refuge to runaways, and desertion on
foreign vessels usually resulted in re-enslavement. However,
pirate raids provided occasion for slaves in Fogo, Santiago
and Santo Antão to elude their owners and settle in the inaccessible highlands of the interior. Escapees could often
count on the assistance of free blacks along the way.
(Barcelos gives a summary of an 1804 Governor's Report on the
problem, 1905 III: 173.)

Fears of a general slave uprising, though mostly unful-
filled, can be understood as reflecting the whites' perceptions of their numerical weakness in comparison to the slaves,
free blacks and land-poor mulattoes. Slave merchants argued
in a 1699 letter to the king that religious instruction for
captives awaiting transshipment was dangerous because it would
lead to a bottleneck of slaves in transit "in a land where

---

[*]This pertains particularly to Santiago.

most of the inhabitants are black" (Carreira 1972:277). Perhaps another cause for alarm lay in the fact that, at least in
Santiago, many slaves bore arms because of the constant inter-
necine warfare between rival landlords. Barcelos writes with
indignation of the "outrages" committed by these small armies
of pistol-bearing slaves, "even in the city" in the early
eighteenth century. "In the houses of prominent families it
was considered unusual if the servants at table were not armed
with one or two pistols . . ." (1900 II: 232). At about the
same period, whites felt threatened by the celebrations of the
feast of the Holy Cross (*Santa Cruz*), in which a ritual "king"
and "officers" rode horseback as their followers came behind,
on foot, all of the participants wearing masks and speaking a
dialect of Crioulo that whites could not understand. Dom
Joao V of Portugal sent an alarmed message to the governor in
1723, urging the prohibition of such festivities because "the
blacks, being superior in numbers" and "more barbarous by
nature," could easily take control of the island (Ibid., p.
244).

The nearest realization of such paranoiac nightmares was
the restiveness that preceded abolition, coinciding with the
liberal rumblings in Portugal that resulted in the Revolution
of 1820. In 1822, slaves and sharecroppers united against a
particularly oppressive landlord, and complained to the authorities (Barcelos 1905 III: 278-79). The year 1835 saw an
aborted slave revolt in Santiago; not long before, two landlords of that island had been killed by their slaves, who had
escaped the death penalty prescribed by law. "Because of this
impunity, now they have attempted a general massacre of whites
and landlords," claimed the principal landlords in a letter to
the governor (reproduced in Carreira 1972:503-4). Their fears
were exacerbated by the fact that soldiers in the colony's rag-
tag army (mostly composed of recruits from the free black and
mulatto peasantry) had known of the plot and maintained its
secrecy. Tied to the slaves by bonds of kinship, and subject
to conditions in the army that were little better than those
of slavery, they had hoped to escape to the interior themselves if the plot had succeeded (Barcelos 1910 IV: 224-25).

Abolition

In 1858, the abolition of slavery was set for twenty
years thence; in 1869, the slaves were formally freed, but in
their new status as *libertos* were obliged to work for their former masters until 1878. This period of indenture actually
ended in 1874 in Cape Verde, and two years later in the other
colonies. No violence or discernible resistance marred this
process in Cape Verde, while in Angola and Mozambique, abolition was met with "consternation, resentment and a grim deter-
mination not to comply" (Duffy 1963:96).

In contrast, the freed slaves of Cape Verde (who numbered only 5,182 in 1856) had no indigenous mode of life, nor any vast, uncolonized interior to which to return. Like those manumitted earlier, they had little alternative but to share-crop or rent from the landlords, who continued to manage local affairs with little outside interference. Genovese's remarks on the peaceful abolition process of Brazil's northeast, where some sugar lords had even supported abolition, are pertinent: "The transition to ostensibly free labour was in fact a tran-sition to various forms of dependency that had long before struck roots alongside slavery itself" (1969:91).

The case for abolition as a form of economic relief for the slaveowners is easier to make for Cabo Verde than for most societies. By the mid-nineteenth century, the large estates of Fogo and Santiago had long been in decline. Cotton was no longer grown in Fogo; drought and the frequently inept admin-istration of properties, along with the other economic prob-lems of the archipelago, had all combined to weaken whatever bases of a plantation system had ever existed. Abolition can hardly be said to have caused an upheaval in Cape Verdean eco-nomic and social structure. Rather, it represented the culmi-nation of the long tradition of frequent manumissions which had enabled the landlords to surmount the contradictions between their seigneurial pretentions and their inadequate means of sustaining them.

Conclusion

If any slavery regime could qualify as mild, the Cape Verdean would merit the title even more readily than that of northeastern Brazil, depicted in Freyre's 1933 classic. The low number of slaves per household, the widespread practice of manumission, and the influence of the Church, however limited, all contrast with the situation that prevailed in the United States. There, where no universalistic religion placed slave and master on the same plane of common humanity, breakup of families by sale was unimpeded by religious teachings and largely unhindered by law (Genovese 1972:52-53); manumission was not given religious sanction as in Catholic societies, and was in fact forbidden or restricted by law in some states (Genovese 1974:399-400). The states varied as to whether, or in what legal contexts, slaves were considered persons rather than things, mere chattels.

As mentioned at the beginning of this chapter, a number of scholars, inspired by Freyre's studies of Brazil, have examined Iberian and Anglo slavery regimes in order to better understand how differences between contemporary racial systems developed. Certain authors have criticized Freyre and his successors in this field for overreliance on religious and cultural explanations, to the neglect of economic factors;

e.g., Degler (1971), Mintz (1971b), and Harris (1974). In a review of Elkins's *Slavery*, Mintz has pointed out the cruelties associated with the sugar boom in nineteenth-century Cuba, so extreme that slaveholders of the American South could take smug satisfaction in the comparison with their own regime (1961; see also Genovese 1974:59). That "Iberian" slavery varied according to local economic circumstances at any given time is also suggested by some of the remarks made in this chapter about differences between some of the Portuguese colonies concerning miscegenation, the rights of mulattoes, and so on. Davis has gone a step further, criticizing the logical bases of the problem as posed: "I suspect that future historians will be less certain about the importance of slavery in understanding post-emancipation patterns of racial oppression" (1974:9). Davis's call for greater emphasis on the comparative study of post-emancipation patterns, such as sharecropping, suggests that we should, at the very least, avoid assuming a deterministic relationship between patterns of slavery and latter-day race relations. Earlier in this chapter, it was noted that the position of manumitted individuals was little different than it had been under slavery, and that their livelihood was often more precarious. Similarly, abolition did not change the fundamental economic and political condition of the former slaves, a theme to which we return in the next chapter.

Notes

1. Freyre's characterization of Cape Verdean culture as "solidly African" under a "veneer" of European institutions evoked criticism from the colony's intellectuals, e.g., Silva (1956). It is interesting that Freyre remarked the "shame" surrounding African cultural traits, without, however, perceiving any connection between this and the Portuguese colonialism he admired.

2. These were called *morgadios* in Santiago, *capelas* [chapels] in Fogo. The two types of grant entailed similar privileges in practice, though the *capelas* were originally associated with various saints, to whom the lands technically belonged. They were given in usufruct to the family responsible for maintaining religious practices in honor of the saint (Carreira 1972:376). The *capelas* extended from a broad base at the shoreline, becoming narrower as they converged at the cone of Fogo's volcano, the gradations of altitude allowing each *capela* to produce a great variety of crops.

3. A magistrate wrote in 1753 of the "abominable and scandalous" practice of passing these lands to "any sort of heir," even those born of adulterous, sacrilegious or incestuous unions (Carreira 1972:379). When Governor Marinho demanded to see the titles of Santiago's *morgadios* in 1835, the landholders were unable to produce them (Chelmiki and Varnhagen 1841:152).

4. Not only mulattoes, but even white outsiders were rigorously excluded: "There rarely exists in the bureaucracy . . . agriculture or commerce . . . any Europeans or even distinguished sons of the other islands" (Martins 1891:101).

5. The "lack and total abandonment" of public education was such that by the nineteenth century, very few had any schooling, "including the whites themselves" (Chelmiki and Varnhagen 1841:192; see also Lima 1844, Part 2: 111-12).

6. Holder of the title to one of Santiago's *morgadios*; often, however, the term was extended to any large landholder.

7. For example, the *limbabo* which gripped the victim fast at the neck, or the *anjinhos* [little angels] that held the hands tightly, crushing the thumbs (Ramos 1951:34).

8. In 1690, the governor reported that several years of drought had claimed some 4,000 victims, most of them slaves (Duncan 1972:235-36).

9.   For a different point of view, see Bastide (1961) and
     Mintz's critique of Hoetink (1971b).

10. Carreira cites the Provision of 1792, which establishes
     the legal rights, long recognized by custom, of the
     heirs of "sacrilegious" unions, i.e., those involving
     priests or friars (1976:23).

11. These were distinguished in the census from "black free-
     men" (cf. Tenreiro 1961:87).

12. According to Carreira (1972:287).

13. A royal letter of 1701 directs that slaveowners should
     cease to obstruct marriages between black freemen and
     slave women, which they had been doing by setting exorbi-
     tant prices for the women's freedom (quoted in Carreira
     1972:282).

14. Nearly identical observations are made by Chelmiki and
     Varnhagen (1841:325).

VI

RACE RELATIONS UNDER COLONIALISM:
THE POST-SLAVERY PERIOD

Introduction

The peaceful and gradual quality of the abolition process
derived, we have argued, from the fact that it posed no immediate threat to the landlord class. Here our examination of
latter-day race relations begins by noting some of the contin-
uities in social and economic patterns persisting from the
slavery era until the end of Portuguese rule. Next, the study
of racial terminology and racial classification in everyday
life brings our comparison of the Cape Verdean racial system
with that of Brazil into the present. In both cases the
racial lexicon is extensive, comprising many different terms
that are applied in various ways according to the circumstances. Yet attention to the specific social contexts of the use
of racial categories indicates that not only phenotype but
sometimes genealogy as well can be an important criterion in
classification, contrary to what some have suggested is the
case in Brazil.

The study of how different racial terms are used and the
valuations attached to them reveals an aesthetic that deni-
grates features considered African, despite the Portuguese
colonizers' well-known appreciation for *mulata* beauty. This
brings us into the realm of the colonial ideology of race,
whereby notions of culture served to legitimize what were in
essence, we argue, racially based judgments of value. The
latter part of the chapter reveals how racial barriers were
subtly but consistently enforced and reaffirmed in social
practice. Such barriers, we propose, were most evident in
areas of behavior such as courtship and marriage, where the
privileges of the mostly white elite were at issue.

The Living Past

Though slavery had been abolished nearly one hundred
twenty years before, it remained a recent and personal memory
even in the last years of colonial rule. In this face-to-face
society, many people could still remember whose ancestors were
the slaves of whom, and a few households still employed the
desdendants of those who had worked there as slaves. In one

such case, a servant girl was seduced by her employer, who initially refused to acknowledge paternity of the child born of this liaison. The irony was that, given the habit of slaves taking the surnames of their masters, the child would have borne the father's name in any case.

The essential continuity of pre-abolition social and economic patterns until independence in 1975 made slavery more than simply a part of a well-remembered past. Sharecropping patterns changed little over the intervening period; up to half of the produce still went to the landlord. The rental system, most common in Santiago where absentee landlordism was often the case, was, if anything, even more prejudicial to the tenant's interests. Until 1969, rent could be extracted even when drought had ruined the harvest; after that date, provision was made for reductions in such cases (*Decreto* No. 47314, *Portaria* No. 7873), but with little practical effect.

By many accounts collected in the field research, destitute tenants and other creditors of the merchant-landlords (who also acted as moneylenders) were subject to intimidation and sometimes violence (cf. Carreira 1972:389). Their aggressors had little to fear from the colonial authorities, most of whom were Cape Verdean sons of the old landlord families. The *administrador* [administrator] of the island or district would be loath to risk offending such respectable citizens, most of them members of the *Câmara* [council] of the principal town of the district, the only body representing citizens under the colonial government. In practice, though no longer by law, civil authorities usually reinforced traditional patterns of race and class differentiation in exercising their power: the black or mulatto peasant or laborer was as vulnerable to brutality from the police, under the direction of the administrator, as from the landlords (as I had several occasions to witness).

The material conditions of daily life had changed little since the end of slavery for the approximately 90 percent of Cape Verdeans working as peasants, laborers or fishermen. Except for Brava, where emigrants supply used clothing sent from the United States, scarcity of clothing was common, most adults owning two or three outer garments and many children, only one. One could see children shivering in burlap sacks in the mountains of Santo Antão, where temperatures are often cool. The normal diet still consisted of the same staples as that of the slaves: yams, beans, maize, manioc and potatoes, with maize flour playing an important role. This was steamed to make *cûs-cûs*, of bread-like consistency; other important dishes included *djagacida*, a corn and beans mixture, and *cachupa*, based on a variety of beans and corn, with meat in its richer versions. For most of the population, meat (including poultry) and fish were too costly for more than occasional consumption. Fish, in fact, was as costly as meat

and just as difficult for inhabitants of the interior to
obtain. Only about six months out of the year are good for
fishing in the waters near shore. During this time, small,
three-man rowboats work these waters and, by custom, one-third
of the catch goes to the owner (usually a local merchant),
another third goes "for the boat," and the remaining third is
divided among the crew. Fishermen rarely use their share for
personal consumption, instead giving it to the women of the
household, who sell it in order to procure more grain, which
better "deceives the mouth" (*enganar a boca*) by relieving hunger more quickly.

Habits of courtesy and propriety signaled the perpetua-
tion of a social hierarchy little changed since abolition.
Peasant men were likely to step aside and tip their hats at an
oncoming car, a custom reminiscent of the deference patterns
of black freemen remarked by earlier observers (see Chapter
V). The kiss of greeting and departure in everyday encounters
between women was accorded only to those of similar status,
however intimate and warm the relationship. A white might
capture a black's attention by touching or more forceful physical contact, whereas the reverse was considered offensive and
impertinent (*atrevido*). "That nigger had the nerve to grab me
by the arm!" exclaimed a merchant -- whose response was a violent cuff. A physician who had once worked in Brava was
widely praised because "he didn't mind touching us colored
people." In Fogo, where the social hierarchy had changed
least since abolition, one elderly *fidalga* (noblewoman), now
living in penury in her crumbling *sobrado*, still adhered to
the custom of her youth by washing her hands after any contact
with an "inferior."

Because of the near-isomorphism of the class and racial
hierarchies, discussed more fully below, these status-
differentiating behaviors tended to serve indirectly as racial
boundaries, in the absence of legalized color bars. Even
during the slavery era, the dominance of Cape Verde's landlord
class was never sustained by segregationist or other racial-
discriminatory laws, nor did there exist a legal hierarchy of
racial types as in Cuba (Martinez-Allier 1974:71-76). Though
travel permits and other legal documents gave racial descriptions, these did not constitute fixed legal identities. The
character of Cape Verdean slavery, as described in the preceding chapter, along with the absence of legal color bars,
might suggest an extremely fluid racial system, and in certain
senses, this was indeed the case. One aspect of this system
was a complex set of racial categories that might be applied
to individuals in differing ways, according to the social context. Until now, we have had recourse to the tripartite
classification of "black" (*preto*), "white" (*branco*) and
"mulatto" (mixed/*mixto*) that prevails not only in historical

descriptions and documents, but also in a number of social situations, some of them specified below. On other occasions, though, a great many other categories might come into play.

Racial Terminology

A picture test devised by Marvin Harris for use in Brazil proved useful in eliciting racial categories.[1] One hundred adults in Brava, evenly divided by sex, were shown 72 full-face drawings that included various combinations of three skin tones, and two each of hair, lip, nose and sex type. After glancing at the deck, participants were asked to name the type (*tipo*) of each person depicted. The nature of the drawings unavoidably affected the testing situation. Being done in black and white, they do not show differences of eye color, a factor that field observations suggest may sometimes be used as a criterion of classification. Sanjek mentions this problem in his use of the same test in a village in northeastern Brazil (1971:3). One may question, as well, how faithfully differences of skin tone can be rendered by shading alone. Although the drawings present faces of uniform, neutral expression (several are reproduced in Harris, 1970, and in Whitten and Szwed, 1970), respondents sometimes personalized them, as certain of the remarks quoted below will bear out. Since they were originally designed for use in Brazil, some of the drawings depict Amerindian physical traits. Interestingly, Cape Verdeans had no difficulty in finding terms for any of the physical types depicted, suggesting a certain extensibility in their racial category system that allows "coverage" of new and unprecedented cases.

Given that the test was fairly time-consuming, the best location for administering it turned out to be near the medical clinic, where people passed the time while friends and relatives awaited the physician's attention inside the building. On a few occasions, other locations were used, mostly private homes, to provide a better cross-section of social class among the respondents. A photograph was taken of each participant, so as to have a record of his/her own physical type and as a reward for taking part in the test.

The drawings, designed to appear impersonal and standardized in expression, were ascribed a personal identity and history by many of the test subjects. Some made elaborate speculations on possible origins. ("Maybe his father was a European and his mother a black or a very dark *mulata*.") Others made humorous, but revealing, commentaries. ("Mother of God, did you ever see such a nose?" "Poor thing, with that hair, he can only be *mulato claro*, not white.") One woman shyly explained, "he's really *negro* but that's not a nice thing to say, so I'm calling him *mulato sucuro*" [from the Portuguese *oscuro*, "dark].[2] Several others made similar allusions to considerations of politeness during the picture test.

In all, 140 different terms for physical types were collected, eliminating duplications based on sex (i.e., *moreno/a*
are counted as one item). This is considerably less than the
492 terms collected by Harris in Brazil, and somewhat more
than the 116 collected by Sanjek, though with a small number
of respondents. The difference in the number of terms collected by Harris and found in Brava probably says less about
differences in the two racial systems than those of procedure
and analysis used in each case. Harris counts male and female
variants as two different terms; by that approach, the number
of terms found in Brava would have been 229.[3] Also, Harris's
findings are based on use of the picture test in several different regions of Brazil; the total number may say very little
about the terminology current in any given locale, and still
less about the relation between racial categories and other
aspects of social structure (cf. Chapter VIII; see also
Machado 1981).

Sanjek (1971) finds it useful to look as base terms (e.g.,
moreno) and their modified forms (e.g., *moreno claro*) as clusters. Labelle, in a study of Haitian racial terminology, suggests that modified forms be considered as referring to subtypes of the basic category (1979:103-4). In Cabo Verde, however, modified forms are not so used. Such terms are always
formed by a term referring to color and a modifying term or
phrase referring either to a gradation of color (e.g., *claro*,
sucuro) or another feature, usually hair type. To presume that
color completely overrides other criteria seems unwarranted in
the Cape Verdean case. *Branco di cabelo crespo* [white with
frizzy hair] does not necessarily refer to a semantic subset of
"white"; rather, it appears, from subjects' remarks while
classifying the drawings, as a possible alternative to terms
such as *mulato claro, mixto*, etc. Respondents often remarked
that *feiçoes* [features, i.e., hair, nose and lip form] are more
important than color for determining a person's "type," though
this was occasionally disputed. The existence of sixty-two
compound forms making reference to hair type, as well as general observations, suggest that hair is seen as a key feature
in racial classification. In all, twenty-one terms for different hair types were collected during the course of the field
work, such as *fino, gudi* or *bom, em grau* [fine, good, and
grainy, respectively]. Noses, another racially significant
feature, may also be described by a number of terms, eleven of
which were collected, such as *tambor* [drum], i.e., large and
full, and *batata* [potato].

Cape Verdean racial classification has an idiosyncratic
aspect; some individuals habitually use the term *bermedjo*
[from the Portuguese *vermelho*, "red"] for persons with fair
skin and frizzy hair. Others said that they knew this term,
but usually used *branco di cabeca seca* [white with dry hair],
and that the two expressions "mean the same thing." Now and
then, some individuals used terms of their own invention; one

man classified some of the drawings as *preto furrado* [freed black], to the amusement of nearby family members, who explained that this was "his name" for a certain type.

Just as important as terminological variety and disagreement is the fact that twenty-five respondents used only three terms in the picture test, though which three and how they were applied could vary. That is, one might use *branco, preto, mixto,* and another, *branco, mulato, negro,* and so on. The high frequency of tripartite classification seems due to the historical importance of three broad racial divisions, particularly in the islands of Sotavento. Brava developed in the shadow of her larger neighbor, Fogo, and was ruled by factors (*feitores*) from that island's landlord class until 1756 (Barcelos 1905 III: 30). Fogo's plantation society was clearly divided into three class/racial groupings until the 1930s (Sousa 1958; Monteiro 1960).

Racial Classification

To describe racial terminology as discussed so far is but the beginning of an understanding of racial classification. Hymes has proposed that understanding any domain of meaning requires examination not only of the structure of language, but also of the context of its use (1964:67). In that light, the picture test situation constitutes but one type of social context for the use of racial terms and, for these subjects, a rather unusual one, defined by factors such as audience, relationship between interviewer and subject, and the subject's prior experience of interview-like situations. (In this case, such experiences had usually occurred in the course of dealings with authority figures, such as government bureaucrats, physicians, and so on.)

Similarly, many factors are likely to influence racial classification in everyday life, besides the various phenotypical criteria. These may include attributes of the individual being categorized (ancestry, wealth, community status), as well as contextual factors (e.g., audience, relationship between the classifier and the individual classified). In Cabo Verde, as in Brazil, a person's status in the community can affect his or her classification, so that a wealthy person of dark complexion may be termed *branco/a* (cf. Harris 1974: 57-59). Just as Brazilians say, "Money whitens," so Cape Verdeans refer to certain persons as *branco de dinheiro* [white by money]. The phrase, in fact, suggests by implication that there are different types of whiteness whose distinction could become pertinent in certain contexts, which is, in fact, the case.

Personal relationships can affect classification, as an occurrence in Brava illustrates. A certain man was walking

from the town of Nova Sintra to an upland hamlet called Mato.
On his way he came upon two small boys who began to harass
him, throwing stones at him. Furious, he shouted imprecations
at the boys, calling them *pretos*. On arriving at his friend's
house in Mato, the traveler learned that one of his young tor-
mentors was the son of his host. "I called your son *preto*,"
he declared, "but for the sake of our friendship I take it
back -- he's *mulato sucuro*! [dark mulatto]."

Politeness usually calls for avoidance of using certain
terms to describe others in their presence that might, however, be used in their absence. Except to tease or insult,
people are rarely called *preto* or *negro* to their faces, and in
the case of friendship, perhaps not even in their absence.
"She's really *preta*, but it's not nice to say so, so we call
her *mulata*," one women said of a friend. As noted earlier,
some mentioned such considerations in response to the picture
test.

Although multi-category systems of racial classification
such as Brazil's have been portrayed as emphasizing the criterion of phenotype to the exclusion of descent (Harris, for
example, speaks of the "absence of a descent rule" in Brazil,
1974:56-59), the latter is far from irrelevant in Cabo Verde.
In any town or village, everyone's genealogy is common knowledge, and slave ancestry remains a social stigma whose importance varies according to context. "So-and-so (phenotypically
and according to prestige/wealth considerations, *branco*), is
not really white, but we don't mention his background." One
man said of his family, "We are really *mixtos*, but we never
served in anyone's *quintal*." [The *quintal* is the interior
courtyard where most heavy domestic labor is done.] Discussions of genealogy are potentially embarrassing and thus to be
avoided, although a few see themselves as having something to
gain in the way of support of a claimed racial identity. Some
descendants of the landlord class maintain a lively interest
in their genealogies, though others mock and sometimes dispute
their claims to "pure" European descent.

Self-classification is a particularly delicate matter,
since the same criteria used to justify classifications may
also be used to discredit them. When categorizing themselves,
as participants in the picture test were asked to do, some
attempted to explain possible discrepancies between their own
categorization and that imputed to me or others. Women would
raise their skirts or their sleeves to show that the suntanned
parts of the body normally in view provide misleading information as to racial categorization. A nose described as
batatinha [little potato] would be used to explain that the
speaker is "not really white," but rather *morena clara*.
Alternatively, nose form would be discounted as unimportant,
since "even metropolitans have noses like this these days.
There aren't many noble noses (*narizes fidalgos*) around these
days."

In self-categorization, the genealogical knowledge of others becomes a mine of potentially discreding information. Several individuals termed themselves *moreno*, though I had only heard them called *branco* by others and would have so categorized them myself, on the basis of phenotype alone. When I mentioned my puzzlement, they responded with references to ancestry; e.g., "My mother is not really white, because her grandmother was *mulata*." In another instance, the wife of a leading merchant took pains to explain that her children were *morenos*, not from African but from Moorish (i.e., Portuguese) ancestry.

A story told in Fogo illustrates the perils of self-categorization. A newly arrived Protestant clergyman was giving his first sermon in the town of São Felipe and began to expound on the love of God for all mankind, "*branco, preto* and *moreno* like myself." This provoked great hilarity among his audience, because the man was of very dark complexion. From then on, he was known as *moreno-como-eu* [*moreno*-like-myself].

If many factors enter into racial classification, what determines which will be decisive? I believe that the answer must be sought in the social function of the particular act of classification. When accurate physical description is called for (as, for example, when I asked for help in locating an individual with whom I was unacquainted), classification is likely to reveal consideration of phenotypical details; e.g., "light mulatto with wiry hair" (*mulato claro di cabeca seca*). Other factors are excluded for the moment, but may become relevant in another context. A phrase such as *gente branca* [white people] can normally be taken as a class designation.

When social exclusivity is at issue, persons normally termed white on the basis of phenotype or community status may be labeled in some other way that takes into account non-white ancestry; e.g., as *mulato, mixto*, or *preto*. As discussed later in this chapter, ancestry was found to be a consideration in situations where the class position of the light-complexioned elite is at stake, such as courtship and marriage.

The social functions of the classifying act affect not only the category used, but the number of racial categories that serve as a frame of reference. Certain individuals who used a great variety of terms to categorize the drawings could be heard on other occasions classifying without regard for fine distinctions of phenotype, using phrases such as "that *mulato*," or "that *preto*." Asked who had attended a party in a nearby house, a young woman who had responded with several dozen different terms in the picture test replied, "oh, just some *pretos and mulatos*." "There are hardly any white folk left here," confided a woman from one of Fogo's old families, "just *negros*." [The closest translation of this term is the

English epithet, "nigger."] In other words, the fact of having access to a racial classification system of many categories does not mean that a "system" of only two or three cannot
be used on certain occasions.

Racial Ideology

It is evident that terms such as *preto* and *branco* do more
than simply describe physical appearance. Racial terms may be
used, for example, to tease or insult, or alternatively, to
show respect. Furthermore, connotations of origin, traits of
character and even moral worth may be associated with racial
terms: the everyday uses and meanings of these terms cannot
be understood without reference to the images, beliefs and
stereotypes that made up part of the dominant racial ideology
under colonialism: that is, the ideology of race that
appeared most prevalent under colonialism, and that was promoted by the colonial apparatus, its press, and its educational
system. It did not enjoy complete or universal acceptance;
Chapter VII takes up the theme of counterideological responses
in popular culture and spontaneous political action.

Certain racial terms make an explicit association between
physical type and place of origin; e.g., *africano*, *preto di
Guinē*, and *tipo europeo* [European type]. The physical features considered diagnostic racial criteria were often explicitly interpreted as signs of African or European origin;
wide lips and frizzy hair were taken as evidence of African
ancestry, however distant, while thin lips and straight hair
indicated at least partially European origins (cf. the discussion of "noble" noses, above). On several occasions, I was
told that my dark hair showed that I, too, must have some
remote African ancestry. Such associations of physical traits
with place are, of course, by no means innocuous. Many popular phrases imply an aesthetic whereby "African" features are
denigrated as intrinsically ugly, and "European" ones are considered "good," "correct," "right," or even "clean." This was
not unequivocally accepted in all cases. "Isn't she pretty?"
a woman was heard to ask of a man looking at the photograph of
a girl in her late teens. "Well," he conceded, "she's white."

"African" features, on the other hand, are "wrong,"
"ugly," "not right," or "not correct." In a household where I
lived for a time, a small boy about four years old petulantly
called his mother "ugly . . . because you're brown" (*castanha*).
His remarks evoked amusement because *castanha* is a color term
normally applied to objects, not people. Yet, even in his
error, he revealed an understanding of the values attached to
racial designations. Popular phrases referring to miscegenation are also illustrative: a light-skinned woman who bears a
child by a darker man is said to be "mixing up the race"

(*trança raça*), while a dark woman who bears a white man's child is "fixing up the race" (*compo raça*).

Terms for racial classification and for describing features considered racially significant do not refer to a neutral continuum of categories, but rather to a value-laden hierarchy in which "white" skin and features are aesthetically superior to "black" ones. Differences of opinion may arise over the place of any one type in the hierarchy of racial categories; for example, some argued that *negro bermedjo* [red nigger] is a "worse" or "uglier" type than *preto* or *negro*, while others argued the contrary. (The first term refers to someone of light or pinkish complexion, whose features are otherwise considered "African.") And, as we have seen, disagreement exists over which feature is most significant for racial categorization.

The fact that color is but one of several traits considered racially diagnostic is crucial for understanding the Cape Verdean appreciation of *morena* beauty. Indeed, the woman of medium-dark complexion is often much admired, a fact that might seem to lend credence to the much-vaunted Portuguese susceptibility to the "dusky enchantress" who makes her appearance in Freyre's work and later, in theoretical fancy-dress, so to speak, in Hoetink's study of race in the Caribbean. But in Cabo Verde, and possibly in Brazil as well, the beauty of the *morena* is seen to rest precisely in the combination of her tawny complexion and "right" features. In other words, the conventional admiration for the *morena* is not necessarily contradictory to the basically anti-African quality of the colonial aesthetic.

Aesthetic valuations of this sort constitute an incursion of political realities into the innermost reaches of privacy, the relationship of persons to their own bodies. Fanon has described eloquently the profound self-denigration of the colonized, who view themselves as well as others through the perspective of a racist aesthetic (1967). As Goffman puts it, "Shame becomes a central possibility, arising from the individual's perception of one of his attributes as being a defiling thing to possess, and one he can readily see himself as not possessing" (1963:7).

Acceptance of a "stigmatized" (to use Goffman's term) identity can take a variety of forms, such as joking about the attribute supposed to be discrediting. "I'm black, but I'm sweet," men might say in a half-flirtatious way, or "I'm black and ugly," delivered with a laugh and spoken in fun. Another way to deal with the undesired attribute is to disguise or minimize it, as some men did with hair they did not like, by keeping it very short. Women might wear theirs in rollers most of the time to make it straighter, or use straightening treatments and complexion-lightening lotions if they could afford them. Photographs, a classic occasion for "impression management" (cf. Goffman 1959:208 passim), can become so in an added sense when color is at issue. Many times I was cautioned when taking a photograph, "Don't let me come out too black!"

The political implications of this racial aesthetic became readily apparent in the few instances that it was defied. Students coming home from university in Lisbon with natural ("Afro") hairstyles risked harassment by police and administrators. Their detractors among the elite qualified them as not only "ugly" but "shameless," a particularly significant epithet in the Portuguese context (see below).

"Culture" and Racial Ideology

The notion of culture was of central ideological importance for Portuguese colonialism. Marcelo Caetano, later to succeed Salazar, expressed the official position when he asserted that

> . . . the Portuguese colonial administration has for its object a spiritual assimilation of its native populations. Although respecting the modus vivendi of the natives, the Portuguese have always endeavoured to impart their faith, their culture and their civilization to them, thus calling them into the Lusitanian community (1951:34).

According to Overseas Minister Silva Cunha, in a passage recalling Freyre (cf. Chapter V):

> While the Portuguese colonial expansion had the predominant character of a crusade, the expansion of other colonising powers was born as a commercial enterprise . . . . The form by which Portuguese colonisation began, the character it took from the beginning and maintained . . . defended us from the vices affecting the colonial projects of other peoples (1960: 59-60).

Such interpretations of Portuguese imperialism invariably refer back to the "Line of Demarcation" decreed by Pope Alexander VI in 1493, giving Portugal rights to exploit and settle certain areas of the world, with Spain receiving such rights to other areas.

The exclusively religious inspiration attributed to Portuguese colonialism, which many writers have called into question (e.g., Boxer 1973; Ferreira 1974), was supposed to explain its allegedly non-racist character. In Cunha's words:

> Never did we see local populations as simply objects of domination and exploitation. Never did we treat them with an overweening concept of racial superiority. We saw them always as a wellspring of souls to conquer, as potential shareholders in the nation needing only to be educated, *policed* . . . to enjoy the status of full citizenship (1960 I: 60; emphasis added).

Such cozy myths of Portugal's "civilizing mission" rest on the tacit assumption that European cultural patterns are superior to African ones, thus establishing an association between African origins, blackness, and cultural inferiority. As one student of Portuguese colonialism in Angola put it, the emphasis on "culture" as a criterion of equality "made it possible to speak of the equality of races and at the same time furnish a theoretical basis for not practicing it" (Santos 1979:23).

Notions about "culture" also held a central place in folk expressions of the dominant racial ideology. Expressions of popular attitudes about Crioulo, the Cape Verdean creole language, provide illustration. Crioulo is explicitly associated with blackness in popular phrases that refer to it as *lingua di preto* or *lingua di negro* [blacks' language or niggers' language].[4] Not only the Portuguese, but also most Cape Verdeans, considered it "only a dialect," a corrupt and inadequate vehicle of expression, while Portuguese, by contrast, was "prettier," "finer," "more agreeable." As Memmi, writing from his experience of French colonialism in Tunisia, sees it, "the colonised's mother tongue, that which is sustained by his feelings, emotions and dreams, that in which his kindness and wonder are expressed . . . is precisely the one which is least valued" (1965:107).

Virtually any cultural form believed to be of African origin constituted a sign of backwardness; at the same time, any form considered primitive was assumed to be African. Cape Verdean women have traditionally smoked clay pipes, a custom said to have been brought by African slaves; some peasant women continue to do so, though today's pipes are likely to be imported from the United States. Except in the most isolated villages, few smoke in public, for this would stigmatize them as *atrasadas* [backward]. Most seemed embarrassed if a stranger came upon them while they were smoking, and would put the pipe out of sight. Similarly, wearing the traditional kerchief (*lenço*) is a sign of slave forbears and low social origins. Most women wear such a head covering while doing household tasks, though some deny this. Many would be ashamed (*ter vergonha*) to be photographed thus. "No one in my family ever wore a kerchief outside the house," declared one. Nevertheless, when I happened upon women wearing kerchiefs who had previously denied doing so, they did not seem particularly discomfited. And when cigarettes were offered, those who had been smoking pipes were content to retrieve them. This suggested that the initial behavior had been stereotyped responses, or related to considerations of propriety, rather than a manifestation of deeply felt valuations.

Use of the *lenço* was uncommon among upper-class women, though its folkloric value was recognized. A much-admired set of postcards printed by the government c. 1964 depicts nine different women, each wearing the kerchief tied in the fashion of her own island. This, along with differences of cuisine and dialect, is seen as a mark of each island's cultural distinctiveness. The postcards were issued to mark the visit of Americo Tomas, the president of Portugal, at a time when the colonial regime began to encourage folkloric manifestations, including some that had previously been suppressed.

Carrying objects on the head and walking barefoot were regarded both as signs of poverty and as African holdovers. Belief in magic and witchcraft, though widely held, were disparaged as "African," as were the wearing of amulets, and such clearly Mediterranean elements as belief in the evil eye (*mal di odjo*)[5] and the seven days of *garda-cabeca* [guarding the head][6] during which the newborn is protected from evil influences by the vigilance and prayers of close relatives. In fact, however, all of these customs, with the exception of pipe-smoking by women, can be found in rural Portugal as well as in Africa. The folk ethnology that ascribed them African origin expressed on the popular level the colonialist ideology whereby civilization was synonymous with metropolitan culture.

One writer has suggested that any dominant racial category faces the dual problem of preventing biological dilution, on the one hand, and cultural dilution on the other (Szwed 1975). Neither was successfully avoided by Cabo Verde's white landlord class. If genealogical amnesia (the selective forgetting of one's ancestors) might disguise the first, the second was all too evident. Crioulo is the first language of all Cape Verdean children, and the only one in which most will ever be fully at ease. Portuguese observers of an earlier day were dismayed to find that not only whites born in the islands, but even recent arrivals from the metropole, had adopted Crioulo (Chelmiki and Varnhagen 1841:196; Lima 1844, Part 2: 109). Symbolic of the cultural borrowing from both Africa and Europe is the fact that corn is ground for the distinctive dishes of Cabo Verde with both the Iberian handmill and the African mortar and pestle.

'Virtual Moral Ascriptions'

Szwed has argued that any stereotype ("a distortion or exaggeration of the facts") involves two forms of typing: first, that based on concrete physical characteristics or behavior, and second, judgments of such a category of people as lazy, stupid, childish, etc., "virtual moral ascriptions" (1975:22). The first kind of typing is subject to verification; the second is not. Guillaumin makes the further point that despite changes over time in the concrete categories of people being stereotyped, and in their social position, the stereotypes may change very little.[7] In other words, stereotypes do not automatically give way to reflect social change, being at the outset a misrepresentation of social reality.

Various authors, such as Nogueira (1959), Banton (1967), and Harris (1974), have argued that the presence of numerous racial categories in a racial system precludes the development of stereotypes, or what Banton calls "prejudice directed in an unreasoning way toward all members of the lower category" (1967:277). In fact, such stereotypes were frequently expressed in colonial Cape Verde, e.g., "blacks need more discipline than whites," or even, "the whip is the only rule they understand." Such statements, it must be emphasized, do not represent widespread beliefs, rather justifications by the elite of social conditions of the time, particularly the abusive treatment of "blacks" (note the collapsing of racial categories) by police, administrators and landlords. Blumer has termed such beliefs a "defensive response to a felt threat to the sense of group position" (1958:4).

Much more common, and more in accord with the official colonial program of "cultural assimilation," were the more explicitly moral stereotypes applied to darker social categories by Portuguese in the colonial administration and the Cape Verdean elite. "Blacks" (i.e., the popular classes) were often described as sexually promiscuous, lazy, improvident, and lacking a sense of time. In such stereotypes, reference is made to behavior, "explaining" it by inherent moral qualities. Such stereotypes might be seen, following Szwed's argument, as a highly condensed form of social myth, wherein the ellipsis -- what Barthes has called the evacuation of social reality (1972) -- is perhaps the most important element.

"Lack of a sense of time," for example, has been ascribed to many subordinate groups, whether ethnic minorities (e.g., Chicanos and Afro-Americans in the United States) or the people of any nation considered less developed than one's own. Such an ascription eliminates from consideration any number of sociogenic factors that might explain tardiness or absenteeism, such as, for example, the fact that (1) such behavior is sometimes a form of passive resistance by those who feel powerless; (2) appointments are usually set by the higher-status

individual in view of his or her self-interest, and may offer
little to the lower-status party; (3) mutual knowledge that
the lower-status individual is seen as "irresponsible" may
become a self-fulfilling prophecy; (4) economic or political
stagnation in the social environment may make it objectively
irrelevant whether a task is accomplished "on time," or may
make it subjectively perceived as such. Certainly, the
classes of Cape Verdeans portrayed as "lacking a sense of
time" were remarkably punctual for events such as the arrival
or departure of an interisland vessel, and extremely attentive
to the proper moment for sowing the next year's crop.

Whites often ascribed others' behavior to the "shamelessness" of blacks or mulattoes. The term "shameless" (*sem vergonha*) constitutes a global moral indictment and a particularly powerful one where Iberian influence is strong, given
the preoccupation with honor and shame in Spanish and Portuguese cultures (cf. Cutileiro 1971:193-94). Honor, as Pitt-
Rivers explains, is "the value of a person in his own eyes,
but also in the eyes of his society" (1966:21). To have shame
is to be "sensitive to one's own reputation, and therefore
honorable" (Ibid., p. 43). By contrast, the shameless individual is "beyond the moral pale" (Ibid., p. 41). The epithet
of shamelessness is often applied to low-status groups; Pitt-
Rivers, for example, mentions that Andalusians consider the
gypsies to be shameless by nature (Ibid.). Calling another
group "shameless" may also define its members politically, as
less than fully adult. In Cabo Verde, it is only small children who are called *sem vergonha* with any indulgence.

Racial Ideology and Social Practice

So far, colonial racial ideology has been discussed in
terms of images, beliefs and values, but, as Rancière suggests
in a critique of Althusser, ideology must be understood as
more than such relatively discrete collective representations,
as also situated in social institutions. That is, ideology
cannot be entirely separated, even analytically, from social
practice (1974:270-71).[8]

Before pursuing the implications of this, a brief description of the class system in Cape Verde as it existed in
the last years of colonial rule is necessary, for in social
relations and institutions "on the ground," race and class
were often confounded, coalescing in the popular notion of
social "level" (*nível*). The following resumé, being intended
primarily for descriptive classification, is not all-inclusive.
Not included, for example, are returned emigrants from America
and Europe, and those households that derive most of their
support from remittances. Most of the old landlord class had,
by the time of the study, emigrated or passed into the bourgeoisie or petite bourgeoisie. Peasants and proletarians are

grouped together in the "popular class" because the division
between the two categories is a fine one on the empirical
level, and to a large extent, they share common class interests, since most peasants rent or sharecrop some of the land
they till. Individuals may pass from one category to the
other by a reversal or some small improvement in circumstances, without a clear change of social placement or identification. In times of famine, both categories depend on state
relief projects or other external aid for survival.

Racial designations are used in a folk sense; that is,
they describe the broad categories of phenotypes found in each
class as Cape Verdeans would describe them.

> Bourgeoisie: *Gente Branca*, in popular
> parlance. This class is represented by
> landowners engaged in market production
> and commerce, with close ties to Portu-
> gal and/or the United States. By class
> origin and interests, a number of colo-
> nial bureaucrats might be placed in this
> class. Most are very light in complex-
> ion and are considered "white," and many
> have ties to the old plantocracy. Some
> of this class emigrated after indepen-
> dence; most remained, though the class
> has lost its politically hegemonic posi-
> tion.

> Petty bourgeoisie: Shopkeepers, clerks,
> most bureaucrats and professionals,
> schoolteachers, owners of small commer-
> cial enterprises based entirely in Cabo
> Verde. Most are mulattoes, lighter in
> color than the general population.

> Popular class: *O povo* [the people].
> This class includes peasants, i.e., agri-
> culturalists whose main source of live-
> lihood comes from the produce of their
> own land, and the rest from renting,
> sharecropping, or practicing a craft. It
> also includes proletarians, such as fish-
> ermen and agricultural laborers or tenants
> who do not own their means of production
> (i.e., boats, land); and domestic servants,
> urban laborers, and others with no stable
> source of livelihood. Most are considered
> black or dark mulatto.

Certain terms used here correspond to a capitalist mode
of production, and thus may appear inappropriate to describe a
society where quasi-feudal relationships persisted and where

barter and communal labor were still practiced to some degree.
However, while social relationships of production were far
from fully capitalized, they were nonetheless largely determined by Cape Verde's position "on the periphery of the periphery" of capitalist development. Labor migrations and the
near-dissolution of the old landlord class, to give but two
examples, reflect her vulnerability to exogenic processes
emanating from the centers of the world market economy.

Race and Class in Everyday Life

At first glance, there appeared to be many social occasions where participants were of homogeneous class and phenotype, especially at certain types of gatherings where sociability was not the primary object. A good example of this are
the visits made to households where serious illness or death
has occurred. These are de rigeur for friends, relatives and
economic dependents of the afflicted household. Death can be
the stimulus for months of visits from persons of all social
"levels." The hosts are expected to provide occasional
refreshments regardless of the caller's social position, and
all visitors are invited to sit in the main room (in larger
houses, in the *sala* or parlor). For some townswomen, these
visits seem to be a major form of leisure activity -- one
might almost call it recreation. The refreshments are an
attraction, especially for some of the poorer visitors, and
behind their backs the motives of some of the habitués of
these gatherings are impugned.

The gossip at such gatherings is as delicious an attraction as the *lanche*, or tea-time snack served in the late
afternoon, or the other, occasional, refreshments. At first,
only an audible sigh breaks the silence of grief and respect;
it then becomes a tentative murmur and finally, a low, continuous buzz that abruptly subsides at the arrival of a new
guest, only to recommence after a few moments. Meanwhile, the
conversation steers gingerly outward from the obviously appropriate topics of sickness and death, to more lively ones such
as the details of a recent party that members of the bereaved
household could not attend but are delighted to hear about.
While men do appear to pay their respects to the family, it
is the women who come more often and for longer periods, as
the obligations of mourning weigh more heavily upon women than
men. Thus, the *sala* is likely to be the site of an all-female
gathering for extended periods in the morning or afternoon,
which facilitates discussions related to marriage and courtship. Though conversational roles tend to reflect gradations
of status, all present may take part, and there is an air of
conspicuous equality about these occasions.

When, however, sociability is the primary object of a
gathering -- such as the dinners and dances held in private

homes during the religious feasts (*festas*), wedding parties,
baptismal celebrations and the like -- a new set of restrictions comes into play. For this type of occasion, and in
general, household layout depicts a mini-geography of social
relations. (This pertains to houses of the first two classes
described, and to the *sobrados* of the old landlord class.)
Invitations to converse in the *sala*, a room rarely used except
for receiving guests, or to eat with the family in the dining
room (*sala de jantar*), are usually tendered only to those of
comparable "level," and here observes marked homogeneity of
class and phenotype.* Invitations for coffee or *lanche* in
the kitchen are extended somewhat more freely. The *quintal*,
or enclosed courtyard behind the main part of the house, is
the only part of the dwelling accessible to those of much
lower standing. Here the numerous clients of a better-off
family enter by a rear entrance to converse and, if offered
food, to eat. Some might, by virtue of long association with
the household, be invited into the kitchen to eat, but in the
instances observed, this was usually declined with apologies.

Fogo's tradition of *canizade* plays upon the symbolism of
household geography. This is a form of dance performed two
evenings before a major saint's feast, and in the past it
seems to have involved some ritual inversion of social roles
between slave and master. Pairs of male slaves, perhaps a few
dozen in all, were dressed in white, their faces powdered a
chalky color. In *canizade* they came to dance in the normally
prohibited *sala*, while the whites watched from a distance. All
but extinct today, *canizade* is now performed out-of-doors. The
performance I witnessed in the town of São Felipe was danced
by six men, agricultural laborers from the rural hinterland,
who wore tall, pointed caps with long tassels, and white garments cut so that streamers whirled as they moved. The dances
include a great deal of pantomime, the significance of which
is no longer known, though some movements appear to simulate
aggression and combat. One of the dances performed until
about a generation ago called for the men to stand in a circle
holding long sticks in the manner of spears (a weapon unknown
in Cabo Verde), and to feint with their partners.

The restrictive nature of most recreational gatherings
made it unlikely that opportunities for courtship would arise
between young people of widely different class and phenotype.
This was somewhat less true for *liceu* (secondary school) students in the two cities, but parental controls and self-selec-
tion tended to produce racial and class homogeneity at those

---

*Until a few decades ago, mulatto friends of Fogo's
white families were issued invitations to watch parties being
given in the *sala* from the home's verandah.

gatherings held outside school hours. The festivities of New
Year's Eve and the Feast of the Three Kings as observed in
Brava seemed to pose an exception to the usual exclusivity of
courtship situations. On these dates, groups of unmarried
girls hold parties to which young men, organized in clubs, are
invited. In principle, each group of boys visits each party
for a specified length of time, and the boys provide hired
musicians and fireworks. In the past, all of the young men
involved must have been fairly homogeneous in respect to class
and color, if only because the lower classes would not have
had the necessary means. However, in recent years, because of
the depletion of the old landlord class and the ascent of some
families from the popular class through remittances from
America, the boys' clubs came to vary considerably in composition.

According to some of the girls, there were only two boys'
clubs "worth anything" anymore, and the rest were composed of
"just anybody." Being curious as to how this unusual "mixture," as the girls referred to it, would be handled, I spent
the evenings of these two feasts at the parties given by the
category commonly referred to as *as meninas da primeira* [the
first-class girls]. When the boys from the clubs deemed "just
anybody" arrived, they met with pleas of fatigue and headaches
(as excuses not to dance), and they made an early exit. Once
the "better" clubs arrived, they were persuaded to stay well
past the usual time limit, blocking the entrance of less
desirable groups.

Social distance in situations such as these is viewed differently, depending on whether one is in the exclusive or the
excluded category. Individuals in a position to exclude
others defined their selections as "people of the same background" or "those of the same level." Members of a certain
social club in Mindelo (one of the casualties of independence)
claimed that they recruited on the basis of community status
and "background." In fact, persons of color who were prominent in local affairs were rarely asked to join, though Portuguese army officers could use the club's facilities with no
question as to their "background." Boys from the clubs
rejected at Brava's New Year's celebrations complained indig-
nantly afterwards of class and color prejudice on the part of
the girls, who, for their part, simply regarded the preferred
group as "people we know well." Similarly, some viewed a public dance as "more lively" and "less pretentious" than the
private ones from which they would be excluded, or where they
would feel out of place. Others disparaged such dances as
being "just black people," "just anyone," or as having too
much "mixture." Women of the upper classes, when asked why
they did not give the customary kiss of greeting and farewell
to certain women with whom they seemed friendly, replied that
such behavior is inappropriate for persons of different
"levels." Those in the lower-status position in such situations

were likely to offer such reasons as "they don't like my color," or, "they don't like to touch dark people." In a study of São Paulo, Brazil, Fernandes found that whites are far less likely than individuals of darker categories to perceive racism (1978 II: 409-11), and this finding seems equally valid when applied to the Cape Verdean case.

The very fact that normative restrictions resulting in a high degree of racial exclusiveness only applied to certain types of contact -- those implying social equality -- was sometimes perceived as an absence of racism. Seeing his wife cuddle a *badiu* child who had been grazed by a passing car, a merchant declared, "You see, there is no racism here." In general, restrictions on social and physical contact tend to be relaxed in the case of small children, and only become more apparent as they move into more adult roles of work and court-ship. Young children sometimes sleep in the same bed as the servant woman who has cared for them since birth. The chil-dren of domestics, and other youngsters taken into the house-hold, receive loving attention and caresses. Only when the child-servant is old enough to do domestic chores, at about five or six years of age, does the distance between him or her and the employer's children begin to show itself.

Sexual Relationships and Marriage

In all of the situations described so far, the rubrics of social level or background allowed considerations of race to remain implicit. In the realm of marriage and courtship, on the other hand, phenotype and ancestry might become explicit matters of concern. It is not the physical intimacy of mar-riage, but the social equality it presumes between spouses and affines, that is at issue. In Cabo Verde, as in Brazil, the young man of good family is expected to sow his wild oats with servant girls and prostitutes, often beginning at the very onset of puberty. It is, of course, the well-chaperoned and sexually unavailable woman of his own class and similar racial type whom he will marry. Upper-class individuals discuss this as a matter of propriety, even honor. Ideally, in the words of a common saying, both spouses should be "clean of skin and past" (*limpo de pele e de passado*). Just as Martinez-Allier has described for nineteenth-century Cuba (1974), a white male is not dishonored by sexual contact with a woman of color, only by marriage to her. But the white woman's chastity ensures that the high-status category is perpetuated in "undi-luted" fashion, so her sexuality must be confined to marriage within that category.

The lower-class girl seduced by an upper-class male, usually when in her early teens, is unlikely to form an endur-ing liaison with him, though exceptions do occur. If she is a virgin at the outset of the affair, she may be supported

through any resulting pregnancy by the father of her child,
though this is not the rule. Once she has a dependent child,
her chances of marriage within her own class (already much
reduced if her loss of virginity is known) are very slim. She
is likely to have a series of sexual partners who provide pit-
tances in the way of gifts, and who will be of progressively
lower economic standing as time goes by and her desirability
fades. In some cases, economic need will lead such a woman to
prostitution in one of the islands' cities.

The case of Lili is a typical story in many respects.
Born of an unknown father in the village of Furna, Brava's
small port, she lived there with her two daughters, aged five
and two. Lili was barely twenty, but her sweet, melodious
voice still sounded like that of a child; with her jet black
skin, green eyes, and delicate features, she was a striking
woman. Lili and her daughters lived in a one-room dwelling
with a floor of packed earth, furnished with a bed, a small
table, a chest of drawers, and a single chair. Wall decorations were those commonly found in houses of this type: several
old calendars and numerous sentimental postcards showing ideal-
ized, radiant parents with immaculate blond infants.

Lili was "lucky," she said, because her mother lived
nearby and could look after the children while Lili carried
stones for a road gang on one of the state construction projects. Even so, life was a struggle, since her earnings
(about U.S. $0.50 per day) were the only regular income for the
household. When she was fifteen, Lili had her first sexual
experience with a man in his twenties, a local government official, whom she professed to "love with all my heart," pointing
to several pictures of him on the bedside table, amidst saints'
images and family photographs. Soon after Lili became pregnant, the man married the daughter of the island's leading
family and shortly thereafter, left with his wife for a post on
another island. For Lili, this experience of betrayal was
apparently no less painful for being a predictable one in this
milieu, and in her account, the emotional loss seemed paramount
even over the economic burden she had to face alone. By comparison, the encounter with a visiting seaman that produced her
younger daughter was recounted with little feeling other than
resignation. Not long afterward, Lili gave up her impossible
struggle and went to Praia, to work in one of the many little
bars on the outskirts of the city.

Lili's history reveals how the class/color hierarchy still
manifested itself in male-female relationships, following patterns developed under four centuries of slavery. If the black
woman was no longer subject to a master's sexual demands, she
could nonetheless be compelled, by poverty and hunger, to sell
herself for a bit of food or a few *escudos*, as often happened
during the famines. In some cases, the line between seduction
and forced prostitution was ambiguous: family need sometimes

put pressure on girls barely in their teens to take advantage
of the fact that virgins could command a higher price (whether
in the form of gifts or outright payment) than women with previous sexual experience.

The weak economic position of men in the popular class --
itself part of the legacy of the slave era -- added to the
likelihood that a girl in Lili's position would be easily persuaded to jeopardize future chances of marriage or cohabita-
tion on a permanent basis with a man of her own class, as
these were limited in any case. It was easy enough for the
upper-class male to incorporate a sort of *droit de seigneur*
into any role of authority; should he do so, his behavior
would likely be explained by his class peers, male and female,
as caused by the alleged promiscuity of the *mulata*. Bastide
has remarked in a critique of Freyre that "the dusky Venus
hides the debasement of the black woman as prostitute . . . it
is not so much love that breaks down barriers and unites human
beings as that racial ideologies extend their conflicts even
into love's embraces" (1961:18).

The Norm of Homogramy

The norm that "like should marry like" was widely sub-
scribed to by Cape Verdeans of every social class. Spouses,
it was held, should be of similar racial type and background
(*formaçao*). Background is normally taken to mean upbringing,
thus including such factors as education, religion, and social
class. But it can also refer to ancestry, at least in cases
involving "white" partners where one of them was known to have
African ancestry. Beside the fear of this manifesting itself
in the offspring, there were moral considerations at stake.
"If anything goes wrong in the marriage, the blame is likely
to be placed on that person's *formaçao*." (In other words,
'blood will tell.') This remark came from the young man,
mentioned earlier, who had described himself as "mixed," despite being generally considered white. His remark was probably based on personal experience; a year before, his sister,
married to a promising young administrator, had caused a scan-
dal when she was caught in *flagrante delictu* with a colleague
of her husband. She herself -- in temporary banishment at her
parents' home -- had lamented her behavior, saying "it's in
the blood."

Outside the elite, where mixed unions were highly
unlikely, phenotype rather than ancestry was the focus of concern in applying the norm of homogamy. One of the grounds for
this was aesthetic appeal. Since African traits were widely
held to be ugly, a visible disparity in racial type also
implied a difference in levels of general physical appearance.
The social consequences of a mixed union had to be taken into
account as well. Relationships between affines could become

conflictual or awkward if one set felt itself socially superior to the other, and parental disapproval could subvert the harmony of the marriage. In effect, the norm of homogamy itself generated an added preoccupation, the fear of social criticism, whether from one's own relatives or the community at large.

For two sisters born of an important landlord family in Brava near the turn of the century, this meant spinsterhood. One of them, Dona Rosa, a handsome woman of alabaster complexion, explained, "There were no cousins our age. But," she added, "we maintained our position and the honor of the family." In Brava and Fogo, the preference for first cousin marriage not only helped keep family lands together, but also assured (or was taken to assure) racial "purity." Though land no longer provided most of their income,* Fogo's former gentry still commonly practiced first cousin marriage.

"Much better someone in the family than some stranger," I was told of one case of first cousin marriage in this class -- albeit in this case, the woman had been jilted by another first cousin, and the bridegroom was a cousin of illegitimate birth, of mixed background, but with the advantage of American citizenship. In this case, the marriage was considered advantageous, it being widely thought that the young woman, nearly thirty and little-educated, was no longer a virgin. In addition, her family's means were no longer what they once were, and her parents seemed more anxious than she herself to see the marriage take place. The preference for first cousin marriage, though born of racial and property considerations, also provided reassurance that the bride would be well treated by her husband.

This marriage gives illustration of the elasticity of norms pertaining to spouse selection. Though ancestry was clearly taken into account, it did not become the determining criterion. The upward mobility over the twentieth century of a number of mulattoes through education or emigration, coinciding with the decline of many "white" landlord families during the Depression, had made such mixed marriages more common than before. Historical accounts give the impression that such unions involving the landlords in the past tended to occur between white men and women of color; e.g., concubines who had borne them heirs who would be legitimized by the marriage. In Brava, emigration to the United States and Holland had resulted in many marriages being arranged by correspondence, usually through the mediation of relatives.[9] While

---

*By the 1970s, they were more likely to be found in commerce or in Portugal's colonial bureaucracy, whether in Cabo Verde or on the African continent, than in agriculture.

stable employment abroad was considered an asset (except in
the bourgeoisie), some engagements were broken off when the
prospective spouse proved darker than he or she had appeared
in photographs. Brava was reputed to be particularly race con-
scious in such matters, though in a different way than Fogo,
with her three clearly delineated color/class categories. Many
of Brava's whites were peasants descended from Azoreans or
Madeirans with little claim to status other than race.

Marriage between individuals considered to be of different
racial type and background (i.e., ancestry) could occur for a
variety of reasons. Among Protestants, religion was often more
important than race as a consideration of marriage partners.
The church-sponsored activities of the Nazarenes (who disap-
prove of dances) provided opportunities for courtship among
mixed couples, though family pressures sometimes impeded marriage. Mixed marriages might also occur when the prospective
fiance was unusually well educated or accomplished. For some
of the daughters of the white families in reduced circumstances, marriage to such a man, even though his racial background
was "imperfect," could provide mutual advantage. The daughter,
her children, and possibly her parents and siblings, would
benefit economically, while her husband's upward mobility was
sealed with a guarantee of respectability that no achievement
of his could assure. Independence, besides creating a new
political climate, has brought a number of highly educated emigrants back from Europe; both factors can be expected to lead
to more marriages where race becomes at most a secondary consideration.

The example of one Senhor Roberto was considered a classic
case of marriage of the type just mentioned. Born early in
this century of an impoverished black mother and a white father
from one of Fogo's leading families, he was taken as an infant
and brought up by maiden aunts on the father's side, as sometimes happened with illegitimate sons (evidently rather more
often than with illegitimate daughters). Problems arose when
the boy entered his teens, because other "good" families feared
that he might become involved with their daughters. The young
man eventually went into business with his father's backing and
became quite wealthy, mostly through his activities as a labor
recruiting agent for planters in São Tomé. His economic ascent
was finally crowned by his marriage to the most sought-after
daughter of the island's leading family, which had lost money
during the Depression and in a series of droughts. His legitimate children are treated as "white."

Ritual and the Racial Hierarchy

Folk ritual offers an opportunity to examine racial patterns in a domain of behavior that is relatively structured and
codified by tradition, where roles are well defined and the

public valuation of roles and performances easily discerned.
The association of ritual roles with racial/class categories
and the differential prestige accorded the various roles was
particularly evident in the feast of St. Philip (São Felipe),
the patron of Fogo, celebrated in early May. The celebration I
witnessed was atypical of Cape Verdean religious feasts
(*festas*) in several ways. Rather than being sponsored by an
individual man or woman, it was organized and financed by a
group of young men from the old landlord families, employees of
the colonial bureaucracy. Sponsorship of this, the island's
major feast, had been a jealously guarded privilege of the
landlord class, but for some fifteen years the *festa* had been
suspended, since no one considered an appropriate sponsor had
felt able to bear the expense. The young men who revived it
c. 1970 did so not from religious motivation but, as some of
them phrased it, "out of civic pride." Normally, sponsors take
on the financial burden of the feasts as part of fulfillment of
a religious vow, or *promessa*, to the saint for a favor hoped-
for or already received. Such a vow may be made publicly or
privately, and the specific petition disclosed or not, according to individual preference. Often such vows are made during
the various processions that are part of each *festa*. These
appear to be spontaneous declarations, whose public expression
has been stimulated by the *festa*'s atmosphere of excitation and
religious fervor.

The feast of São Felipe, unusual for its degree of secu-
larization, had been made a legal holiday, and most of the
highest-ranking dignitaries of the colonial bureaucracy were on
hand, with most of the festivities compressed into two days to
accommodate their schedules. However, this feast possessed the
major elements found in other saints' feasts, including a Mass,
several processions, equestrian events, drumming, singing of the
call-and-response type, and a banner (*bandeira*). This last is
carried at the head of the processions and serves as a symbol
of sponsorship. At the last, climactic moment of the *festa*,
the banner is passed to the next year's sponsor, who will keep
it until it is passed on once again. If no sponsor is forthcoming, the banner is "buried"; i.e., left in the parish
church, with funereal solemnity.

Roles that had once been taken by slaves eventually came
to be assumed by blacks and mulattoes of the popular class.
These include the grinding of corn for communal meals, *canizade*, and providing the music that is essential for many activities of the feast, in the form of drumming and call-and-
response singing. The singing is usually performed by women,
called *coladeiras*, with occasional contributions from the men.
One *coladeira* improvises a verse, typical subjects being peti-
tions to the saint, descriptions of the celebration taking
place, and humorous, often satirical, references to individuals
present -- including anthropologists. Meanwhile, one or two
men play goatskin drums, with a score or so of women providing

a background chant. Eventually another woman takes up the improvisation, and there is friendly rivalry among the more gifted *coladeiras* to produce the wittiest or the most risqué verses.

Since the sponsor (*dono/a*) is expected to provide food to all comers on the saint's day, large quantities of corn must be ground for the traditional dishes that will be served. For a week before the feast of Saint Philip, female peasants and laborers spend their evenings in the *quintal* of the principal organizer's house, grinding and sifting corn. The corn is ground using a large mortar and pestle to the accompaniment of *coladeiras*, drummers, and men who beat the sides of the mortar with pairs of sticks, in tempo to the music. It is these evenings of *pilon* [mortar] that mark the beginning and establish the ambience of the *festa*.

Ideally, the participants are well primed for their work with *aguardente*, or *grog* as it is termed in Crioulo, provided by the sponsor, though on this occasion a few complaints were heard about the less-than-plentiful supply of drink. The normally drudgerous female task becomes an exuberant, competitive demonstration of endurance and skill, as two or three women seize pestles and time their strokes to the quickening crescendo of percussion. Sometimes a man joins in, which adds a humorous note to the proceedings. All of this creates a thunderous cadence that overwhelms the voices of the *coladeiras* and attracts onlookers of every age and station.

The sponsor takes responsibility for the major expenses of the feast, including the meal offered on the saint's day, the collation served the evening before, the fee for having Mass said in the saint's honor (for major feasts such as this one, a high Mass), *grog* for the *coladeiras* and drummers, decorations, and fireworks. Though a single individual bears most of these costs, others may make a more limited contribution, such as offering a communal meal on the eve of the feast, or, as is traditional in Fogo's feast of Saint Philip, offering a midday meal to the horsemen (*cavalheiros*). The latter lead the several processions of the feast, with one of them acting as standard-bearer, a particularly prestigious role. In the past, horsemen were recruited from the sons of landlord families; at this celebration, they were members of the sponsoring committee who had, as mentioned earlier, close kin ties with the old gentry class. At the meals offered during this *festa* and that of St. John the Baptist, Brava's patron saint, the usual etiquette of status was observed. Though all were offered the same meal, guests considered *de categoria*, that is, those described by one of the sponsoring committee as "having sufficient background" (*formaçao*), were invited into the dining room and served a variety of imported whiskies, besides the *grog* given those who ate outside in the courtyard.

The horsemen are honored guests at a miniature, less costly or elaborate, celebration of St. Philip that has its own sponsors from the popular class. This is the *bandeira da praia* [banner of the beach], the main celebration being known as the *bandeira da vila* [banner of the town].[10] It commences with a procession from the outskirts of São Felipe down to the part of the shore that lies below the fortifications built centuries ago to repel invading pirates. There the horsemen consume a light meal served under a canopy formed by knotting together several of the *panos* that women of the popular class commonly wear tied around the waist and draped over the hips.

Except for the horsemen, all of those present at the *bandeira da praia* that I witnessed were peasants and day laborers. While the prestigious roles of the elite in the *festa* were performed in public as the focus of general attention (e.g., horse races, displays of horsemanship, carrying the banner into the church), former "slave" roles and activities attracted only casual spectators from the upper classes, or none at all. Due to this lack of interest, along with role segregation by social level, the few individuals who still know all of the details of ritual procedure are to be found in the popular classes. A certain drummer known locally as Tchitchiti was indispensable for the celebration of the feast of St. Philip, since only he knew the proper drumbeat and exact procedure for certain parts of the *festa*.

Although the activities of singing, drumming, and grinding corn are considered essential to the *festa*, no recompense or public recognition was accorded those who performed them, save for the fee of 150 *escudos* (about $8.00) paid to Tchitchiti. No prestige was attached to these activities, even when performed with considerable skill. Thus, no one with any claims to community status or lineage would perform them except as a kind of minstrelization, that is, the emulation of lower-status persons within a carefully regulated and socially approved context (Szwed 1975:27). For example, white men of good families might take a turn at grinding corn or improvising a verse or two, to the great amusement of bystanders. Sponsorship of Brava's feasts has been mostly taken over by returned emigrants from America, that island's elite having declined more rapidly than Fogo's. But, significantly, it had become difficult to find people to perform the less prestigious ritual roles, and on several occasions, there was doubt as to whether drummers or *coladeiras* could be found.[11]

The *festas* not only incorporated status distinctions between slave and master, black and white, but also dramatized them in ritual. This is clear in the inversion of slave and master roles in *canizade*, a form of ritual license that, by contrast and by its very burlesque quality, reaffirms the social roles of everyday life. Until parish priests forbade the practice a few decades ago, the standard-bearers for Fogo's

and Brava's patron saints entered the church on horseback,
riding up to the altar and pausing there as their mounts performed special dancing feats, before depositing the banner as
the Mass was beginning. This flaunting of elite privileges
(both sponsorship and horsemanship) in the divine presence
might be interpreted as a dramatic affirmation of the heavenly
charter claimed for such prerogatives.

The various *festas* themselves enjoy differing degrees of
prestige, with one in particular being regarded as pertaining
to the slaves and their descendants: *Santa Cruz*, or the Holy
Cross, observed on May 3. Commonly known as "blacks' day,"
(*dia do preto, dia do negro*), this was, according to oral tradition, a special day of liberty for the slaves, when they
might wear the cast-off finery of their owners. In preparation
for this feast as celebrated in São Felipe, Fogo, a novena of
evening prayers is held in the house of the sponsor, beginning
eight days before the feast. In this instance, the sponsor was
Tinani, a fragile woman in her eighties, of weathered skin the
color of café au lait, and eyes still lively with intelligence.
For most of her life, Tinani had toiled as a servant and as a
carrier on the waterfront. The feast had been inherited from
her mother, and from her mother's mother before her, but the
duties and expenses were shared with an *irmandade* [brotherhood]
of some ten men and women, each of whom had had a parent or
other close relative in the brotherhood before them. It is
interesting that the similarly popular feast of Saint Anne
(*Santana*) that I observed in Brava was also the responsibility
of a brotherhood, together with a sponsor who had acquired the
feast from his mother.[12] In both cases, the *irmandades* are
bound by patterns of mutual aid among the members, including
special religious observances as well as material assistance on
the occasion of a death in any of their households.

Tinani's two-room stone cottage, with its dirt floor and
sparse furnishings older then their owner, was just large
enough to accommodate the several dozen people who appeared on
the eve of *Santa Cruz*. On this night, the prayers of the
novena are followed by a procession, lit by makeshift torches,
to a small roadside shrine to the Holy Cross, where the torches
are planted in the ground and left to burn through the night.
The group returns to the sponsor's house, where a *batuque* takes
place, consisting of call-and-response singing during which the
women providing the background chorus beat the wadded-up cloths
usually worn around the waist as they though were drums. Pairs
of individuals, on this occasion including both men and women
in mixed and single-sex couples, begin to move in a sensuous
pantomime-dance, urged on to more and more explicit gestures by
the laughter, clapping and comments of the onlookers. *Grog* is
passed around to "liven up the singing," though little was to
be had that year, one of drought and scarcity. Finally, the
chicken soup (*canja*) served at all Cape Verdean *festas* appears
at about 2 a.m. Due to a shortage of bowls and spoons, these

were passed from one person to another until all had been
served. Then the tired participants, most of whom would be
working "on the road" (in state-sponsored construction projects) in a few hours' time, bade each other goodnight. Those
of the brotherhood who can do so attend Mass the next day, and
most return for the completion of the novena.

Felix Monteiro, a student of the history and folklore of
his archipelago, witnessed the same feast in 1947, under the
same sponsor. He found, from listening to my recordings, that
many of the traditional Crioulo litanies had been replaced by
Portuguese prayers since then, probably as a result of certain
priests' efforts to regulate the ritual in recent years.
Except for the priests' concern, the feast was of little
interest to Fogo's upper classes. "So you're going to watch
the savages!" one man joked as I departed for Titani's. Others
expressed apprehension that I might consider such "African"
goings-on typical of Cape Verde. As far as Tinani was concerned, this was nothing but a dangerous lack of piety on
their part. That year, after nearly three decades of sponsoring the feast, she passed the banner to her daughter-in-law,
since she had no living daughters of her own and she believed
that this would be her last *Santa Cruz*. Six months later, I
received notification of her death.

Tinani's castigation of elite disdain for "her" feast was
echoed by Deka, as the sponsor of *Santana* was popularly known.
A cook and household servant about sixty years old, he complained loudly during the festivities of the lack of faith and
piety evinced by the spectators' hesitation to join in the
singing and procession. "You have to play seriously for the
saint," he remonstrated, and probably by sheer force of per-
sonality, he succeeded in mobilizing many members of his audience.

Community and Hierarchy

All of the saints' feasts celebrated in the fashion
described here fall between May and August, a "dead" period in
the agricultural cycle and one of considerable anxiety, since
it is during this time that rain must fall on the newly sown
fields. Most peasants still consider celebration of the
saints' feasts -- especially that of their own island's
patron -- as necessary if not sufficient protection from the
catastrophe of drought. Though they involve a great deal of
apparently wasteful expense,[13] the *festas* remain important as
a focus of community, attracting the visits of many emigrants,
who often contribute financial support, especially in Brava.

But even as the *festas* have united participants in a community of belief and shared devotion, they have also reaffirmed

the seigneurial prerogatives of the elite, thus reinforcing
divisions of class and color. The possible contradiction
between the values of community and those of hierarchy are
evident in the remarks quoted above by the sponsors of *Santana*
and *Santa Cruz*. To "play seriously," as Deka put it, meant to
reject, at least for the occasion, the denigration of these
"African" celebrations, to shake off, for the moment at least,
any status pretensions of one's own for the sake of honoring
the saint. In Brava particularly, changes in the social order
brought about by emigration posed a threat to the continuity
of the *festas*. Remittances had created many potential sponsors, but they had also depleted the ranks of those willing to
participate in the prestigious roles.

What of social changes brought about by the ending of
colonial rule? Videotapes of several major *festas* held since
independence[14] give the impression that they are still celebrated with enthusiasm, and with greater public recognition
accorded the contributions of musicians, cooks, and so on,
under the encouragement of the representatives of the new
regime. The very fact that the *festas* incorporated so vividly
the central contradiction of Cape Verdean society as it existed
under colonial rule, the racially based class hierarchy, may
make them a particularly eloquent vehicle for dramatizing and
reinforcing social change in the future.

Race and 'Culture'

In colonial Cape Verde, ancestry and phenotype were taken
as signifiers of different background (*formação*), an ambiguous
notion, since the term's primary meaning of "upbringing" had,
in actual usage, acquired a secondary connotation of "ancestry." *Formação* was seen to lie at the root of certain moral
qualities that could be discerned from the observed behavior
of persons of different social levels. The fact that a few
outside the white elite had always been able to move into its
ranks, a process accentuated over the twentieth century for
reasons discussed in the next chapter, was not taken as contradiction of the importance of background, but as offering
exceptions that proved the rule, bringing to mind Guillaumin's
remarks on the "elasticity" of stereotypes. The very fact
that a few persons of color had so succeeded gave evidence
that others had not because of moral deficiency. Indeed, the
"real" place of blacks or mulattoes who improved their standing was constantly reaffirmed, as when the colony's most eminent scholar was referred to as "that black professor" among
whites. If such a person failed in some aspect of demeanor --
a hint of standoffishness, a lack of deference to those who
considered themselves superior -- his or her racial characteristics became the focus of criticism. "There's nothing worse
than a black with schooling" is an example.

The belief among the elite that social differentiation was based on moral (i.e., cultural) qualities rather than race, along with the absence of legalized racial barriers -- unnecessary, as we have seen, to maintain pre-abolition class structure -- were taken as evidence of the absence of racism. Yet despite the apparent fluidity of the Cape Verdean racial system, both phenotype and ancestry could become criteria of exclusion in certain contexts. A later chapter pursues, in greater depth, the theoretical implications of this for the comparative study of race relations.

In the last two decades of Portuguese rule, Cape Verde became something of a showcase of Lusotropicalism in colonialist propaganda. The next chapter examines the issue of racial ideology and practice in the wider context of Portuguese colonialism. There we take up the relationship of the dominant ideology of race, as described in this chapter, to the colonial apparatus, the shaping of Cape Verdean race relations by the colony's role in the empire, and also the roots of counter-ideological challenges to colonialist racial doctrine in Cape Verdean popular culture.

Notes

1. Professor Harris very kindly furnished me with a set of the drawings and explained their use.

2. Racial terms are given in Crioulo, using Portuguese orthography.

3. In Harris's words, "In a strictly lexical count the sample responded with 492 different categorisations" (1972: 2). However, the increased number of terms obtained by counting male and female forms as separate terms is due to the nature of the Portuguese and Crioulo languages rather than to that of the racial system under study in each case.

4. Crioulo term.

5. Crioulo term.

6. Crioulo term.

7. "There is a mechanism of perpetual reintegration of old elements in function of the current situation and the concrete relations between majority and minority groups" (Guillaumin 1972:209).

8. Rancière invokes Marx's preface to *Contribution to the Critique of Political Economy* to assert that "ideology does not exist merely in discourse, nor merely in systems, signals, images, etc. . . the ideology of a class exists primarily in institutions" (1974:270-71).

9. Of the several dozen marriage ceremonies I witnessed in Brava, only one was not by proxy. All of the others involved emigrants residing abroad for whom the time and expense of a visit home were not feasible. In most of these cases, the spouses had not met as adults. Nonetheless, most of the fiancées displayed happy excitement at the prospect of marriage and emigration, and looked forward to joining not only their new husbands, but also friends and relatives in the United States or Holland.

10. There is also the *bandeira do campo* [banner of the countryside], a smaller celebration of the patron saint's feast day held in rural villages and hamlets.

11. For the feast of St. John the Baptist, *pilon* was omitted, to the disappointment of many, because, according to the sponsor, it was "too wild and noisy."

12. One *festa* I encountered was passed on patrilineally. This was the feast of St. Peter in São Felipe, Fogo.

According to the current sponsor, his father had been a
ship's captain who made frequent trips to the United
States. On one such voyage, his vessel began to sink in
a storm, but at the last moment St. Peter appeared and
promised to save those aboard, who were rescued shortly
thereafter. The captain made a vow that the banner of
St. Peter would never leave his family, that it would be
passed from father to son. Much of the financial support
for the *festa* comes from a brotherhood of the crew and
their male descendants whose headquarters is in New Jer-
sey. Each year, the members observe the feast and send
donations for the celebration in Cabo Verde.

13. The feast of St. John the Baptist (*São João Baptista*) in
    Brava, for example, costs some $8000 for decorations,
    fireworks, food, and offerings to the priests who cele-
    brate Masses in the saint's honor. But the actual cost
    is more than double this figure, if one considers the
    fact that the sponsor's adult daughter lost a year's pay
    from her job in the United States, having spent the year
    before the feast in Brava overseeing household repairs
    and other preparations necessary for the event.

14. These were produced by Tony Ramos of New Bedford, Massa-
    chusetts, a filmmaker and video artist who has shot many
    hours of footage in Cabo Verde since independence, and
    who has generously allowed me to view them.

VII

COLONIZERS AND COLONIZED:
CAPE VERDEANS IN THE EMPIRE

As presented in the preceding chapter, the dominant, or
hegemonic, racial ideology served as a prop for local class
structure, legitimizing and perpetuating a social hierarchy
wherein class and racial status were closely associated. At
the same time, this ideology was embedded in a wider political
context, that of Portuguese colonialism; one of its central
premises, the transmutation of racial issues into cultural
ones, was also a cornerstone of Portugal's colonial program.
Here we look at the Cape Verdean racial system from the perspective of this wider context, beginning with an historical
examination of the islands' somewhat ambiguous role in the
empire.

Because of Cape Verde's dual role as both a colony and a
source of intermediaries for Portugal in Africa, the racial
policies of the Salazar period were applied somewhat differently there than in other African colonies. On one hand, Cape
Verdeans were considered assimilated to Portuguese culture and
were thus spared the indignities of the indigenous status
ascribed to other Africans. On the other, they were far from
enjoying a standing of equality with metropolitans, something
that became all too evident during the colonial wars that
marked the last fifteen-odd years of Portuguese rule. Oppressive cultural policies, along with greatly increased police
surveillance and the massive deployment of Portuguese military
forces to the archipelago, all served to heighten Cape
Verdeans' awareness of their colonized status.

Under the tense conditions of a virtual occupation by
Portuguese forces, colonial cultural policies met with considerable resistance. Religion and language became arenas of
protest where state control of cultural expression and social
institutions was contested, and where the ideological premises
of Portugal's colonial rule were sometimes challenged.

These examples of cultural resistance give evidence that
acceptance of colonialist notions of race and culture was less
than complete and wholehearted. In the last part of the chapter, I argue that certain folk beliefs, stereotypes, and
notions of group identity constituted something of a counter-
current to the prevailing racial ideology that was to provide

128

a base in the popular culture for the nationalism promoted by the PAIGC.

The 'Indigenato' Policies

The installation of a Republican government in Portugal in 1910 had immediate political consequences in Cape Verde. That year, peasants took control of the Riberão Manuel Machado area in Santiago with such efficacy that the governor was forced to appeal to Lisbon for reinforcements. Any hopes of revolution were dashed by the arriving troops' swift "pacification" of the rebels (N. Cabral 1980:22). However, the first Republic's policy of decentralized colonial administration did allow scope for the occasional reformer, such as Governor Fontura da Costa, who founded Cape Verde's first *liceu* [secondary school] in 1917, and who greatly expanded primary education (Silva 1929:184). This governor is still remembered with affection for his disdain toward the pomp of office. Fontura da Costa was known to disguise himself as a pauper to check on the practices of Mindelo's merchants. A number of periodicals, some of them dating from the last half-century of the monarchy, flourished during the Republican period (1910-26), only to wither and die under the press controls of the New State (N. Cabral 1980:109; Ferreira 1974:132; cf. Gonçalves 1972:141-49).

The *Estado Novo* was the creation of Antonio de Oliveira Salazar, prime minister of Portugal from 1932 to 1968. Every important cultural and economic activity fell under the purview of one or another state corporation in a regime characterized by authoritarianism, rigorous censorship, and xenophobia -- for modern, liberal influences were anathema to Salazar.[*]

While he was yet Minister of the Colonies pro tem, Salazar drew up the Colonial Act of 1930. This, along with other policy statements such as the Organic Charter of 1933 and the Missionary Statute of 1941, effectively incorporated the colonies into the fascist regime being created in Portugal. By the Act of 1930, all but a miniscule proportion of the African population were assigned the status of *indigenas* [natives or indigenous persons], wards of the State. Cape Verdeans, however, were considered assimilated (*assimilados*) and therefore were citizens of Portugal. In the words of Marcelo Caetano, who was to succeed Salazar in 1968, "the law regards as aborigines (*indigenas*) the members of the black

[*] See Marques 1974 II: 291-310 for a description of what he calls the "authoritarian-corporate state."

race or those descending from it who continue to live in their
traditional way of life and do not by education acquire the
outlook or manner of life of civilized men" (1951:32).

Useful explanations of what was meant in practice by the
distinction between *indigena* and *assimilado* status have been
given by Duffy (1963:160-66) and Bender (1978:149-55). *Indígenas* were not allowed to vote, were restricted to inferior
schools, and had to obtain official permission for a wide
range of economically significant activities such as traveling, buying power tools, and selling their crops. Perhaps
worst of all, they were subjected to a head tax and vagrancy
laws (subsistence cultivation being defined as "vagrancy" for
males) that made them vulnerable to labor conscription. In
effect, *indigenas* were confined to low-paying occupations and
even in these could legally be paid less than "civilized" persons performing the same type of work (Duffy 1963:165). In
addition, *indigenas* were liable to corporal punishment or
labor sentences for minor crimes that might draw a fine for a
Portuguese (Ibid., p. 167). And, at least in Mozambique,
indigenas were separated from whites in public entertainment
facilities and excluded from white restaurants and residential
areas (Harris 1966:159). In brief, the status of *indigenas*
implied a denial of civil rights, serious economic disadvan-
tages, and a politically infantile status.

Indigenato policies amounted to institutionalized racism,
a virtual color bar legitimized in the name of culture. Only
Africans had to demonstrate worthiness for civilized status,
just as in the American South, where Blacks have had to demonstrate recondite knowledge of American history and government
to gain voting rights that were automatically accorded to
whites. Portugal's slave trade of an earlier day had been
justified in the name of bringing pagan African souls into the
Christian fold. The *Indigenato* policies that effectively
designated Africans as a reserve of cheap labor were phrased
less in terms of Christianization than as part of a policy of
assimilation to *portugalidade* [portuguese-ness] in culture and
in group identity. In the revealing words of a former Overseas Minister, *portugalidade* would bring national unity to
"various races, various religions, various levels of evolution"
(Cunha 1960:123, emphasis added; see also Cunha 1960:148).

The stated goal of assimilation was belied by the rigorous criteria applied to Africans for obtaining "civilized"
status. To become assimilated, Africans had to be fluent in
written and spoken Portuguese, over eighteen years of age,
with no police record, and with a standard of living and life-
style similar to those of Europeans (Bender 1978:150). Indeed,
many metropolitans would not have qualified as *assimilados*;
45 percent of the Portuguese population was illiterate in 1950
(Marques 1974 II: 323). Given the wage scale applied to
indigenas and the limited education allowed them, several of

these criteria proved insurmountable obstacles. From 1940 to 1950, the percentage of Africans (excluding *mestiços*) considered assimilated remained a mere .7 percent (Bender 1978: 151).[1]

The outbreak of guerilla warfare in Angola in March, 1961 brought the *Indigenato* to a speedy end, and only months later, this was followed by numerous other reforms in health services, education, and labor policy. Though important indicators of a shift in Portugal's colonial policy, these changes did not necessarily change the racist treatment of Africans in social practice, as Harris has pointed out (1966).

Cape Verdeans as *Assimilados*

According to Bender, even the few Angolans who managed to qualify as *assimilados* did not enjoy the same status as whites; *assimilados* were paid less in both the public and private sectors, the rationale being that black labor was less productive than white labor (1978:153).[2] Similarly, the classification of Cape Verdeans as *assimilados* by no means exempted them from the conditions that were given legal underpinnings in the other colonies by the *Indigenato* policies. Allegedly, Cape Verdeans were considered assimilated because of their cultural similarity to the Portuguese. If so, it was also true that Cape Verde had little in the way of desirable land and natural resources, one function of the *Indigenato* being to facilitate expropriation of valuable African land by metropolitans (Idib., p. 136). Nor was there any shortage of labor in the colony. Such was not the case in São Tomé, for example, where plantation agriculture made land valuable and created high labor demands. There, a creole population came to be defined as largely "black" and "indigenous."

Most Cape Verdeans -- the ninety or so percent working as peasants, fishermen or laborers, most of them illiterate -- lived in political and economic circumstances that closely approached those of the *indigenas* in other colonies. Famine and the threat of famine made them vulnerable to labor conscription for the cacao islands, where they worked under the same conditions as the *indigenas* brought from Angola. Travel from one island to another could be restricted by an administrator's whim. (I encountered several cases where this prerogative was exercised; in one, the father of a boy beaten by the police was prevented from leaving Brava to lodge a complaint in Praia.) Use of force by administrators and police to punish or intimidate was common enough, even though not sanctioned by law. Voting, admittedly a dubious privilege in Portugal herself at the time, was an outright sham. Peasants were simply convened to drop folded ballots into a designated receptacle, and the deceased were enumerated as electors as a matter of course.[3] Under the *Estado Novo*, until the colonial wars, Cape Verdean army recruits were allotted food and quarters inferior to those given Portuguese soldiers, and were not allowed promotion above the rank of private first class (*primeiro cabo*).[4] In sum, the privileges of *assimilado* status were of little practical meaning in Cape Verde, only becoming pertinent for those who went to other colonies in the role of "proxy colonizers."

Proxy Colonizers

The slave traders' agents, or *lançados*, described in Chapter III were the most effective promoters of Portuguese language (in its creolized version) and culture in the Africa of their time. The *lançados* were something of a prototype for the Cape Verdeans who would function as middlemen for Portugal in Africa, especially Guinea, in one capacity or another -- as missionaries, traders, settlers, and government administrators. Use of Cape Verdeans in the work of colonization was expedient for several reasons, one of them being climate. From May or June through September, the rainy season and the contagions associated with it made life nearly intolerable for Europeans on the coast. Cape Verdeans, though used to a dry climate, were accustomed to heat and to occasional humid periods, and had been exposed to many of the diseases that plagued the African mainland. Also, it was believed that their African antecedents allowed them greater resistance than the Portuguese had to tropical diseases. This was not entirely without foundation; it is now known that the sickle-cell genetic trait prevalent in African populations, which causes a deadly anemia when dominant, protects carriers from malaria, thus giving a survival advantage to those in whom it is a recessive trait. Besides such physical advantages, Cape Verdeans were familiar with many African customs, which added to their value as intermediaries.

Cape Verdeans were particularly active in colonizing Guinea, since that territory was administered from Santiago for over two centuries (from 1640 to 1879). Governors rarely visited the colony, "confining themselves to the mediocre administration of the Islands," as Barreto puts it (1938:102). Santiago herself being a hardship post, only a prelate as unusually zealous as Portuense,[5] bishop from 1688 to 1705, took a serious interest in the spiritual welfare of the mainland colony. The few missionaries who did go to Guinea were more likely to engage in commercial endeavors than pastoral ones, according to a Jesuit report of 1627 (Rodney 1970:76). Portuguese missionaries seem to have been primarily concerned with forming useful alliances with African groups in order to stem the incursions of French and English traders.[6]

Clerical education in Cape Verde declined greatly after its first flowering in the early sixteenth century, which

helps to account for the "shameful" state of Catholicism in
Guinea at mid-nineteenth century (Lima 1844, Part 2: 76).
Owing to the lack of clergy, primary education was non-
existent in the Guinea of Lima's day; ironically, given the
avowed civilizing mission of Portugal in Africa, such literacy
as Lima did encounter was due to the Islamicization of groups
such as the Mandinka (Part I: 86). Little improvement was
made over the following century; in 1950, the illiteracy rate
in Guinea was 98.85 percent (Ferreira 1974:71). Access to
education was enlarged after the revocation of the *Indigenato*
in 1961, but soon the PAIGC was setting up schools in the
liberated zone, and by 1972, it was providing education for
14,531 students (Andréini and Lambert 1978:135). Amilcar
Cabral, founder of the PAIGC, was one of only fourteen individuals from Guinea in five centuries of Portuguese rule to
have received a university education (Ibid., p. 132).

Unlike the case in Cape Verde, Portugal's presence in
Guinea was minimal and ineffective until the Berlin Conference
(1884-85) made it imperative that she occupy the territories
she claimed in Africa. Guinea-Bissau's earlier role as a
dependency of Santiago, and her lack of trained personnel, is
reflected even today in the sizable numbers of Cape Verdean-
born civil employees. Amilcar Cabral himself was born of a
Cape Verdean father and and educated at the *liceu* in São
Vicente. Though the PAIGC's armed struggle against Portugal
was waged in Guinea, the party's leadership during the war
was composed primarily of Cape Verdeans. Portugal apparently
hoped to manipulate ethnic differences to divide Cape Verdeans
and Guineans in the PAIGC, though how much this succeeded is
not clear. When Cabral was assassinated by a former Party
colleague, later believed to have turned collaborator with
the Portuguese, this was thought by some to indicate ethnic
rivalries. However, both elements worked together in the
Party until December, 1980, when the Cape Verdean and Guinean
wings separated after a relatively peaceful coup d'etat in
Conakry. Again, the question of ethnic rivalries was widely
raised, though Chabal argues that the coup was in fact the
outcome of a political struggle between the "first generation"
of nationalists (mostly urban-based intellectuals, bureaucrats and professionals, many of them Cape Verdeans), and a
"second generation," all Guineans, who had risen through the
Party ranks and spread throughout the country (1982:14-15).

During the colonial period, Guinea served Cape Verde as
something of a social safety valve, much as more promising
parts of the empire did for Portugal. Guinea absorbed younger
sons (and illegitimate sons) of landlords, and offered the
ambitious a means to achievement and gain in the name of
service to empire. An illustrious early example was André
Alvares de Almada, a mulatto born in Santiago, who distinguished himself as a military officer, scholar, and proponent
of missionary activity in Guinea. Almada's treatise on the

riverine regions of the Guinea coast, *Tratado Breve dos Rios de Guiné*, published in 1594, survives as a valuable historical record and merited him the Order of Christ, despite his "defect" of having a black grandmother.[7]

A new phase in the relationship between Cape Verde and Guinea began with the founding of a *liceu* [seminary] in São Nicolau in 1866. This institution was of remarkably high quality and produced several generations of missionaries, teachers, and civil servants, many from humble backgrounds (Araujo 1966:12-13). A former professor from this school related in an interview that priests educated there were required to spend several years in Guinea after graduation.

The seminary was succeeded in 1971 by the *Liceu* Gil Eanes in São Vicente. The *liceu* offered a secular secondary education to many who would later work in Guinea. Antonio Carreira, who spent many years as a colonial administrator in that colony, estimates that between 1920 and 1940, some 70 percent of Guinea's civil employees were Cape Verdeans (1977: 114-15).

Many Cape Verdeans went to Guinea without the advantages of family background or formal education. In 1857, a year of famine in Santiago, 57 individuals were sent to Guinea to settle the region of the Bulola River (Barreto 1938:240-41). Other Cape Verdeans established numerous settlements along the Farim River in a region where the Portuguese had as yet no control. There they prospered for some time as sugar cane planters. Carreira compares them to the *lançados*, for like them, the planters established peaceful relations with neighboring Africans, trading and sometimes intermarrying with them. When the area was brought under Portuguese control early in the twentieth century, most descendants of these colonists became skilled laborers, rural shopkeepers, and petty civil employees (1977:114-15).

More recently, Cape Verdeans were settled in Angola, but with very different results. Beginning in 1961, Angola's colonial government established nine planned agricultural settlements, called *colonatos*, that were to be multiracial in composition. Many other *colonatos* were designed to be racially homogeneous; Bender lists thirty-five (1978:117). At this critical moment in Angola's history, when anti-colonialist warfare had just begun, the new *colonatos* were designed as a demonstration of the racial harmony possible under Portugal's rule where Cape Verdeans would play an intermediary role between Portuguese and African settlers. The *colonatos* were to embody, as Duffy explains, Salazar's ideals of "Africans and Portuguese holding rural Portuguese values, industrious, dedicated to the land and politically conservative" (1963:169).

Eventually, 594 Cape Verdeans were recruited to the
colonatos (both multiracial and homogeneous), along with
1,824 Europeans and 693 Africans (Bender 1978:116). Bender
gives a copiously documented account of this doomed enterprise. Besides many practical errors of planning and recruitment (for example, many of the Cape Verdeans had been fishermen, not peasants), only four of the settlements were truly
multiracial. As it happened, these were the very places where
conflict was most acute and white attrition highest. Most of
the Cape Verdeans were too poor to leave, even if they wished
to do so. Rather than apostles of harmony, all too often they
became agents of conflict. Relations with neighboring
Africans were so hostile that Cape Verdeans became a political
liability; their recruitment was ended in 1968 (Ibid., pp.
107-31).

Bender attributes the view of Cape Verdeans as potential
buffers between the races to the Social Darwinist influences
on Portugal's policymakers. This crude variant of nineteenth
century social evolutionism saw all human cultural development
as unilineal, with all people on the same path, where they had
eventually to pass through the same stages. Race was considered to be an indicator of cultural level; thus, it could
"logically" be assumed that Cape Verdeans, being of mixed
European and African background, would function as intermediaries on the social and cultural levels (Ibid., p. 225).

We have seen that in certain instances, Cape Verdeans
did indeed establish pacific relations with Africans on the
continent. But significantly, this occurred in situations
where Portuguese control was minimal or nonexistent. In the
colonial context, Cape Verdeans tended to cling to the precarious advantages of *assimilado* status. A peasant woman
returned to Fogo from Angola, where she had worked as a cook,
expressed it simply: "Here I'm nobody but in Angola I was
somebody!" Not surprisingly, after April of 1974, many Cape
Verdeans joined the exodus of the Portuguese from the mainland colonies.

Education in Cabo Verde:
Myth and Reality

In large part because of Cape Verde's administrative and
religious jurisdiction over Guinea, education was somewhat
more developed there than elsewhere in Portuguese Africa
through most of the colonial period. Under the *Indigenato*,
Cape Verdeans also enjoyed a certain advantage over the peoples of the other colonies, since *indígenas* were confined to
substandard mission schools offering three years of rudimen-
tary education (*ensino rudimentor*), from which it was almost
impossible to transfer into the state system (Ferreira 1974:
66-67).

Nonetheless, access to schooling remained hypothetical
for most Cape Verdeans. Early nineteenth century reports converge in their descriptions of the lamentable state of public
education (e.g., Pusitch's account in Ribeiro 1956:16;
Chelmiki and Varnhagen 1841:195-294; Lima 1844, Part 1: 79).
A report to the Ministry of the Colonies in 1913 estimates
illiteracy at 85 to 95 percent, and urges the opening of more
primary schools in order that Cape Verdeans emigrating to the
United States will be able to fulfill the literacy requirements that were becoming a condition for entry into the
country (Anonymous 1913:40). The *liceu* in São Vicente
(founded in 1917) offered a course in teacher training, in
accord with Fontura da Costa's aim of increasing primary
schools in the rural areas. Carreira reports that many adults
and adolescents took advantage of the new facilities to learn
to read and write, with the view of emigrating to America
(personal communication).

The rise of fascism in Portugal had drastic consequences
for education in Cape Verde. Antonio Salazar's policies,
begun during his tenure as Minister of Finance (1928-32) and
continued during most of his rule (1932-68), resulted in the
closing of many small primary schools throughout Portuguese
territory.

The "virtues" of illiteracy and the "dangers" of extending education to the masses were the subject of fatuous
declamations in Portugal's National Assembly in the early
years of the New State (Mónica 1979).[8] In 1936 the normal
schools were abolished, cutting off the supply of primary-
level teachers for Portugal as well as her colonies (Marques
1974 II: 323). Primary school enrollment in Cape Verde
dropped from 6,693 in 1926 to 4,977 in 1946, while the population increased from 160,000 to 169,000. In the same two
decades, the number of primary schools declined from 150 to
only 62 (1926 figures from Silva 1929:189; 1946 figures from
Serviços da Estatística do Cabo Verde 1947:105). Thus, Cape
Verdean illiteracy was high, though somewhat less so than in
the other African colonies, at about 80 percent by various
calculations made between 1958 and 1975. In 1958, government
figures showed Cape Verdean illiteracy at 78.5 percent, as
compared with 98.85 percent in Guinea, and 96.97 percent in
Angola (Ferreira 1974:71). In fact, these figures probably
erred on the side of optimism, at least with respect to Cape
Verde. Educational administrators estimated truly functional
literacy at only about 15 percent in 1972; various sources
give similar figures at the time of independence (e.g.,
Decraene 1977), and this after a decade of educational expansion stimulated by the colonial wars. While doing a socio-
linguistic study of 23 households, I found some half-dozen in
which the elderly were able to read and write, whereas their
adult children could not, though their grandchildren were
enrolled in school. These families reflected in miniature the

vicissitudes of public education in the colony since the turn
of the century.

Despite the severely underdeveloped state of the Cape
Verdean educational system, it was widely believed, by metropolitans as well as by Cape Verdeans themselves, that the
inhabitants of the archipelago were a highly literate, educated people. Portuguese newcomers were often shocked at the
contrast of the reality of the colony to their image of Cape
Verde as an intellectual oasis in the tropics, where even
lowly shops' clerks had *liceu* degrees and stevedores could
read, write, and speak several languages. Illiterate Cape
Verdean peasants who had never ventured beyond their island
of birth held that Cape Verdeans were *mais culta* [more cul-
tured] than Angolans or Guineans, who were imagined to be a
savage, primitive lot (*selvagens, primitivos*), a stereotype
likely to be reinforced by ex-*colonos* and others returning
from the mainland colonies.

What was the historical basis for this image of Cape
Verdeans, so much at variance with the realities of illiteracy
and lack of educational facilities? It seems probable that
the abysmal state of education in Portugal herself, which did
not begin to improve until the 1950s, was a factor. The
accessibility of education at both the primary and secondary
levels that existed under Governor Fontura da Costa had no
parallel at that time in Portugal, so it is likely that Duarte
Silva (first rector of the *liceu*) is correct in claiming a
lower rate of illiteracy in Cape Verde c. 1926 than in the
metropole. Also, those who did pass through the *liceu* produced an unusually rich literature, in proportion to their
numbers (see Araujo 1966; Hamilton 1979). Despite the press
censorship of the Salazar regime, and often at some risk, Cape
Verdean writers produced the journal *Certeza* in 1944, the confiscation of whose third issue led to its demise. Another
periodical, *Claridade*, produced only eight issues between its
founding in 1938 and 1958, but these were remarkable collec-
tions of poetry, essays, and short stories expressing the
literary voice of several generations of writers who had
passed through Duarte Silva's *liceu* (N. Cabral 1980:110-11).

The propaganda of the colonial regime tended to exagger-
ate any of its accomplishments; since Cape Verde was the only
African colony with an educational system "worthy of the
name" (Marques 1974 II: 394), it is not surprising that metropolitans should have had unrealistic notions about the colony.
Furthermore, until large numbers of Cape Verdean laborers
began to arrive in Lisbon in the early 1970s, the few Cape
Verdeans who went to live there were usually university students or graduates.

An important contribution to metropolitans' perceptions
of Cape Verdeans was the limitation on upward mobility that

weighed more heavily on Cape Verde's *liceu* graduates than on
their metropolitan counterparts. Unlike the *liceus* in
Portugal, the *Liceu* Gil Eanes in Mindelo was open to anyone
who could pay. However, appropriate employment for the
schools's graduates was often lacking. The stories of *liceu*
graduates starving in the famines of the 1940s -- nearly
unthinkable in the Portuguese context -- are probably based on
fact. Similarly, the accounts of Cape Verdean army recruits
said to have tutored some of their metropolitan fellow-
soliders during World War II are probably true. Certainly one
could find, at the end of the colonial era, poets and literati
of various types employed in menial clerking jobs, a factor of
the meager opportunities of their youth. Finally, the exaggerated impressions of Cape Verdeans' educational levels may
have been abetted by a subtle type of racism, whereby any dis-
play of intelligence or intellectual achievement by people of
color was to be viewed with wonder.[9]

While the stereotype of Cape Verdeans as well educated
did not conform to reality, it certainly expressed a meaningful ideal, for most Cape Verdeans possess an almost palpable
longing for education. Parents often toiled desperately to
realize this dream for their children, and even charwomen in
Mindelo sometimes managed to send their sons to the *liceu*.
Where state schools did not exist, parents sometimes organized
informal classes so that their children might learn to read
and write. But, as Nelson Cabral points out, these skills
were often forgotten for want of opportunities to use them
afterward. By way of exception, in rural Santiago, certain
folk religious practices requiring the use of sacred texts
allowed students to retain their ability to read into adult-
hood (1980:98). Except in Brava, where emigration to the
United States replaced education as the avenue to upward mobility, schooling provided the only hope of economic security for
the popular classes. The escape from poverty it symbolized
cast an aura of respectability upon even the humblest village
letter-writer.

The economic significance of schooling is still only part
of the story. Wit and intelligence have always been prized in
Cabo Verde, since the important popular forms are primarily
verbal ones that require mental agility and articulate use of
language: the improvised songs of *batuque* and religious
feasts; the mournful ballads (*guizas*), also improvised, that
are as much wept as sung by women in mourning; the poetic
lyrics of the *morna*; anecdotes and folk tales. The best known
of the folk tales are the stories of Nhô Lobo, an anthropo-
morphized wolf whose greed and other antisocial traits invariably lead him to an ignominious end.* Some of these tales

---

*Interestingly, there are no wolves in Cabo Verde.

appear in Elsie Clews Parsons' study of Cape Verdean folklore
among immigrants in Massachusetts, Rhode Island and Connecticut (1923). The paramount importance of oral performances,
along with the general desire for learning, has produced poets
and autodidacts amidst widespread illiteracy, persons much
esteemed in their local communities.

Cultural Controls:
1930 - 1974

Despite their status as assimilated, the *portugalidade*
of Cape Verdeans was ever open to question, and especially so
after war had broken out in Angola, Guinea, and Mozambique.
While the civil administration of the colony came to include
more and more Cape Verdeans in ministerial positions, the
metropolitan policy and military presence was greater than
ever before. A crossroads of the seas in the days of sailing
ships, Cape Verde was now, by virtue of her geographical
position, an aerial springboard to the African continent,
serving as a military base and refueling station of the first
importance. Tens of thousands of Portuguese troops poured
into São Vicente and Santiago, while the security police
force (PIDE, later known as the DGS[10]) was greatly strengthened and took over some functions from the local police. On
the one hand, colonial officials bravely affirmed Cape Verde
"more Portuguese than ever," and the single newspaper allowed
to circulate, *O Arquipelago*, bore on its masthead the words
of Adriano Moreira, Overseas Minister in 1961-62, pronouncing
the Cape Verdes as "islands asleep since the eve of time,
waiting to be able to be Portugal." On the other hand, suspicion of Cape Verdeans' loyalties was evident in the day-to-
day encounters between Portuguese police and military and the
people they were allegedly protecting from "terrorists" (i.e.,
nationalists). The Portuguese army captain who lay awake at
night expecting "terrorists to crawl over his windowsill" cut
a ridiculous figure even among his own subordinates, yet paranoia was generalized enough to provoke such incidents as one
that occurred in Praia in September, 1972. Following a personal quarrel between a Cape Verdean and a low-ranking
Portuguese officer, the central *praça* [square] was surrounded
by Portuguese troops, convinced that a rebellion had broken
out. In the panic that ensued, many evening strollers were
beaten while trying to escape. ("Now you see who the real
'terrorists' are," commented a bystander.)

That Cape Verdeans were less than full-fledged Portuguese
citizens was demonstrated by the cultural policies instituted
over the war period (1961-74), such as special press controls,
changes in the educational system, and restrictions on the
use of Crioulo and on other forms of cultural expression.
Designed to further *portugalidade*, these measures were at the
same time aimed at denigrating and eliminating what one is

tempted to call *africanidade*; that is, African cultural traits and identity. Cultural policy was so embedded in assumptions of European cultural superiority that they amounted to a kind of racial policy.

If the overall aim was to further Portuguese culture and identity, thereby to assure popular loyalty to Portugal, cultural policy was also shaped by considerations of political expediency, giving rise to a number of ironies and apparent contradictions. A folk religious tradition passed down from the slaves, called *tabanca*, had been suppressed under Salazar, only to be revived and folklorized by the state when this seemed useful for promoting an image of racial tolerance and multicultural harmony. Access to education, once restricted in order to keep a docile and politically conservative base of support for Salazar's regime, was now expanded, with roughly the same rationale. That is, once Portugal was at war in Africa, educating the populace to be culturally Portuguese came to be seen as a means of assuring her allegiance. Expanding the educational system also served to demonstrate that Portugal was developing her colonies. To give another example, at the very time when Crioulo was prohibited on state property in Cape Verde, its use was being encouraged in Guinea,[*] where only one percent of the population spoke Portuguese. There, fluency in Crioulo was accepted as fulfilling the linguistic criterion of "civilized" status (N. Cabral 1980:120).

Press censorship was rigorous, with only one newspaper, a government mouthpiece, permitted; local intellectuals circulated their poems and other writings in a kind of *samidzat*. Carreira's *Cabo Verde*, published in 1972 under (indirect) government auspices in Lisbon, was judged too volatile for readers in the islands, since it documented several nineteenth-century slave rebellions. The book would therefore regularly disappear from shop windows, having been confiscated by the security police, only to reappear and disappear again.

Censorship was "abolished" in 1972. That is, before that time all publications had to bear certification of having been reviewed by the censor (*visado pela censura*); after that, so-called "pre-censorship," a kind of self-censorship, was instituted. At the same time, any printed reference to censorship or pre-censorship was made illegal!

---

[*]Cape Verdean Crioulo had been brought to Guinea by the *lançados* and served thereafter as a lingua franca in the territory.

Between 1960 and 1970, primary school enrollment
increased from 9,383 to 40,685; during the same period, the
total population increased from 200,000 to 270,000. Secondary
enrollment nearly doubled during that decade, from 1,637 to
3,107. A normal school was opened, and by 1972, primary-level
enrollment had increased to 55,062.[11] However, this signified
less a fundamental political change than a shift of tactics
away from Salazar's attempt to cultivate illiteracy, or at
least restrict literacy. Maintaining the political status quo
(restricted access to schooling's supposed aim) now became the
goal and raison d'être of educational development. Silva
Cunha, the Overseas Minister, asserted that "the mere spreading of knowledge" could not be the goal of education; rather,
the ultimate objective should be "the continuation of the
Nation" (*Diario de Noticias*, Sept. 6, 1966; quoted in Ferreira
1974:80-85). Decades earlier, before the proponents of illiteracy won the day, a Portuguese security inspector had argued
that primary schools could be "the most diligent and disci-
plined State security police" (*Diarios de Noticias*, Sept. 23,
1931; quoted in Mónica 1979:6). Now, it seemed, policy had
shifted back to this premise, probably because of the fact
that the high level of illiteracy in Portugal, and the even
higher ones in her colonies, had come to constitute embarrassing evidence of underdevelopment.

Oblique recognition was paid to nationalist movements in
the African colonies by introducing textbooks that gave
greater attention to the *provincias ultramarinas* [overseas
provinces]. But, as Ferreira observes, the "africanization"
of textbooks was superficial and misleading (1974:85-86).
"History" still meant Portuguese history, and issues were
invariably approached from a Portuguese and colonialist point
of view. The message was everywhere *Nos somos todos Portu-
guêses* [We are all Portuguese].

In any case, the attempt to introduce greater African
content backfired in Cape Verde. Students keenly resented
the fact that references to Africa pertained mostly to the
larger and more economically valuable colonies of Angola and
Mozambique. While some were dismayed at being given books
for "tribal peoples," as they put it, most took the new texts
as yet another indication that for Portugal, Cape Verdeans
were as African as Angolans or Mozambicans.

One of the major aims of colonial education was to pro-
mote the use of Portuguese; again, Silva Cunha is explicit:
"We must be obstinate, intransigent, and insatiable in the
intensification of the use of the Portuguese language" (*Diario
de Noticias*, Sept. 3, 1967; quoted in Ferreira 1974:85). By
law, all education was in Portuguese, in Cape Verde as in the
other colonies, even though this was not the students' mother
tongue. A year of *pre-primaria* was instituted c. 1970 to
combat what the Portuguese superintendent called the "ill

effects" of their speaking Crioulo at home. Unfortunately,
the metropolitan educators who came to predominate in the
secondary levels and the administration of the Cape Verdean
school system after 1961 believed that Crioulo was merely a
corrupted version of Portuguese, a "bad habit," as one such
teacher put it, to be cured by increased exposure to the
metropolitan tongue. *Liceu* students were forbidden to use
Crioulo on school grounds in 1959 (N. Cabral 1980:120), a
highly impracticable measure, since even well-educated,
bilingual Cape Verdeans use Crioulo in personal conversation
between intimates or equals, to tell jokes, or to express
strong emotions (see Machado 1977). In village schools, practical necessity, as well as common sense, obliged teachers to
violate the language policy of the colonial state.

Fluency in Portuguese carried prestige not only because
of its association with formal schooling, but also because it
was a legal prerequisite for most white collar employment.
Moreover, the law required Portuguese for all public occasions
and government affairs; even radio programs in Crioulo, once
permitted, were now verboten. A district administrator con-
ducting a petty judicial proceeding was expected to employ a
translator when a witness could not speak Portuguese, even
though the administrator's own mother tongue was Crioulo. In
fact, during the last decade or so before independence,
Crioulo was expressly prohibited in all government buildings
-- a regulation constantly flouted by necessity.

The impracticability of colonial language policy, as well
as the obvious ignorance on the part of those charged with
implementing it, of Crioulo as a language and its place in
Cape Verdean culture, made this a particularly vulnerable
aspect of Portugal's cultural policy. Moreover, language
policies (like those governing educational programs and the
media) affected most directly the small but politically significant petty bourgeoisie class, in particular the intellectuals, in Gramsci's sense of the term; i.e., those involved in
the day-to-day technical and ideological functions of the
political-economic order, such as writers, teachers, and civil
service employees (Gramsci 1972; Macchiocchi 1974:202-20).
Amilcar Cabral, the chief ideologue of the PAIGC, held that
"it is from the indigenous petite bourgeoisie, a social class
which grows from colonialism itself, that arise the first
important steps toward mobilizing and organizing the masses
for struggle against the colonial powers" (1973:69).

The other social category that became a special target of
colonial cultural policies was the *badius*, the peasants of
Santiago. It can be argued that, on the level of radical/
cultural ideology, the *badius* served as a symbolic counterpart
to the *indigenas* of other colonies. Even the name is revela-
tory, deriving from a term originally used to denote the
escaped slaves who fled to remote, inaccessible areas of

Santiago's hinterland. *Badius* comprise a substantial proportion of the Cape Verdean population; in 1969, the rural population of Santiago was about 40 percent of the total (based
on figures in Agência Geral do Ultramar 1970:22).

Because absentee landlordship was more common in Santiago
than elsewhere, social distance between white landlords and
their tenants was greater there than in the other islands.
Owner/slave and landlord/tenant relations were relatively less
paternalistic in Santiago, and it seems not by chance that the
few known instances of slave and peasant rebellion in Cabo
Verde were the work of *badius*. Because of their social isolation and physical distance from the centers of white settlements, *badius* retained a certain cultural autonomy in relation
to urban and metropolitan influences; thus, in their dialect
of Crioulo, their folklore, religious practices and other customs, one finds many archaisms, both Portuguese and African in
origin, that are unknown outside of Santiago.

Badius formed the backbone of the labor migrations to
the dreaded cacao islands (São Tomé and Príncipe), for reasons
that are not altogether clear. It seems likely that the
greater prevalence of large, absentee landholdings in Santiago, along with cash rents (rather than sharecropping), and
the fact that *badius* were a denigrated social category, rendered the latter particularly vulnerable to labor conscription.

The cultural distinctiveness of the *badius* made them the
subject of negative stereotypes that tended to legitimize
racist treatment at the hands of authority figures such as
landlords, administrators, and police. Both colonial authorities and other Cape Verdeans perceived *badius* as the bearers
and representatives of an African heritage, and thus as the
most "backward" sector of Cape Verdean society. However, they
seemed to strike a chord of ambivalence in the popular imagination, at least at the time of the field work. On one
hand, *badius* were seen, in Brava, Fogo, and the more distant
Leeward (Barlavento) islands, as somewhat mythical, knife-
wielding savages. On the other hand, *badius* were often the
protagonists of anecdotes (true or apocryphal) in which the
Portuguese came out the losers.[12] *Badius*, then, represented
something both opposite to and opposed to "Portuguese-ness,"
something disdained and yet, on occasion, admired. Thus,
while *badius* were normally seen as "other," as different from
normal, civilized Cape Verdeans, they could also serve, on
the symbolic level, as representatives of Cape Verdeans.

Certain cultural forms distinctive of the *badius* were
matters of concern to the colonial regime. The Portuguese
administration considered the folk religion festivities of the
tabancas as nothing more than "a disgusting association among
savages" (N. Cabral 1980:124). These were, in fact, mutual

aid associations with a territorial base; the term *tabanca* is
a West African one meaning "place" or "settlement" (Monteiro
1949). The feasts of *tabanca* as described by N. Cabral (1980:
124-32) and Monteiro (1949) include singing, drumming, dancing, processions, and simulated possession. Celebrations are
presided over by a "king," who is attended by a court including soldiers, thieves, witches, executioners, and "daughters
of the saint" (these last being subject to sexual taboos).
During most of Salazar's rule, *tabanca* was discouraged, and
at times suppressed; in one case, the "king" of a *tabanca* was
imprisoned (N. Cabral 1980:126). In 1965, on the occasion of
a much-publicized tour by Portugal's president on the nation's
African colonies, an attempt was made to revive the *tabanca*
as a demonstration of Portugal's new-found tolerance for local
cultural forms.

As supposedly the most "African" of Cape Verdeans, *badius*
were regarded with suspicion during the war period. Suspicion
became paranoia with the emergence of a religious movement in
the early 1960s. The movement, which arose in Santiago's hinterland, had roots going back several decades, to the 1941
arrival of Portuguese missionaries belonging to the Congregation of the Holy Spirit, a Catholic religious order. These
missionaries attempted to control and regularize the religious
practices of a population habituated to a great deal of autonomy in their religious practices (Monteiro 1974:92-94). As
Monteiro explains it, before the arrival of these new missionaries, the few priests ministering to the inhabitants of rural
Santiago were extremely permissive about folk religious practices, such as those connected with births, weddings, and
funerals, and delegated many priestly functions to laymen and
women. It was in the early 1960s, however, that the movement
took on political significance, and its members came to be
labeled *os rebelados* [the rebels] by the authorities, quick to
sense the incipient communism in some of its precepts; formerly, the adherents of the movement had been called simply
increntes [unbelievers].

Among their precepts was a refusal to accept religious
rituals performed by priests; members performed their own
baptisms and weddings, and venerated, in particular, a copy of
the Bible brought from the United States some years earlier.
Adherents worked land communally, refused contact with outsiders, and forbade the killing of any living creature. It was
their refusal to deal with money, have contact with priests,
or allow their homes to be fumigated in an anti-malaria campaign that brought *os rebelados* to the government's attention.
Some of the accusations leveled against them are revealing;
for example: they refused "all that is civilized and has anything to do with whites" (Portuguese priest); they were hostile to authority, "which they confuse with the white man"
(Portuguese priest); they hated organized society and authority, and inculcated this hatred in small children, and they

made subversive statements regarding private property (municipal administrator); and they made allusions to famines
during which their relatives were alleged to have died (public
health official) (J. Monteiro 1974:107-8; see also N. Cabral
1980:99-100). The movement's leaders were eventually
arrested, brutally interrogated, and finally dispersed among
the other islands.

Religion as Cultural Challenge

Neither the *tabancas* of the twentieth century nor the
movements of the so-called *rebelados* were characterized by
explicitly political motivations or objectives. The same can
be said of the Church of the Nazarene, a Protestant sect first
introduced in Brava by emigrants returning from the United
States around the turn of the century, which in 1972 numbered
some 1,000 active members and another several thousand occasional participants. Leadership of the Cape Verdean branch of
the church was American until sometime in the early 1970s,
when a Cape Verdean became its director. A large proportion
of the Nazarenes was drawn from the petty bourgeoisie of
teachers, public employees, shopkeepers and so on, who were
attracted by the sect's emphasis on honesty, hard work, and
sobriety (drinking and dancing being forbidden). Many had
been converted because of their disillusionment with the
corruption among the Catholic clergy.

In the mid-1960s, a number of Nazarenes in Santiago were
subjected to surveillance and police interrogation about their
political activities, according to accounts given by the
church members involved and several Nazarene clergymen. This
probably resulted from the fact that, during the early years
of the war in Angola, colonial authorities attributed the
guerrillas' successes to their supposed collaboration with
Protestant missionaries. It was easily ascertained that the
Nazarenes were not functioning as a revolutionary cell; in
fact, some considered themselves defenders of the Portuguese
rule.

Why were three such different religious manifestations as
the Nazarenes, the *rebelados*, and *tabanca* ascribed a political
significance by the colonial regime? I would suggest that
each in its own way constituted by its very existence a challenge to the social order of the colonial state; each proposed, in one form or another, a model of social organization
that stood outside the Church-state structures of Salazarian
Portugal. The *tabancas*, for example, were localized social
units, each with its own hierarchy of elected king and queen,
as well as soldiers, slaves, etc., and its own chapel, prison,
infirmary, and dance floor constructed for the duration of the
tabanca festivities (N. Cabral 1980:127). The social order

proposed by *tabanca* was a ritual one, an imaginary one from the perspective of the outsider; the *tabanca* king arrested in 1942 defended himself in front of the Portuguese administrator by saying that his kingship and indeed, *tabanca* itself, was a "game," a *jeu d'esprit*, as Cabral translates it (Ibid., p. 126). The ritual quality of *tabanca* roles is underscored by the fact that the "queen" may not be the wife of the "king" in everyday life.

Nelson Cabral proposes that the social organization of *tabanca* was at some unconscious level a reaction to, perhaps even a parody of, the imposed hierarchy and the seemingly arbitrary rulings of the colonial regime (Ibid.). If only in the ritual domain (and it appears that some of the administrators did not grasp the distinction between this and the everyday, secular sphere), *tabanca* violated the organizing principle of Salazar's *Estado Novo*, whereby the state was by right in control of all social relations of public significance.

In an earlier day, the *tabanca* may have expressed a more direct challenge to the colonial social order. In 1723, the Castilian king ordered Cape Verde's governor to cease tolerating the existence of "armies of black freemen and slaves" who were wont to absent themselves from work and even attack white slaveowners if their own "governor" (i.e., *tabanca* king) so ordered (Barcelos 1900 II: 244). The "king's soldiers" of *tabanca* carried arms and appear, from Barcelos's account, to have constituted a threat to the property, if not the persons, of the landlords during the celebrations of the feasts of the Holy Cross and St. James (*Sant' Iago*, the island's patron).

In the case of the *rebelados*, religious convictions inspired the creation of a social order designed to approximate what was believed to be the *status quo antes*, led by individuals who had taken prominent roles in folk-religious practices. What began as a rejection of the modern Catholic Church as represented by the new Portuguese missionaries, came to be viewed as a rejection of the State, since the *rebelados* considered the civil authorities in charge of the anti-malaria campaign that began in 1961 to be agents of the false priests. It is worth noting, though, that even before 1960, the *increntes* [unbelievers], as the movement's adherents were then called, were arrested for continuing traditional religious practices in the privacy of their homes. Even before 1960, allegations were made by the missionaries to the effect that the unbelievers were being led from the outside and constituted a political-social danger (Monteiro 1974:96-97). Thus, by the time of the anti-malaria campaign, the stage had been set for a violent reaction. The *rebelados'* refusal to permit the fumigation of their homes, along with their pattern of communal labor (which, in fact, is traditional in Cabo Verde),[13] was assumed to be subversive, perhaps even indicative of communist influence, as far as the security police were concerned, resulting in brutal treatment of the movement's leaders. For more educated and privileged dissenters, the *rebelados* took on the aura of political martyrs (N. Cabral 1980:100).

For their part, the *rebelados* professed to accept civil authority, except for what they deemed its "satanic" works (e.g., fumigation), supposedly engineered by the "false priests." In the view of Júlio Monteiro, the only person to study the *rebelados* systematically, while the movement was not a political one, its underlying causes were economic and political. "Its present members ought not exceed 2,000 persons. But the same 'mentality' exists among thousands (in Santiago)" (1974:80). Those "thousands" were the land-poor and illiterate who felt themselves vulnerable to seemingly arbitrary and invasive changes imposed by Church and state, changes over which they had no control. Monteiro's study, produced before independence under conditions of considerable difficulty, makes the courageous affirmation that the political problem posed by the *rebelados* was not the communist tendencies of which they were accused, but rather their exclusion from all structures of decision making and power. It was for that reason, he believed, that the movement could yet evolve into a more politicized struggle (Ibid., pp. 179-83).

As for the Nazarenes, I suggest that their particularly delicate position at the time the colonial wars broke out derived from the fact that theirs was the only formal organization of any importance outside the control of the state. The Catholic Church, by contrast, was heavily subsidized by the state; her priests were considered employees of the state, which paid their salaries, and which reserved the right of veto over the selection of her bishops (Ferreira 1974:78). In Praia, Mindelo, and the island of Brava, the sect was large enough in number to provide its members with "cradle to grave" alternatives to the monolithic Church-state structures. For example, Nazarene adolescents had their own organization instead of *Mocidade Portuguesa*, a Catholic, fascist organization originally modeled after the Hitler Youth (Marques 1974 II: 298-99). In the repressive context of the last years of Portuguese rule, the very existence of the Nazarenes constituted a subtle challenge to the regime; it is perhaps not surprising that the sect has gained many more adherents since independence.

Cultural Resistance

The absence of armed struggle against the colonial power in Cape Verde was more a matter of physical geography than of political consciousness. The small size of the islands and the lack of any natural shelter for guerrillas made them easy to control, given the deployment of large numbers of Portuguese troops there. One of the PIDE's most dreaded prisons, where political detainees from the various Portuguese territories were sent, was located in Tarrafal, Santiago. The Cape Verdean struggle for independence took place abroad, in large part. The PAIGC attracted Cape Verdean supporters and guerrilla fighters from among emigrant workers in Holland, deserters from the Portuguese army in Guinea, students studying in Lisbon (some of whom proceeded to Belgium and France), as well as from among those who had left Cape Verde for political reasons.

Moreover, support for the colonial regime was far from unqualified in Cape Verde herself. Little more than a year after Caetano's government was overthrown by liberal and socialist elements within the Portuguese army, Cape Verdeans voted overwhelmingly for independence under PAIGC leadership, and this despite efforts by the short-lived administration of General António da Spinola to muster support in Cape Verde for continued affiliation with Portugal. The PAIGC's success, I suggest, was in large part due to the fact that its ideological program of nationalism and anti-colonialism found a fertile soil in Cape Verdean popular culture.

Intimations of nationalism in Cape Verdean intellectual circles can be traced to the beginning of the twentieth century (N. Cabral 1980:109). Here, however, we are concerned with more broadly based, popular expressions of Cape Verdean identity that challenged, however subtly and implicitly, the legitimacy of Portuguese rule. I will argue here that even before the sudden end of Caetano's regime, there was much evidence to suggest that acceptance of the hegemonic ideology of race and culture described in the preceding chapter was far from unambiguous.

Chapter I described some of the difficulties I experienced in my attempts to discover what individuals really believed when they expressed seemingly contradictory notions of race, culture, or Cape Verdean identity. As Gramsci has written, "bad faith" is not a very satisfying explanation when such contradictory expressions are frequent and widespread in a society. In that case, he asserts,

> . . . this contradiction must be the expression of deeper contradictions at a historical and sociological level . . . because of social and intellectual subordination a class borrows a world view from another class and asserts this borrowed world view in words, although in action a contradictory world view is manifested (quoted in Genovese 1969:117).

A contradictory world view was sometimes expressed in action -- as when Portuguese police were met with taunts and flying rocks when they entered the slums of Praia or Mindelo to make an arrest. But even in more normal circumstances, everyday speech offered many hints of what Gramsci would call a different world view from the "borrowed" one. For several reasons -- the fact that Cape Verdean culture is primarily an oral one, the ease with which the military and police apparatus could control other means of political expression, the fact that Crioulo offered a clear marker of Cape Verdean cultural distinctiveness that was shared by all Cape Verdeans -- the Crioulo language had become, at least by the early 1970s, a symbol of Cape Verdeans' identity as a people and, without much exaggeration, a political battleground.

Crioulo is the mother tongue of all Cape Verdeans and, for all but an educated minority, the only language spoken fluently. Although some 90 percent of the vocabulary is of Portuguese etymology (the rest originating from various West African languages), these derivations take on new meanings, and many archaisms now extinct in Portugal have been retained. The grammar of Crioulo is quite different from that of Portuguese; the tense of verbs is less important than their "aspect," such that Crioulo conveys an entirely different sense of time and action (Almada 1958; Meintel 1975; see also N. Cabral 1980:115-24).

Crioulo is a largely unwritten language with no single recognized orthography, though several grammars do exist, the best known being that of Balthasar Lopes da Silva (1957). Several poets, including Eugenio Tavares of Brava and, more recently, Ovidio Martins and Jorge Pedro Barbosa, have published poetry in Crioulo. Since independence, short stores in Crioulo have been published regularly in the newpaper *Voz de Cabo Verde*. For the most part, though, linguistic creativity has been channeled into the spoken word; neologisms, inventive nicknames (such as *mîl e un* [1001] for a boy with two front teeth missing), expressive and idiosymcratic usages all make a playing field of everyday speech. In the stagnant, claustrophobic political atmosphere of the last years of colonial rule, the popular spoken language sparkled with irreverent life, in vibrant contrast to the vacuous complacency of official public discourse.

Laden with imagery obscure to the outsider, spoken Crioulo is unintelligible to the untutored Lusophone. Interestingly enough, it is nearly mutually intelligible with the Papiamento of Curaçao in the Caribbean, as migrants from Cape Verde and Curaçao working in Holland have discovered. Since the two places have no history of direct contact, it seems likely that this is due to common West African bases in phonology (sounds) and morphology (language structure), as well as to heavy Portuguese influence on vocabulary in both cases.

In circumstances when Portuguese would normally be used by bilingual individuals (that is, with persons "of respect" such as schoolteachers, or government administrators in formal contexts), unilinguals speak what is called *Crioulo mas levi* [lighter Crioulo]. Simplified grammar and syntactical structures are employed, and individual words made to sound as much like Portuguese as the speaker's knowledge of that language allows. Metropolitans usually respond in simplified Portuguese, often without realizing how much the Crioulo speakers have adapted their speech to the occasion. Sometimes, in the sort of *mesentente* so typical of colonial intergroup relationships, metropolitans will respond in what they call *portuguēs do preto* [nigger Portuguese], that is, grammatically incorrect Portuguese, in the belief that they are speaking Crioulo.

Crioulo was usually considered something of a vice by Portuguese commentators, from Lopes da Lima, who deemed it a "monstrous" hodgepodge (1844, Part 1: 81), to the Portuguese school superintendent who claimed, in 1972, that it was not a suitable vehicle for abstract concepts, a position all too common among Portuguese educators in Cape Verde. In reaction, some of the *liceu* students and their Cape Verdean professors made a point of discussing mathematics and philosophy in Crioulo.

Even those who did not consider themselves politically nationalistic asserted the importance of Crioulo as a marker of Cape Verdean cultural distinctiveness. Bilinguals who preferred to speak Portuguese most of the time still held that Crioulo was more suitable for telling jokes and stories, making love, or expressing any strong emotion. I was often told that the verses of the *mornas*, haunting melodies played on the violin, viola, and other stringed instruments, were always in Crioulo. The fact that Tavares composed several *mornas* in Portuguese was discussed as an aberration that simply proved the rule.

Unilingual Crioulo speakers were more likely than bilinguals to profess unqualified acceptance of the superiority of the Portuguese language, disparaging their own tongue as "only a dialect," "not as pretty" or as "fine" as Portuguese. Even so, such assertions were often nuanced by a note of ambiguity: "It's a messed-up language (*lingua deturpada*)," laughed an old peasant woman in Brava, "but we think it's nice (*sabi*)!"

The possible eradication of Crioulo, however dear a project it might have been to some metropolitans in the colonial administration, was so unlikely as to seem unthinkable for Cape Verdeans, who saw this as tantamount to the destruction of their culture. By way of argument, bilinguals would point out Crioulo words that have no counterparts in Portuguese and that, in their eyes, refer to distinctively Cape Verdean qualities or experiences. For example, *morabeza* [possibly derived from the Portuguese *amor*] denotes what is seen as a peculiarly Cape Verdean quality of character, roughly translated as "a kind and tender disposition toward others" (adjective form: *morabi*). Other examples include *sabi*, perhaps originating from the Portuguese *saboroso/a* [tasty], meaning "delightful, delicious," and *cretcheu* [beloved one]. Cape Verdeans could find no Portuguese equivalent for this word; the *cretcheu* may or may not know of one's feelings of love, or reciprocate them. He or she may or may not be one's lover (Portuguese: *amante*) or one's boyfriend/girlfriend (*namorado/a*), but is by definition the exclusive object of one's tender, romantic affection.

Under the conditions of military occupation after 1961, Crioulo took on an important political function for bilingual Cape Verdeans. They began to use Crioulo deliberately in order to demarcate Cape Verdeans from Portuguese and to socially exclude metropolitans in the parks, streets, cafes, and other public places where they could not be physically excluded. This linguistic tactic for demonstrating resentment at the monopoly of local facilities by outsiders acquired an added measure of political significance insofar as, at the same time, the government was promoting the use of Portuguese at the expense of Crioulo.

The cultural uniqueness embodied by Crioulo was now manifested in interaction as distinctiveness from Portuguese culture and identity. "That's 15 kilo *na lingua 'strangeira* [the foreign language]," the baggage attendant at Praia's airport told me, "or 10 kilo in *caboverdeano* [i.e., Crioulo]." Bilinguals frequently asserted, "We use their language only when we have to." In government offices, bilinguals normally reverted to speaking Crioulo with each other when no metropolitans were present, underscoring, in this violation of regulations, in-group solidarity vis à vis the absent outsiders.

Crioulo was also used by Cape Verdeans, whether unilingual or bilingual, as a means of camouflaging politically dangerous statements. In such cases, "heavier Crioulo" (*crioulo mas fundo*) was used; that is, Crioulo more difficult for the outsider to understand. This defensive use of Crioulo is a traditional one; the improvised verses sung by the *coladeiras* for saints' feasts and in *batuques* often contained veiled political content, e.g., references to exploitation by landlords or to the cruelty of overseers in São Tomé. The popular song about labor recruitment in Fogo, quoted in Chapter IV, exemplifies what is called rather picturesquely *radfodja* in Crioulo: "to cover in layers of wrapping," from the Portuguese *refolhar*. According to Barcelos, the "armies" of *tabanca* that vandalized plantations in the late nineteenth century used "a Crioulo dialect of Guiné" and "obscure phrases, in order that they might not be understood" (1899 II: 245).

After independence, the status of Crioulo became a matter of debate. Amilcar Cabral had encouraged the study of Portuguese in the liberated zones of Guinea, with an eye toward its future utility for international relationships with the other Lusophone nations of Africa as well as with Brazil. At the same time, the PAIGC made radio broadcasts in Cape Verdean Crioulo from Senegal. Though listening to them was illegal, the programs found a wide audience in Cape Verde, partly because of their novelty value as the only radio broadcasts in Crioulo at the time. Given the political significance of Crioulo during the last decade or so of colonial rule, it seemed ironic that nearly all the public speeches made by the nation's new leaders on Independence Day (July 5, 1975) were in Portuguese. Since then, Crioulo has been made an official national language along with Portuguese, and is widely employed both in elementary school texts and by the mass media.

Race and Group Identity

Chapter VI describes the values and stereotypes of the prevailing, hegemonic racial ideology under colonialism. Side by side with these subsisted images, beliefs, and values that in some way contradicted them. While the *badius* were generally denigrated as primitive, even somewhat savage, they could still represent Cape Verdeans in symbolic opposition to the Portuguese and *portugalidade*. Similarly, while white or European racial features were generally considered "finer" or "prettier" than African ones, certain racial terms suggest an identification of African racial characteristics with Cape Verdean-ness. Various types of wiry hair, for example, are described by terms pertaining to the distinctive dishes of Cape Verdean cuisine, such as *xerem* or *cus-cus*. Wide noses may be qualified as *maduc*, a kind of stucco traditionally used in house construction, or *tambor* [drum], an important instrument in the music of folk-religious celebrations. Occasionally, the conventional racial aesthetic was contradicted outright: one may who described a woman as "white, pretty" (*branca, bonita*) added, "well, here we say someone is pretty if they're white but it's not really so -- there are ugly whites, too." Likewise, recall the case mentioned earlier, of the man who described a girl in a photograph as "white" rather than "pretty."

Negative stereotypes of metropolitans appear to be of long standing. Chelmiki and Varnhagen write of metropolitans in Cape Verde that "the natives despise them and with good reason" (1841:195). Crioulo terms applied to the Portuguese were varied, colorful, and usually pejorative in some degree.

Nyam bobo, a term of African origin whose original meaning is uncertain, was current in São Vicente in the late nineteenth century; today it survives among Cape Verdean-Americans as a mildly derogatory designation for Azorean and continenal Portuguese. *Mondrong* was so commonly used at the time of the research that its literal meaning [white pig] had lost much of its force of insult. *Tchico* [pig, from the archaic Portuguese *chico*], and *dago*, perhaps borrowed from American slang through the influence of returned emigrants, were also common epithets.

Folk conceptions of Portuguese national character shared general agreement on certain points. Above all, metropolitans were supposed to be *cinicos*; i.e., unfeeling, a highly unfavorable quality in Cape Verdean judgment, that is the moral opposite of the *morabeza* seen as both normal and normative for the Cape Verdean character. (That is, individuals are likely to describe some of their near neighbors as lacking in this quality they "ought" to have; at the same time, Cape Verdeans as a people are frequently described as *morabi*). Furthermore, metropolitans were castigated as avaricious, obsessed with money and money-making, and in the eyes of some, careless about personal hygiene.

The quasi-mythical image of Cape Verdeans as highly literate was clearly a politically convenient one for the colonial regime. To metropolitans, it presented Portuguese rule in a beneficial light, and perhaps added credence to racist stereotypes by suggesting an association between intellectual achievements and mulatto racial characteristics, with an implied correspondence between ignorance and black Africans. That Cape Verdeans shared the myth was all to the good, in colonial terms; Cape Verdeans could thus see themselves as different from and superior to "tribal" Africans from Guinea and the rest of the continent. However, if this favorable stereotype of Cape Verdeans coincided with colonial interests in some ways, it also rebounded against the Portuguese, who were themselves widely regarded as "more ignorant" and "less cultivated" (*menos cultos*) than Cape Verdeans.

Negative stereotypes of metropolitans date back to well before the 1960s, but they seem to have become much strengthened and more widely generalized during the military occupation of the war years. Most Cape Verdeans were having their first direct contact with large numbers of metropolitans during this particularly repressive period. Moreoever, it was also a time, at least after 1968, of scarce food and water resources on which the occupiers constituted an added burden. City dwellers often remarked on the contradictions between Portugal's claims to be saving Cape Verdeans from starvation, and the fact that fresh meat, fish, and vegetables were being bought up by the metropolitans whenever they became available.

Significantly, anti-Portuguese stereotypes were not
extended to other foreigners. In fact, Portuguese neglect and
ineptitude were frequently contrasted with aid received from
the United States in the past and with the British commercial
success in Mindelo. In 1941 the administrator of Fogo, the
son of one of the island's oldest landlord families, was
forced out of his position after having threatened to call
upon the United States for famine relief assistance (N. Cabral
1980:150-51). More recently, a bartender in Fogo evoked laughter -- and a stern warning from the administrator -- when he
referred to a price as "25 Portuguese (*escudos*), or one American (dollar)." The British-founded and -owned telegraph company in Mindelo was being taken over by the Portuguese government in the early 1970s: "Now," people laughed, "we'll be
sending telegrams by boat!"

Epilogue

In 1975, the newly independent Republic of Cabo Verde
faced a formidable array of economic problems, many of which
have been described in this book. These difficulties were
compounded by the fact that many areas of the archipelago were
in their tenth year of drought, and a world recession was
underway. Though satisfying immediate subsistence needs has
had to take priority, a certain degree of progress has been
made in the long-term projects of developing agricultural and
fishing resources. This has only been possible through substantial amounts of foreign aid; such aid normally totals more
than the national budget. In 1979, for example, over $860
million was received from various sources.

Such extensive reliance on foreign aid has created a new
set of problems; it poses a possible threat to political autonomy, and at the same time is likely to create a class of
dependent beneficiaries in the receiving country. The presence of such a category encourages corruption and fosters a
mentality of dependency, as was encouraged during the famine
of the last decade or so of Portuguese rule. Cabo Verde has
so far managed to avoid accepting aid with political conditions attached to it, striving to rely as much as possible on
multilateral sources such as the European Economic Community
and OPEC. A number of measures have been taken to forestall
the internal political dangers that large sums of foreign aid
might present. Austerity is observed at every level of
government, beginning with the prime minister, who earns only
$7,000 a year. (Foreign aid goes into an "extraordinary"
budget; it is used exclusively for development, and not to
balance the "ordinary" budget.) Food sent from abroad is sold
at state-controlled prices, rather than distributed gratis,
except for that given to children, the aged, and the infirm.
Jobs created by development programs are distributed by locale
and then by household, according to need. For the most part,

small-scale projects at the village level are emphasized
rather than vast, centralized forms of development. Coopera-
tives are encouraged by the government, which provides advi-
sors upon request, but the societies remain the responsibility
of their members. Finally, all development projects funded
from abroad are worked out in close collaboration with the
Cape Verdean Solidarity Institute, which is directly responsible to the PAIGC (*Partido Africano da Independencia de Cabo
Verde*), as the ruling political party came to be called after
the 1980 break with Guinea-Bissau.

It seems evident that political and ideological change
has taken priority even over the urgent goal of increasing
production. This is well in keeping with Amilcar Cabral's
perception of the process of national liberation, in which
overthrow of the colonial power is but a movement. Essential
to this process, as he saw it, is the construction of a
"national culture," which includes not only scientific and
technical progress needed for economic development, but "a
new moral and political awareness" (1973b:55). Cabral's
recognition of the importance of culture in the development
of the nation was no uncritical form of "negritude" or "pan-
Africanism," theories he regarded as the "means whereby the
alienated, educated petite bourgeoisie had sought to articulate their new consciousness of the culture and history from
which they had been severed," theories with little meaning
for the popular masses of peasants and laborers (Chabal 1981:
54). Rather, developing national culture was a much more
complex undertaking, involving the recognition of positive
elements in the popular cultural tradition, while encouraging
the aforementioned new awareness. Nor should the more negative elements of popular culture be ignored, for the moral
and psychological precepts of popular culture could also be
"a source of obstacles and difficulties," of "erroneous conceptions" and "limitations" (A. Cabral 1973b:53).

By way of example, the traditional pattern of cooperative
labor (*juntamão*) seems to offer a promising traditional precedent for new forms of cooperative effort, such as have been
attempted in recent years among seamstresses, agricultural-
ists, stonemasons, and other workers. On the other hand,
the welfare mentality encouraged by Portuguese propaganda and
relief programs, as well as the longstanding dependence on
emigrants' remittances in certain areas, would seem to constitute potential obstacles to the development of civic responsibility and initiative.

If one considers the ethnic stereotypes described earlier, the question might be raised as to whether some of these
did not hold what Saul terms the "negative political potential" of ethnicity (1979:412-20), e.g., for anti-white racism,
or chauvinism in regard to other Africans for the post-
colonial era. Neither possibility seems to have materialized.

Negative stereotypes of the Portuguese were never extended to
all whites, though they might have become so under certain
circumstances. The belief in Cape Verdeans' cultural and
intellectual superiority to other Africans seems not to have
manifested itself in international relations, since Cabo Verde
maintains close ties with Senegal and various other African
nations. To what extent new experiences -- such as Cabo
Verdean students pursuing higher degrees at the University of
Dakar -- and the new political context have affected such
notions on the popular level would have to be verified by
further research. Development of a national culture should,
in Amilcar Cabral's view, release peasants and the working
masses in general from narrow local prejudices such as ethnic
chauvinism, and bring them to an awareness of their role in
larger processes transcending the boundaries of their hereto-
fore circumscribed social universe. At the same time, the
intellectuals (in Gramsci's sense of the word) of the petty
bourgeoisie should come to discover the valuable elements of
their own tradition, and develop greater understanding and
appreciation of groups in their society that have been
socially invisible, even denigrated, under the colonial regime.
(Here, the *badius* come to mind.)

The role of the petty bourgeoisie was a crucial one in
Cabral's political program, because under colonial conditions
only this class would have both the means and the motivation
to lead the struggle against the colonizers. Yet, after political independence, this class would constitute a potential
danger to the long-term process of "national liberation."
(See Cabral 1969a, 1969b, 1973a and 1973b.) It was in this
educated class of clerks, civil employees and the like that
the contractions of colonial policy would be most keenly felt,
since here the false nature of the purported goal of assimilation to the metropole would be most evident. Much of the discussion in this chapter, e.g., of language policies, would
seem to bear out Cabral's assessment, which was based partly
on his own experience as an *assimilado* in Guinea:

> To take my own case as a member of the
> petty bourgeois group which launched the
> struggle in Guinea, I was an agronomist
> working under a European who everybody
> knew was one of the biggest idiots in
> Guinea; I could have taught him his job
> with my eyes shut, but he was the boss
> . . . . (1969a:63).

After independence, the petty bourgeoisie faces a
dilemma: either it promotes a new form of domination based on
its own class interests, or it "commits suicide as a class";
that is, through ideological conviction undergoes a gradual
and voluntary loss of privileged status (A. Cabral 1969b:110;
see also 1973b). Many would consider this latter a highly

unlikely possibility, and indeed Cabral himself once referred
to it as a "miracle," albeit a possible one (1969b:70). A
propos of this issue, Chabal offers an interesting analysis of
the moral/ethical aspects of Cabral's political thought
(1981:46-48; 54-56).

To date, the Cabo Verdean government has proceeded cau-
tiously in any attempts to mandate changes in class relations,
e.g., by expropriations, arrests, or "peoples' tribunals"
(Dumont and Mottin 1980:229).[14] At the same time, its policies favoring initiative and decision making on the local
level and imposing austerity in its own ranks may encourage,
through community pressure and example, the moral transforma-
tion of the petty bourgeoisie that Cabral saw not as inevitable, but as eminently possible.

Notes

1. During the same period, the number of *assimilados* among *mestiços* increased by 5.9 percent, that is, by less than 3,000 persons; the "assimilated" proportion of the population as a whole remained nearly constant during this decade. (See figures in Bender 1978:151.)

2. Bender (1978:153, note 79) cites Alphonso Mendes, Director of the Angolan Labour Institute from 1962 to 1970 and of that in Mozambique from 1970 to 1974, to this effect.

3. According to a Portuguese lieutenant who, astonished, watched this being done in a district headquarters in rural Santiago.

4. Djunga (João Cleofas Martins, 1901-1970), a popular poet and satirist from Mindelo, protested this by refusing his promotion to *primeiro cabo*, to the consternation of his superiors.

5. Portuense, mentioned in Chapter IV, was a formidably righteous prelate, his moral stance honed all the sharper, surely, by the appalling corruption and laxity typical of the clergy in the colony. He impressed king and populace both with his zeal to Christianize Guinea and his many achievements, including completion of the cathedral at Ribeira Grande, Santiago. In his quarrels with Santiago's notables, the energetic bishop invoked the threat of excommunication liberally, and with the king, that of resignation. Neither appears to have been carried out, and Portuense died in office in 1705 (Barcelos 1900 II: 110-74).

6. Three Spanish Capuchins working in Bissau, 1683-86, were ejected in favor of Portuguese Franciscans at the behest of a local Portuguese priest, on the grounds that the Spaniards had not attempted to form commercial ties with local groups but had "only" tried to convert them (Rodney 1970:143).

7. This fact came to light when Almada presented the information on his filiation required for receiving the habit of the order and the 15 *mil reis* pension that went with it. It was decided that his service to the king, as well as the compensating nobility of his father's lineage, should provide dispensation, and so the honor was duly conferred (Barcelos 1899 I: 176-77).

8. In this vein, the Minister of Instruction, one A. Magalhães, noted with some irony (perhaps unintended) that his was not a position in which one could easily

praise illiteracy; however, he went on to say that he "trusted illiterates completely" (Mónica 1979:9).

9. Macedo mentions a debate current among Lisbon intellectuals of his day as to whether blacks <u>could</u> be educated (1901).

10. The PIDE (*Policia International e da Defesa do Estado*), known as the DGS (*Direcçao Geral da Segurança*) under Marcelo Caetano's government (1968-74), was established in the 1930s with considerable assistance from the Gestapo and Mussolini's secret police. Its methods included refined and sophisticated methods of torture; its penetration of all spheres of social life and government made the PIDE virtually a "state within a state" under Salazar's rule (Marques 1974 II:301-2).

11. Figures provided by *Serviços da Estatistica do Cabo Verde* (personal communication, 1972).

12. I was told the following story in Mindelo, in the home of an upper-class family generally considered "white." After some discussion of *badius'* "primitive" culture, one person remarked, "but they're clever, too," and told this story:

> Not long ago a Portuguese soldier was walking with a woman on a street in Praia. On seeing a *badiu*, he called out, "Hey, nigger (*preto*), come here. I have an errand for you to do." The *badiu* needed money of course, so he did it. When he returned and asked for a tip, they just laughed at him. So he turned as if to go, but instead drew his knife and stabbed the man. The *metropolitano* died, but the *badiu* got away . . . they never caught him . . . you know, they think we're all *pretos*, *pretos obedientes* (Machado 1977:62).

13. Among relatives and sometimes neighbors, communal labor, *juntamão* [putting hands together] in Crioulo, was common for tasks such as harvesting and housebuilding. Usually those who contributed labor were rewarded with food and drink, and could expect similar help when they needed it.

14. In 1981, measures were taken to eliminate sharecropping (*parceria*) and to redistribute large absentee landholdings (Legum 1983:B405).

VIII

RACE AND CULTURE IN COLONIAL CAPE VERDE:
A COMPARATIVE VIEW

A number of references were made in Chapter VI to various
points of similarity between the Cape Verdean and Brazilian
racial systems. Here these resemblances will be examined in
greater detail and I will argue, on the basis of the Cape
Verdean case, that the contrasts between multi-category racial
systems such as the Brazilian and the binary one of the United
States, often made in comparative studies of race, are somewhat overdrawn. I argue that terminological fluidity and the
absence of legal color bars do not necessarily imply lack of
racism. "Race," understood as a type of social classification
based on alleged ancestry and phenotype, may still constitute
a social distinction of paramount importance, and racial barriers may still function in social practice, despite the apparent flexibility of racial categories. The last part of the
chapter returns to the original point of departure for this
study, as described in Chapter I, and examines the significance of the present anaysis of the race relations in colonial
Cape Verde for understanding the experience of Cape Verdean
immigrants in the United States.

Racial Categories and Race Relations:
Brazil and Cabo Verde

Chapter VI presented the findings from a projective test
designed to elicit racial terms. Marvin Harris, who designed
the test, found 492 such terms in Brazil; the same test, when
used in Cape Verde, produced a corpus of 140. However, as
mentioned earlier, this difference can be attributed, in part,
to different modes of procedure and criteria of analysis.
Harris administered the test to 100 subjects in five different
states in Brazil, as well as in the city of Brazilia (1970:2),
while in Cape Verde, the same number of subjects was drawn
from a single locale. In addition, Harris counted the terms
in "strictly lexical" fashion (Ibid.), apparently treating
male and female variants such as *mulato/mulata* as two different terms. Thus, a part of the "lexical productivity" Harris
calls attention to is due simply to the structure of the
Portuguese language.

Roger Sanjek's use of the same test in a single village in Bahia, with 60 subjects, produced a corpus of 116 terms (1971:1,127). Sanjek, however, appears to have counted male and female variants of the type mentioned above as single terms. He also offers convincing evidence to show that there is considerable organization of this cognitive domain. Ten terms accounted for nearly 85 percent of all responses (Ibid., p. 1,129). Eleven terms and their modified forms (e.g., *mulato, mulato claro, mulato oscuro*, etc.) comprised 86 of the terms collected, or 74 percent of the corpus (Ibid., p. 1,130). This modifies somewhat Harris's contention that no "intersubjective uniformity" exists in the domain of Brazilian racial terminology (1970:12).

Results from the use of the test in Cape Verde also tend to support Sanjek's position. In this second instance of a Portuguese-influenced multicategory terminology, more "organization" seems to be the case than Harris would lead us to believe in the presentation of his Brazilian findings. Fifteen base terms and their modified forms account for 125 terms (89 percent) of the corpus. Four base terms and their modified forms account for 95 (67.8 percent) of the 140 terms collected. And, as mentioned in Chapter VI, 25 subjects used only three terms, corresponding roughly to " black," "white," and "mixed" divisions, though which three terms were used varied among these subjects. However, it was also noted that in at least some cases, it could not be presumed that a modified form (e.g., *branca de cabeça seca*, "white with 'dry' hair") constituted a <u>semantic</u> subset of a more general category denoted by the root term (in this case, *branco/a*), judging from the subject's remarks while responding to the drawings and general field observations. *Branca de cabeça seca*, for example, was described as a possible alternative to *mulato claro* [light mulatto] or *negro bermedjo* [red nigger]. Such was most clearly the case for modifications of *branco*, though not necessarily true of other root terms and modifiers. *Mulato claro* may be a semantic subset of *mulato*, in that someone called *mulato claro* might conceivably be termed, on occasion, simply *mulato*. It is, however, inconceivable that an individual termed *branca de cabeça seca* or *branco de cabelo crespo* would ever be termed "white." Thus it is possible, though not demonstrated here, that the most basic semantic distinction is that between *branco/a* and other categories.

The reservations expressed so far in regard to Harris's analysis notwithstanding, it remains indisputable that Brazilian, as well as Cape Verdean, terminology pertaining to racial types is much richer, more varied, and indeterminate in application than the American. What remains problematic is the relation between terminology and behavior. Harris has rightfully pointed out that the indeterminate ("ambiguous") quality of Brazilian racial terminology, along with its variability from one subject to another, poses problems for the

"New Ethnography."[1] This approach to the study of cultural
categories through careful collection of linguistic data pertaining to a given domain of meaning, such as kinship, has
usually relied on one or several informants as representatives
of an entire population.[2] Yet Harris himself seems to assume
a high degree of correspondence between language (in this
case, racial terminology), social relations, and cultural
meanings.

In his comprehensive study of Brazilian slavery and race
relations, Harris takes eloquent issue with Freyre's Lusotropicalism (1974:65-69). However, like Freyre (1961), Elkins
(1959), Tannenbaum (1946), and many others, he conceptualizes
Brazilian race relations as radically different from those
found in the United States, though this is explained by economic factors (e.g., the presence of economic niches for
mulattoes) rather than cultural or psychological ones. What
is more, Harris argues that the very character of the Brazilian terminology system -- its many categories, the multiple
criteria for classification, disagreement among individuals
about how to classify in any given case -- obviates any possibility of racial segregation and makes discrimination on the
basis of race difficult or impossible. Descent is seen as
irrelevant for classification. The fact that an individual of
dark color who becomes wealthy will be termed "white" (as the
Brazilian saying goes, "money whitens") is taken to mean that
in Brazil, persons can change racial identity without the
"passing" required for such a change in the United States,
where friends and family must be cut off in order to do this
(1974:59).

Due to the many criteria that may be invoked for classification, according to Harris, "there are no subjectively
meaningful social groupings based exclusively upon racial criteria" (1974:59). Class, not race, is the basis of pervasive
and enduring social inequalities; whatever racial discrimination does occur is "mild and equivocal" (Ibid., p. 61). This
last statement seems at variance with the findings of many
other students, e.g., Bastide and Fernandes (1959), Ianni
(1972), Azevedo (1975). Fernandes (1969) gives ample evidence
of race prejudice and discrimination in Brazil. The findings
from Cabo Verde presented in this chapter allow us to question
certain of Harris's assertions.

We have seen that Cape Verdean racial terminology is
similar to the findings made in Brazil. As pointed out in
Chapter VI, though, the criteria which determine classification may vary by social context. In contexts where class
exclusivity is a paramount concern (e.g., marriage), the number of categories governing classification can be greatly
reduced from the number available, and ancestry can be invoked
as the determining criterion. Furthermore, phenotypical criteria (those referring to visible physical traits) are not

innocuous data but value-laden attributes. Racial terms comprise not merely a varied ensemble but instead form a hierarchy, though admittedly one whose particulars are disputed.
That is, individuals disagree on which of several categories
is "worst," yet do not question that some categories are
"worse" than others.

If most of our criticism concerns Harris's discussion of
the Brazilian racial system, this is only because his is the
most comprehensive and articulate among those of several
writers who take similar positions. In Banton's widely used
text, *Race Relations*, for example, the author cites the work
of a Brazilian scholar, Oracy Nogueira (1959) to argue that
what prejudice may be found in multicategory racial systems
is of the "intellectual," "aesthetic" type, rather than the
more "emotional" kinds found in two-category systems such as
the American (1967:277). In an integrated racial order such
as Brazil's, Banton argues, "the negative value attributed to
a dark complexion is much greater than that attaching to a
small stature, but the kind of social reckoning is the same"
(Ibid., p. 281). Harris goes even further than Banton, dis-
missing whatever racial stereotypes do exist in Brazil as
"ideological phenomena" that "do not seriously affect actual
behavior" (1974:60). Harris treats ideology more or less
synonymously with attitudes, a usage that may well be questioned. But even as he uses the term, one can only wonder
what sort of ideology it is that has no bearing on behavior.

In Brazil, as in colonial Cape Verde, I would suggest, a
key element of the dominant ideology of race is the notion
that racism does not exist. In fact, Fernandes asserts, even
raising the question of whether it exists is likely to be
itself deemed racist (1978, Vol. 2: 414). Rather than race,
"culture" is supposed to be the most important form of social
distinction; thus, individuals "try to compensate for their
demerits by copying the behavior of their social superiors"
(Banton 1967:277, paraphrasing Nogueira). Similarly, Harris
insists that discrimination is based on class, with race
being incidental. Yet in Cabo Verde, it was found that discrimination presented as a distinction of "level" (*nível*) or
background is experienced as racism by those who are its
object. Social exclusion of those considered to be of a
lower level has the function, intended or not, of effecting
informal but real racial barriers.

Manuel Ferreira, a Portuguese author of numerous works
of fiction set in Cabo Verde, writes that "from the social,
cultural and psychological points of view there are no black
Cape Verdeans, no white Cape Verdeans, and no *mestiço* Cape
Verdeans. There are, yes, rich Cape Verdeans, poor ones, the
well-off and the wretched . . . ." (1967:59). This formula-
tion, if more simplistically stated, approximates Harris's
portrait of Brazil. Let us look, then, at the exceptional

163

individual who surmounts the dual obstacles of poverty and race and becomes "white" -- or *branco de dinheiro*, [white by money], as Cape Verdeans put it. Chapter VI demonstrated that such upward mobility did not ensure white status in all social contexts, and that any false step could ensure a racial "demotion" in the form of a cutting remark, or worse. Things do not seem so different in Brazil. As one "upwardly mobile" black man sees it:

> The black commits a gross error when he
> thinks that education, clothing, reputa-
> tion and money make him somebody. Sure,
> all this makes life better, and gives one
> a lot of pleasure, but on the other hand
> it shows that what we thought was fabri-
> cation or rumour really does exist --
> race prejudice (Ferreira 1967:261).

Indeed, it would seem from this man's remarks that such an individual is confronted with the contradictions of what Banton (1967:277) and Nogueira (1959) term the "assimilationist" ideology supposed to characterize the Brazilian racial order. This occurs in much the same way that Cape Verdeans as *assimilados*, especially the petty bourgeoisie "intellectuals," had to confront those of the Portuguese colonial program of assimilation. In both cases, assimilation is presented as a cultural (i.e., behavioral) matter, and it is precisely those individuals who surmount the obstacles built into the system and assimilate culturally, by the criteria of the dominant class, who discover for themselves that their status as assimilated is never complete and always precarious. In conclusion, I would suggest that it is misleading to oppose race and class as two entirely separate "determinants of stratification" of the social placement of individuals. Rather, the racial hierarchy and the ideology that supports it must be seen as bulwarks of a given class order. In colonial Cape Verde, the "ruling class," to put it broadly, was only partly based in the archipelago; it was not only a local class order that was at stake, but the Portuguese colonial system as well.

Harris concludes that no meaningful racial groupings exist in Brazil (1974:61), and further suggests that a racial category system such as Brazil's precludes the development of racial consciousness among the darker lower classes (1970:12). This seems contradicted by the appearance of the groups and movements described by Fernandes (1978, Vol. II: 7-115). Even if these can be dismissed as lacking a broad popular base, Harris's position would seem precipitous at best. On the question of whether, in the future, Brazil's blacks and mulattoes will mobilize against the dominant ideology of race that is an integral support of Brazilian class structure

(Ianni 1978:132-42), and that keeps black workers in a position inferior to that of white workers (Ibid., pp. 79-80), the jury is still out.

From Cabo Verde to America

Cape Verdeans left a society characterized by an Iberian system of race relations, and then had to adapt themselves to an Anglo racial system, that of the United States. I suggest that the similarities between the two types of systems allowed for a certain continuity of experience, but one that was not readily apparent; this continuity, and its somewhat hidden quality, had, I believe, important effects on how the Cape Verdean community developed in the United States. Quite naturally, it is the contrasts between American society and the one they left that are paramount in the perceptions of most immigrants. Here, though, I will focus on some of the resemblances and parallels between these two parts of their experience.

Certain broad themes bridge the history of Cabo Verde and that of Cape Verdeans in the United States. The social invisibility Cape Verdean-Americans experience as a small, Afro-American ethnic group, is nothing new to them. Time and again the insignificance of the archipelago in Portugal's empire was made clear; for example, by the lack of maritime contact with the metropole for years on end, the indifference of the Portuguese government to the plight of the islands during droughts, and even by the new social science texts, introduced during the colonial wars, that were oriented to the larger, more economically valuable, mainland colonies.

The marginal position of Cape Verdeans as exploited and dominated, but yet traditionally identifying with their exploiters, had its equivalent in the United States. Cape Verdeans who were accepted in the ethnic community in New England and who identified themselves with it, tended to shun association with American Blacks, even while they themselves suffered racial discrimination. In both cases, the exploitation suffered by Cape Verdeans was viewed as aberrant. In Cabo Verde, it was lamented that Portugal did not trust Cape Verdeans, that the Portuguese didn't understand that Cape Verdeans were "just as Portuguese as they"; in the United States, mistreatment by whites was viewed as a mistake: "they don't know that we are not the same as Negroes." In both cases, the ideology of the dominant category was transmitted to spheres of intimacy: "African" customs were considered backward, a sign of ignorance, and physical resemblances between individual Cape Verdeans and Africans or Afro-Americans were cases for teasing, insults, or commiseration by others.

Close examination of the dominant ideology of race in
Cabo Verde shows it to have been far more like that in the
United States than most descriptions of multicategory racial
systems would have us believe. But there is a deeper, complex
resemblance between the dominant ideology of colonial Cape
Verde and the one the immigrants encountered in the U.S. The
myth of racial equality in Cabo Verde is paralleled by the
myth of upward class mobility in the United States. It is
widely believed that upward mobility is a frequent occurrence,
though this notion has been roundly contradicted by empirical
studies (e.g., Lipset and Bendix 1959; see also Bottomore
1966:52). Yet the myth flourishes, along with its corolar-
ries, such as the belief that education guarantees the worthy
individual much more interesting, better paid, and less rou-
tinized work than he would otherwise obtain (Sennett and Cobb
1973:173-88).

In Cabo Verde it was, supposedly, not "race" (phenotype
and ancestry) that accounted for disparities of political
power and economic status, but "background" or "culture" (in
the double sense of customs, values, etc. and refinement,
learning, and so on). Habits of work, notions of time, ability to defer gratification, along with other personal attributes, were adduced to explain the social position of darker
categories of persons. The latter often appeared to accept
such designations by describing themselves as "stupid," by
referring to their own ignorance as the reason for their
exclusion from positions of power. Similarly, the popular
American notion holds that people don't "get ahead" because of
values and mores incompatible with upward mobility, a folk
explanation sometimes allowed the blessing of social science.
In both cases, the individual who makes a spectacular social
ascent is held forth as an example of what others could be or
might have been. In both cases, inequities are explained by
such factors as abilities, values, acquired "culture"; in
short, by merit.

From the perspective of colonial Cape Verde, Cape
Verdean-Americans' marginality vis-à-vis both blacks and
whites seems to replicate their experience as colonized *assimilados*. In general, when Cape Verdeans entered societies
whose dominant ideologies pertaining to race were similar to
the one that prevailed in Cape Verde, they were likely to
retain the notions of race that were dominant under Portuguese
colonialism, and to become a marginal category, neither fully
Portuguese nor African. Cape Verdean immigrants in Senegal
(Andrade 1972), Angola (Bender 1978:203, note 6), and the
United States show certain broad similarities, in that they
tended to keep social distance from and attitudes of superiority toward Blacks, and to be politically conservative. Cape
Verdeans in the Netherlands offer a case in contrast. There,
Cape Verdeans had opportunities to acquire a new perspective
on race and on colonialism, since the Dutch government

tolerated the presence of African revolutionary movements,
whose associations and publications (e.g., *Nôs Vida*) flourished in the emigrant community. Also important was the
relative lack of racism Cape Verdeans experienced there, as
recounted by emigrants on their visits back to Cabo Verde.

In America, the Cape Verdean-American community[3] has been
a successful one from the point of view of the wider American
society and from that of the immigrants as well. They avoided
welfare, became homeowners, and gained a reputation for hard
work and dependability. At the same time, in the Atlantic
coastal communities where Cape Verdean enclaves developed, the
immigrants managed to make great strides toward imposing their
own self-image as different from and better than American
Blacks.

In some ways, the alienation produced by the colonial
racist ideology and the ambiguity of Cape Verdeans' position
in the empire served the immigrants well in the American context. They were able, for example, to accept the ideology of
white supremacy while remaining detached from blackness. "We
are all white under the skin"; "I look black but I think
white, and that's what counts." Such comments give evidence
of belief in spiritual and intellectual equality, along with
acceptance of social inequities that, in a profound way, are
not believed to touch the self. What is needed is culture
(*cultura*), in the double sense of refinement and norms,
beliefs, and values, to allow inner "whiteness" to become
manifest. Rejection by white Portuguese did not convince Cape
Verdean-Americans of their inferiority, perhaps in part
because of Cape Verdeans' traditional stereotype of themselves
as superior in education and intellect to the Portuguese.
Instead, such discrimination contributed to the development of
parallel, ethnically exclusive institutions that, in turn,
contributed to the cohesion of the Cape Verdean-American community and placed Cape Verdeans in leadership roles.

Culture (in the sense of norms, customs, language) became
an arm for defending Cape Verdean distinctiveness on both a
racial and a cultural level. Here we see the confusion of the
two spheres, so charactertistic of Portuguese colonial ideology, perpetuated and used in new contexts. The cultural
traits that became Cape Verdean ethnic "markers" in the new
setting were not simply survivals from the homeland, though
Cape Verdean-Americans usually viewed them as such. Rather,
their form and meaning changed in the new society. Musical
forms considered African, such as *batuque* or the call-and-
response singing typical of religious feasts in the islands,
did not become part of the tradition passed on to children
born in America, though new, sophisticated recorded versions
have been gaining in popularity since Cabo Verde's independence. Customs considered African, such as *pilon* [grinding
corn with a large mortar and pestle before major feasts], were

either abandoned or carried out privately; that of the *mastro* [mast] for the larger feasts has been performed publicly on numerous occasions, being considered part of the Portuguese heritage. *Crioulo*, considered a sign of backwardness and Afrcican-ness in the Cape Verdes, became a mark of distinctiveness from American Blacks, though it was often passed off as Portuguese.

The costs of success, though, have been extremely high if we consider the many Cape Verdeans excluded from the community, in the early days, on the basis of color -- notably the darker immigrants from Fogo and Santiago -- and later, because of marriage to American Blacks. More than this, the quality of life within the community has suffered. The pressures of proving one's respectability in a racist milieu have often required rigid and severe parental controls over children, much as they have for America's traditional black bourgeoisie, or would-be bourgeoisie (Marx 1973:146). The community's ideology of race and its encapsulated quality have made it claustrophobic, especially for those who have moved beyond it because of educational or other achievements. Many such individuals have distanced themselves from it, with considerable loss to the community.

The independence of Cabo Verde presents a new set of opportunities to Cape Verdean-Americans. Some who have been long removed from the community because of their identification with American Blacks have found in Cape Verdean independence an occasion for reintegration into the community, and have become involved in its organizations and publications. No longer is "Cape Verdean" incompatible with "African" or "Afro-American." Some individuals have come full circle in their search for identity to see that, as Cape Verdeans, they have not far or long to search for their roots. Their new appreciation of Cape Verdean identity is certainly timely, since more and more of the community's youths are faced with questions and challenges to its traditional norms of race and culture.

Notes

1. This approach was pioneered by Goodenough (1956) and
    Lounsbury (1956), and developed by a number of others,
    e.g., Sturtevant (1964). As Sanjek has pointed out, not
    all of the proponents of the New Ethnography assume the
    psychological validity of the semantic categories that
    can be isolated through the study of linguistic data
    (e.g., Hymes 1965), arguing instead for criteria such as
    elegance and prediction (1971:1,126).

2. Sanjek has argued, using Brazilian racial terminology as
    his example, that such difficulties can be resolved
    within the parameters of the New Ethnography with the aid
    of quantitative methods using a greater number of
    informants and appropriate sampling procedures (1970:
    1,127).

3. Here, the word "community" refers not to a single, geo-
    graphically localized group of people, but rather to a
    network of people joined across various locales along the
    Eastern seaboard by links of kinship and friendship;
    these ties imply regular contact and mutual aid.

Appendix 1

Area and Population
of Cabo Verde

Island	Area (in sq. mi.)	Population (1960 Census)	Population Density (1960)
Santiago	382.5	88,900	232
Santo Antão	300.7	34,600	115
Boa Vista	239.3		14
Fogo	183.7	25,500	139
São Nicolau	132.4	13,900	105
Maio	103.8	2,700	
São Vicente	87.6	21,400	306
Sal	83.3	2,600	31
Brava	24.7	8,600	348
Santa Luzia	13.5	uninhabited	–
Raso	2.7	uninhabited	–
Branco	1.1	uninhabited	–
Grande	.7	uninhabited	–
Cima	.4	uninhabited	–

Figures are taken from Duncan 1972:253-56. Those for population and population density are based on reports published by the Portuguese National Institute of Statistics.

Appendix 2

Emigration to São Tomé and Principé
from Cabo Verde:
Recorded Departures

	São Tomé	Principé	Total
1902 - 1922	12,942	11,036	23,978
1923 - 1940	n.a.	n.a.	n.a.
1941 - 1949	n.a.	n.a.	20,884
1950 - 1970	30,435	4,095	34,530

From figures provided by Carreira (1977:248).

GLOSSARY[*]

administrador (Cr. *dimistrador*)
Colonial government administrator in charge of a district.

aguardente (Cr. *grog*)
Sugar cane whiskey.

americanos
Cape Verdeans who have lived or are living in the United States.

arroba[1]
Measure of weight equivalent to about 32 pounds.

assimilado
African considered "assimilated" rather than "native," and who is therefore a citizen of Portugal.

atrevido
Impertinent, bold.

badiu
Peasant inhabitants of Santiago's interior, believed to be largely descended from runaway slaves (from Ptg. *vadio*

bandeira
Banner, flag. In the context of saints' feasts, the banner depicting the saint is carried at the head of processions. The term is often extended to refer to an entire feast or celebration within a feast.

barafula[2]
A unit of exchange in the Cape Verdes and on the Guinea coast. An ordinary Cape Verdean cloth was known as a *barafula*; one standard iron bar could be traded for two *barafula* cloths c. 1680.

---

[*]"Cr." indicates that the Crioulo term has no equivalent in Portuguese or is markedly different from its Portuguese etymon. "Ptg." designates Portuguese forms.

[1]See Duncan's useful appendix on Portuguese weights and measures.

[2]See Duncan 1972:218.

batuque
> Traditional musical form handed down from the slaves. Originally, only the clapping or beating of a wadded cloth, used as a drum, accompanied women singing in call-and-response. Nowadays, percussion may also be provided by striking an iron bar or metal triangle.

bermedjo, negro bermedjo (Cr.)
> (From Ptg. *vermelho*, red) Racial designation referring to individuals with fair skin.

branco
> Racial term meaning "white." May be extended to include the well-off: *branco de dinheiro* [white by money].

cachupa (Cr.)
> Festive dish prepared from corn, beans, lard, pork, and other ingredients.

Câmara
> City hall; town council.

canizade
> Dance performed by pairs of men (formerly these were slaves) two nights before a saint's feast day. Dancers wearing white and with powdered faces performed in the parlors of white landlords.

canja
> Rich chicken broth served at all saints' feasts.

capela
> (From Ptg. *capela*, chapel) One of Fogo's hereditary tracts of land granted to her founding families. These extended from the shore up to the cone of the island's volcano. Each *capela* was associated with certain religious devotions performed by the landlord family and passed on to succeeding generations.

cavalheiro
> Horseman. Selected *cavalheiros*, traditionally from leading families, head the major processions of important religious feasts.

claro
> Racial term meaning "light."

coladeira
> Women who sing in the call-and-response pattern; e.g., in *batuque*. Also, a musical form, light in tone and fairly rapid in tempo.

colonatos
  Planned agricultural settlements in Angola. Some of
  these were intended to be multiracial and included Cape
  Verdean settlers.

conto
  Monetary unit equivalent to 1000 *escudos*.

crise
  Often used in reference to drought, but more specifically
  denotes the social upheaval caused by drought.

decreto
  Edict; act.

degredado
  Criminal or political prisoner exiled to Cape Verde.

djagacida (Cr.)
  Popular dish based on a mixture of corn and beans.

dona
  Respectful term of address, placed before the first name,
  applied to women on the basis of age and/or social standing.

dono/a
  Owner; also used in reference to the sponsor of a religious feast.

escudo[3]
  Unit of currency equivalent to 1000 *reis* (singular *real*)
  or a *milreis*.

Estado Novo
  The so-called "New State" instituted by Antonio Salazar.

feitor
  Property administrator; land steward.

festa
  Party; religious feast.

fidalgo
  Aristocrat.

---

[3]See Duncan's discussion of Portuguese money (1972:
263-66).

formaçao
   Background; training.

funco (Cr.)
   Round dwelling made of stones and with a thatched roof.

garda-cabeça
   Prayers said for a week after a child is born by friends
   and relatives. This is believed to protect the newborn
   from malevolent forces.

grog (Cr.)
   Sugar cane whiskey (*aguardente*)

indigena
   African classified as "native." This status implied
   special constraints, such as the head tax, and ineligi-
   lity for the rights of Portuguese citizenship.

Indigenato
   Policy whereby Africans were defined as "indigenous" or
   assimilated, the latter being a restricted category
   which few were allowed to enter.

irmandade
   Religious fraternity of men and women devoted to a particular saint.

lançado
   Cape Verdea, usually a mulatto or a black freeman, working in the Guinea coastal regions as a trading repre-
   sentative of a Santiago merchant.

lanche
   Late afternoon snack.

lenço
   Headkerchief traditionally worn by peasant women.

liceu
   Secondary school.

mal di odjo (Cr.)
   Evil eye.

mestiço/a
   Individual of mixed racial background.

milreis[3]
> One thousand *reis*; one *escudo*.

mondrong (Cr.)
> Mildly pejorative term applied to the Portuguese.

morabeza (Cr.)
> Kindness, tenderness toward others.

morabi (Cr.)
> Characterized by *morabeza*.

morgadios
> In Santiago, tracts of land ceded by the Crown to individuals, to be passed to succeeding generations by the rule of primogeniture.

morna (Cr.)
> Slow, often doleful sounding musical form played on guitars, violas and violins. Lyrics are often considered poems in their own right, and usually concern love, loss, longing, and nostalgia.

nhô, nhâ (Cr.)
> Crioulo forms of Ptg. *senhor, senhora* [Mr., Mrs.]

nyam bobo (Cr.)
> Pejorative term applied to metropolitans.

pano
> Cloth; here refers to the woven textiles exported from the Cape Verdes during the slave trade era.

pano de bicho
> Cloth with woven designs resembling the markings on animal hides; these were highly valued in the Guinea trade.

pilon (Cr.)
> Mortar. Interestingly, the term is derived from Ptg. *pilão*, meaning "pestle." (In Crioulo, "pestle" is called *po di pilão*, literally, "pestle-stick.") *Pilon* also refers to the ceremonial corn grinding that precedes major saints' feasts.

---

[3] See Duncan's discussion of Portuguese money (1972: 263-66).

portaria
 Official document.

promessa
 Vow or solemn promise made to a saint in return for a
 favor asked or already granted.

quintal
 Interior courtyard where much heavy domestic work is
 done.

rebelados
 Literally, "rebels." Applied to adherents of a religious
 sect that developed among Santiago's *badius* in the 1960s.

sabi (Cr.)
 Delightful, delicious.

sala
 Parlor where respected guests are received.

seca
 Drought.

sobrado
 Large, two-story house with interior courtyard and
 veranda, the typical dwelling of white landlord families.

sucuro
 From Ptg. *oscuro*, dark. Used as a racial designation,
 as in *mulato sucuro* [dark mulatto].

tabanca
 Localized social-religious organizations in Santiago.

tchico
 Term of insult, meaning "white pig," applied to metropolitans.

tipo
 Physical type.

urzela
 Orchil, a dye-bearing lichen.

xerem
 Dish made from coarsely ground maize.

References

Agar, Michael H.
1980   *The Professional Stranger: An Informal Introduction
        to Ethnography*. New York: Academic Press.

Agência Geral do Ultramar
1970   *Cabo Verde: Pequena Monografia*. Lisbon: Agência
        Geral do Ultramar.

Albouy, Yves and Bruno Boulenger
1975   Les facteurs Climatiques. In *Sécheresses et Famines
        du Sahel*. Jean Copans, ed. Pp. 41-59. Paris:
        Maspero.

Almada, André Alvares de
1946   *Tratado Breve dos Rios de Guiné*. Lisbon: Ediçao de
[1594] Luis Silveira.

Almada, Dulce
1961   *Cabo Verde: Contribuição para o Estudo do Dialecto
        Falado no Seu Arquipelago*. Lisbon: Junta de Inves-
        tigações do Ultramar, Estudos de Ciências Políticas
        e Sociais, No. 55.

Andrade, E. Silva
1972   Les Migrations Capverdiennes à Dakar. Paper pre-
        sented at the Eleventh International Seminar: Les
        Migrations Modernes en Afrique Occidentale, Dakar,
        Senegal.

Andréini, Jean Claude and Marie-Claude Lambert
1978   *La Guinée-Bissau: d'Amilcar Cabral à la Reconstruc-
        tion Nationale*. Paris: L'Harmattan.

Anonymous
1784   *Nota Coragráphica e Cronológica do Bispado de Cabo
        Verde - 1784*. Ediçao da Revista Diogo Cão, Inéditos
        Coloniais, Série A, No. II.

Anonymous
1913   O Analfabetismo em Cabo Verde. *Revista de Educação
        Geral e Tecnica*. II:140-42.

Araujo, Norman
1966   *A Study of Cape Verdean Literature*. Chestnut Hill,
        MA: Boston College.

Asad, Talal
1973   *Anthropology and the Colonial Encounter*. London:
        Ithaca Press.

180

Azevedo, Thales
1975   *Democracia Racial: Ideologia e Realidade*. Patró-
polis, Brazil: Vozes.

Bailyn, Bernard
1955   *The New England Merchants in the Seventeenth Century*. Cambridge: Harvard University Press.

Bannick, Christian John
1917   *Portuguese Immigration to the United States: Its
Distribution and Status*. Berkeley: University of
California. (Printed in 1971 by A. and E. Assoc.,
San Francisco.)

Banton, Michael
1967   *Race Relations*. New York: Basic Books.

Barbosa, Jorge
1961   Crianças. In *Modernos Poetas Cabo-Verdianos*. Jaime
de Figueiredo, ed. Pp. 29-32. Praia, Cabo Verde:
Edições Henriquinas Achamento de Cabo Verde.

Barcelos, Cristiano José de Sena
1899-   *Subsidios para a História de Cabo Verde e Guiné*.
1913   7 vols. Lisbon: Tipografia da Academia Real das
Ciências de Lisboa.

Barnes, John
1966   Comment. *Current Anthropology* 7:554.

Barreto, João
1938   *História da Guiné*. Lisbon: Edição do Autor.

Barros, Simão
1936   *Ensaio Sobre a História Econômica de Cabo Verde*.
Lisbon: Edições Herpiritanias, 3° Faisiculo.

Barthes, Roland
1972   *Mythologies*. Frogmore, St. Albans: Paladin.

Bastide, Roger
1961   Dusky Venus, Black Apollo. *Race* 3:10-18.

Bastide, Roger and Florestan Fernandes
1959   *Brancos e Negros em São Paulo*. São Paulo: Editora
Nacional.

Bender, Gerald J.
1978   *Angola Under the Portuguese: the Myth and the
Reality*. Los Angeles: University of California.

Bennett, Norman R. and George E. Brooks, Jr.
1965   *New England Merchants in Africa: A History Through Documents, 1802-1865*. Boston: Boston University Press.

Berreman, Gerald D.
1962   *Behind Many Masks*. The Society for Applied Anthropology, monograph no. 4.

Blake, John William
1937   *European Beginnings in West Africa*. Westport, CT: Greenwood Press.

1942   *Europeans in West Africa, 1450-1560*. London: Haklyut Society Publications, Series 2, Vol. I.

Blumer, Herbert
1958   Race as a Sense of Group Position. *Pacific Sociological Review* I:3-7.

Bottomore, Tom
1966   *Classes in Modern Society*. New York: Vintage.

Boxer, Charles
1961   The Colour Question in the Portuguese Empire, 1415-1825. *Proceedings of the British Academy* 1961:1-138.

1963   *Race Relations in the Portuguese Colonial Empire, 1415-1825*. Oxford University Press.

Brace, C. Loring
1967   *The Stages of Human Evolution: Human and Cultural Origins*. Englewood Cliffs, NJ: Prentice-Hall.

Braroe, Neils
1975   *Indian and White: Self-Image and Interaction in a Canadian Plains Community*. Stanford: Stanford University Press.

Brásio, António
1964   *Monumenta Missionaria* (Africa Ocidental), Série 2, Vol. III. Lisbon: Agência Geral do Ultramar.

1968   *Monumenta Missionaria* (Africa Ocidental), Série 2, Vol. IV. Lisbon: Agência Geral do Ultramar.

Bridge, Horatio
1968   *Journal of an African Cruiser*. London: Dawson of
[1845] Pall Mall.

Brooks, George E., Jr.
1970   *Yankee Traders, Old Coasters and African Middlemen:*
        A History of American Legitimate Trade with West
        Africa in the Nineteenth Century. Boston: Boston
        University Press.

Brown, Richard
1973   Anthropology and Colonial Rule: Godfrey Wilson and
        the Rhodes-Livingstone Institute, Northern Rhodesia.
        In *Anthropology and the Colonial Encounter.* Talal
        Asad, ed. Pp. 173-98. London: Ithaca Press.

Bryson, R.A.
1973   Drought in Sahelia: Who or What is to Blame? *The*
        Ecologist 3:377-71.

Cabral, Amilcar
1969a   Brief Analysis of the Social Structure in Guinea.
        In *Revolution in Guinea: Selected Texts.* Amilcar
        Cabral, ed. Pp. 56-75. New York: Monthly Review
        Press.

1969b   The Weapon of Theory. In *Revolution in Guinea:*
        Selected Texts. Amilcar Cabral, ed. Pp. 90-111.
        New York: Monthly Review Press.

1973a   Identity and Dignity in the Context of the National
        Liberation Struggle. In *Return to the Source.*
        African Information Service, ed. Pp. 57-74. New
        York: Monthly Review Press.

1973b   National Liberation and Culture. In *Return to the*
        Source. African Information Service, ed. Pp. 39-
        56. New York: Monthly Review Press.

Cabral, Nelson E.
1980   *Le Moulin et le Pilon: les Iles du Cap-Vert.* Paris:
        L'Harmattan.

Caetano, Marcelo
1951   *Colonizing Traditions, Principles and Methods of*
        the Portuguese. Lisbōn: Agência Geral do Ultramar.

Carreira, Antόnio
1968   *Panaria Cabo-Verdiano-Guinéense. Aspectos Histό-*
        ricos e Socio-Econόmicos. Lisbon: Junta de Inves-
        tigacões do Ultramar.

1969   *As Companhias Pombalinas de Navegação, Comércio e*
        Trafico de Escravos do Occidente Africano Para o
        Nordeste Brasileiro. Porto: Imprensa Portuguesa.

1971 A Ilha do Maio: Demografia e Problemas Sociais e Econômicos. Separata do No. 19. *Revista do Centro de Estudos Demográficos.* Lisbon: Instituto Nacional de Estatística.

1972 *Cabo Verde: Formação e Extinção de Uma Sociedade Escravocrata (1460-1878).* Lisbon.

1976 *Cabo Verde: Classes Sociais, Estrutura Familiar, Migrações.* Lisbon: Bibliotheca Ulmeiro.

1977 *Migrações nas Ilhas de Cabo Verde.* Lisbon: Universidad Nova de Lisboa, Ciências Humanas e Sociais. Série Investigação.

Carvalho, Eduardo de
1931 *Os Portuguese na Nova Inglaterra.* Rio de Janeiro: Teixeira e Ca., Lta.

Casmiro, Augusto
1940 *Portugal Crioulo.* Lisbon: Edições Cosmos.

Chabal, Patrick
1981 The Social and Political Thought of Amilcar Cabral: a Reassessment. *Journal of Modern African Studies* 19:31-56.

1982 Party, State and Socialism in Guinea-Bissau. Paper presented to the Canadian Association of African Studies, Toronto, Ontario, Canada.

Chelmiki, José Carlos Conrado de and Francisco Adolpho de Varnhagen
1841 *Córografia Cabo-Verdiana, ou Descripção Geográfica-histórica da Provincia das Ilhas de Cabo Verde e Guiné, Vol. II.* Lisbon.

Cohn, Michael and Michael K.H. Platzer
1978 *Black Men of the Sea.* New York: Dodd, Mead and Co.

Cunha, J.M. da Silva
1960 *Questões Ultramarinas e Internacionais (Direito e Politica), Vol. I.* Lisbon: Edições Atica.

Curtin, Philip D.
1969 *The Atlantic Slave Trade.* Madison: University of Wisconsin Press.

Cutileiro, José
1971 *A Portuguese Rural Society.* Oxford: Clarendon.

Davis, David Brion
    1974   Slavery and the Post World War II Historians. In
           Slavery Colonialism and Racism. Sidney Mintz, ed.
           Pp. 1-16. New York: Norton.

Decraene, Phillippe
    1977   Facing up to Drought -- and Independence. *The Man-
           chester Guardian Weekly*. September 18, p. 12.

Degler, Carl
    1971   *Neither Black nor White: Slavery and Race Relations
           in Brazil and the United States*. New York: Macmillan.

Donnan, Elizabeth
    1940   *Documents Related to the History of the Slave Trade*.
           4 vols. Washington: Carnegie Institute, Publica-
           tion No. 409.

Dow, George Francis
    1927   *Slave Ships and Slaving*. Salem, MA: Marine Research
           Society.

DuBois, W.E. Burghardt
    1969   *The Suppression of the African Slave Trade to the
    [1896] United States of America 1638-1870*. Baton Rouge:
           Louisiana State University Press.

Duffy, James
    1963   *Portugal in Africa*. Baltimore: Penguin.

Dujardin, Richard C.
    1979   Synagogue Becomes Cape Verdean Church. *Providence
           Journal-Bulletin*. August 11, p. A9.

Dumont, René and Marie-France Mottin
    1980   *L'Afrique Etranglée*. Paris: Seuil.

Duncan, T. Bentley
    1972   *Atlantic Islands: Madeira, the Azores and the Cape
           Verdes in Seventeenth Century Commerce and Naviga-
           tion*. Chicago: University of Chicago Press.

Edgerton, Robert B. and L.L. Langness
    1974   *Methods and Styles in the Study of Culture*. San
           Francisco: Chandler and Sharp.

Elkins, Stanley
    1959   *Slavery, a Problem in American Institutional and
           Intellectual Life*. Chicago: University of Chicago
           Press.

Fanon, Franz
    1967   *Black Skin, White Masks*. New York: Grove Press.

Feijó, João de Silva
1815 *Ensaio Econômico sobre as Ilhas de Cabo Verde, 1797.*
      Lisbon: Memórias Econômicas da Academia das Ciências
      de Lisboa, Tome V.

Fernandes, Florestan
1969 *The Negro in Brazilian Society.* Phyllis B. Eveleth,
      ed. New York: Columbia University Press.

1978 *A Integração do Negro na Sociedade de Classes.* 2
      vols. São Paulo, Brazil: Editora Atica.

Ferreira, Eduardo de Sousa
1974 *Portuguese Colonialism in Africa: The End of an Era.*
      Paris: UNESCO Press.

Ferreira, Manuel
1967 *A Aventura Crioulo ou Cabo Verde.* Lisbon: Platano
      Editora.

Firth, Raymond
1977 Whose Frame of Reference: One Anthropologist's
      Experience. *Anthropological Forum* IV:145-67.

Fonseca, Humberto Duarte
1961 *Considerações em Torno da Problematica das Crises em
      Cabo Verde.* 9:17-29. Lisbon: Garcia da Orta.

Freyre, Gilberto
1933 *Casa Grande e Senzala.* Rio de Janeiro: Maia e Schmidt.

1940 *O Mundo Que o Portugues Criou.* Rio de Janeiro.

1953 *Aventura e Rotina.* Lisbon: Livros do Brasil, Lda.

1959 *New World in the Tropics: The Culture of Modern
      Brazil.* New York: Knopf.

1961 *The Portuguese and the Tropics.* Lisbon: Executive
      Committee for the Commemoration of the Death of
      Henry the Navigator.

1966 *The Masters and the Slave.* New York: Knopf.

Galvão, Henrique
1950 *O Imperio Ultramarina Português.* Lisbon: Emprêsa
      Nacional de Publicadade.

Genovese, Eugene D.
1969 *The World the Slaveholders Made: Two Essays in
      Interpretation.* New York: Vintage Books.

1974 *Roll, Jordan, Roll: The World the Slaves Made.*
      New York: Pantheon.

Goffman, Erving
1959   *The Presentation of Self in Everyday Life*. New
York: Anchor.

1963   *Stigma: Notes on the Management of Spoiled Identity*.
Englewood Cliffs, NJ: Prentice-Hall.

Gonçalves, José Júlio
1972   *Portugueses Dispersos Pelo Mundo*. Lisbon: Agência
Geral do Ultramar.

Goodenough, Ward H.
1956   Componential Analysis and the Study of Meaning.
Language 32:195-216.

Gough, Kathleen
1968   New Proposals for Anthropologists. *Current Anthropology* 9:403-6.

Governo de Cabo Verde
1864a   *Boletim Oficial de Cabo Verde*. No. 3. Praia, Cabo
Verde.

1864b   *Boletim Oficial de Cabo Verde*. No. 150. Praia,
Cebo Verde.

1972   *Recensamento Populational de Cabo Verde*. Lisbon:
Agência Geral do Ultramar.

Gramsci, Antonio
1972   *A Formação dos Intelectuais, Rodrigues Xavier, Venda
Nova-Amadora*. Portugal.

Guillaumin, Colette
1972   *L'Idéologie Raciste: Genèse et Langage Actuel*.
Paris: Mouton.

Gutkind, Peter
1969   The Social Researcher in the Context of African
National Development: Reflections on an Encounter.
In *Stress and Response in Fieldwork*. Francis Henry
and Satish Saberwal, eds. Pp. 20-34. New York:
Holt, Rinehart and Winston.

Gutterres, Jorge de Brito, Jorge Eduardo da Costa Oliveira,
and Fernando Correia da Costa
1961   Estudos das Pescas em Cabo Verde. *Estudos de Econômia* 47:1:43-150. Junta de Investigações do Ultramar, Est dos de Ciências Politicas e Sociais.

Hamilton, Russell G.
1975   *Voices from an Empire: A History of Afro-Portuguese
Literature*. Minnesota Monographs in the Humanities,
vol. 8. Minneapolis: University of Minnesota.

187

Harris, Marvin
1958 *Portugal's African Wards: A First-Hand Report on
      Labor and Education in Mozambique*. New York:
      American Committee on Africa.

1966 Race, Conflict and Reform in Mozambique. In *The
      Transformation of East Africa*. S. Diamond and F.
      Burke, eds. Pp. 156-83. New York: Basic Books.

1970 Referential Ambiguity in the Calculus of Brazilian
      Racial Identity. *Southwestern Journal of Anthropo-
      logy* 26:1-14.

1974 *Patterns of Race in the Americas*. New York: Norton.
[1964]

Henry, Frances
1966 The Role of the Fieldworker in an Explosive Politi-
      cal Situation. *Current Anthropology* 7:552-54.

1969 Stress and Strategy in Three Field Situations. In
      Stress and Response in Fieldwork. Frances Henry and
      Satish Saberwal, eds. Pp. 35-46. New York: Holt,
      Rinehart and Winston.

Henry, Frances and Satish Saberwal
1969 Introduction. In *Stress and Response in Fieldwork*.
      Frances Henry and Satish Saberwal, eds. Pp. 1-5.
      New York: Holt, Rinehart and Winston.

Hoetink, H.
1967 *The Two Variants in Caribbean Race Relations: A
      Contribution to the Study of Segmented Societies*.
      New York: Oxford University Press.

Hymes, Dell
1964 A Perspective for Linguistic Anthropology. In
      Horizons of Anthropology. Sol Tax, ed. Pp. 92-107.
      Chicago: Aldine.

Ianni, Octavio
1972 *Raças e Classes no Brasil*. Rio de Janeiro: Editora
      Civilização Brasileira.

1978 *Escravidaõ e Racismo*. São Paulo: Editora Hucitec.

Innes, Harold
1940 *The Cod Fisheries: The History of an International
      Economy*. New York: Yale University Press.

Jamieson, E. Franklin
1908 *Winthrop's Journal, Vol. I*. New York.

Labelle, Micheline
1978 *Idéologie de Couleur et Classes Sociales en Haiti*.
      Montréal: Université de Montréal.

188

Leclerc, Gérard
1972   *Anthropologie et Colonialisme: Essai sur l'Histoire de l'Africanisme.* Paris: Fayard.

Legum, Colin
1983   Cape Verde Islands. In *Africa Contemporary Records 1981-2.* Pp. B405-9. New York: Africana Publishing Co.

Lessa, Almerindo
1959   O Homen Cabo-Verdiano. In *Colóquios Cabo-Verdianos.* Lisbon: Junta de Investigações do Ultramar.

Levi-Strauss, Claude
1970   *Tristes Tropiques.* New York: Athenum.

Lewis, I.M.
1977   Confessions of a 'Government' Anthropologist. *Anthropological Forum* IV:90-102.

Lima, José Joaquim Lopes de
1844   *Ensaio Sobre a Estatística das Ilhas de Cabo Verde no Mar Atlântico e Suas Dependências na Guiné Portuguesa ao Norte do Equador.* Lisbon.

Lipset, Seymour and Reinhard Bendix
1959   *Social Mobility in Industrial Society.* Berkeley: University of California Press.

Lounsbury, Floyd G.
1956   A Semantic Analysis of the Pawnee Kinship Usage. *Language* 32:158-94.

Lyall, Archibald
1938   *Black and White Make Brown: An Account of a Journey to the Cape Verde Islands and Portuguese Guinea.* London: Heinemann.

Macciocchi, Maria-Antoinetta
1974   *Pour Gramsci.* Paris: Seuil.

Macedo, José de
1901   A Educação do Negro. *Revista Portuguesa Colonial e Marítima.* Ano 4, 1° Semestre, pp. 287-97.

Machado, Deirdre A. Meintel
1977   Language and Interethnic Relations in a Portuguese Colony. In *Ethnic Encounters.* George Hicks and Philip Leis, eds. Pp. 49-62. North Scituate, MA: Duxbury Press.

1981a   Idéologie et Terminologie Raciales: les Brésil et l'Archipel du Cap-Vert. *Culture* I:123-29.

1981b   Cape Verdean-Americans. In *Hidden Minorities: the Pursuit of Ethnicity in American Life.* Joan Rollins, ed. Pp. 233-56. Washington: University Press of America.

Malinowski, Bronislaw
1961   *Argonauts of the Western Pacific.* New York: E.P.
[1922]   Dutton.

Mariano, Gabriel
1959   De Funca ao Sobrado, ou o 'Mundo' que o Mulato Criou.
         In *Coloquios Cabo Verdianos.* Pp. 23-50. Lisbon:
         Agência Geral do Ultramar.

Marques, A.H. de Oliveira
1972   *História de Portugal.* 2 vols. Lisbon: Palas Edi-
         tores.

Martinez-Allier, Verena
1974   *Marriage, Class and Colour in Nineteenth-Century
         Cuba: A Study of Racial Attitudes and Sexual Values
         in a Slave Society.* Cambridge University Press.

Martins, João Augusto
1891   *Cabo Verde, Madeira e Guiné.* Lisbon: Livraria de
         Antonio M. Pereira.

Marx, Gary
1973   The White Negro and the Negro White. In *Social Psy-
         chology and Everyday Life.* Billy J. Franklin and
         Frank H. Kohout, eds.   Pp. 137-48. New York: David
         B. McKay.

Marx, Karl
1971   *Contribution to the Critique of Political Economy.*
[1859]   Maurice Dobb, ed.   New York and London: Inter-
         national Publishing Company.

Masefield, John
1906   *The Voyages of Captain William Dampier.* 2 vols.
         London: E. Grant Richards.

McManus, Edgar J.
1973   *Black Bondage in the North.* Syracuse: Syracuse
         University Press.

Meintel, Deirdre A.
1975   The Creole Dialect of the Island of Brava.   In
         Miscelânea Luso-Africana. Marius Volkhoff, ed.
         Pp. 205-56. Lisbon: Junta de Investigações
         Cientificas do Ultramar.

1983   Cabo Verde: Survival Without Self-Sufficiency.   In
         Islands and Enclaves in Africa. Robin Cohen, ed.
         Pp. 68-78. Beverly Hills: Sage Publications.

forthcoming
         Cape Verdean Emigration: Solution or Problem?
         Revista Internacional de Estudos Africanos. Lisbon.

190

Melville, Herman
    1856   The 'Gees. *Harper's New Monthly Magazine* XII:507-9.

Memmi, Albert
    1965   *The Colonizer and the Colonized.* Boston: Beacon Press.

Minter, William
    1972   *Portuguese Africa and the West.* New York: Monthly
            Review Press.

Mintz, Sidney
    1971a   The Caribbean as a Socio-Cultural Area. In *Peoples
            and Cultures of the Caribbean.* Michael M. Horowitz,
            ed. Pp. 17-46. New York: Natural History Press.

    1971b   Groups, Group Boundaries and the Perception of Race.
            Contemporary Studies in Science and History 13:437-50.

Mónica, Maria Filomena
    1979   Moulding the Minds of the People: Views on Popular
            Education in Twentieth Century Portugal. Paper pre-
            sented at the International Conference on Modern
            Portugal, Durham, NH.

Monteiro, Felix
    1948   Tabanca. *Claridade* 6:14-18.

    1960   Cantiagas de Ana Procôpio. *Claridade* 9:15-23.

Monteiro, Julio, Jr.
    1974   *Os Rebelados da Ilha de Santiago.* Praia, Cabo Verde:
            Centro de Estudos.

Moone, Janet R.
    1973   The Best-Laid Plans: Research Pre-Designs and Field
            Revision. *Anthropological Quarterly* 46:7-14.

Mörner, Magnus
    1967   *Race, Mixture in the History of Latin America.*
            Boston: Little, Brown.

Morris, Patrick
    1973   Problems of Research in a Stratified Little Commu-
            nity. *Anthropological Quarterly* 46:38-46.

Mota, Avelino Teixeira da
    1970   A Malograda Viagem de Diogo Carreiro a Timbuctu em
            1565. *Boletim Cultural da Guiné Portuguêsa* XXV:97.

Nevinson, Henry Wood
    1968   *A Modern Slavery.* New York: Schocken Books.
    [1906]

Nogueira, Oracy
    1959   Skin Color and Social Class. In *Plantation Systems
            of the New World.* Papers and discussion summaries
            of the seminar held in San Juan, Puerto Rico.
            Washington: Pan American Union.

Pares, Richard
1956   *Yankees and Creoles*. Cambridge: Harvard University
       Press.

Parsons, Elsie Clews
1923   *Folk-lore from the Cape Verde Islands*. 2 vols. New
       York: American Folklore Society.

Pereira, João Batista Borges
1967   *Côr, Profissão e Mobilidade: O Negro e° Rádio em
       São Paulo*. São Paulo: Biblioteca Pioniera.

Pitt-Rivers, Julian
1966   Honour and Social Status. In *Honour and Shame*.
       J.G. Peristiany, ed. Pp. 19-78. Chicago: Univer-
       sity of Chicago Press.

Platzer, David and Deirdre Meintel Machado
1978   *Cape Verdeans in America: Our Story*. Boston:
       American Committee for Cape Verde, Inc.

Powdermaker, Hortense
1966   *Stranger and Friend*. New York: W.W. Norton.

Pusitch, António
1810   *Memoria ou Descrição Fisico-politica das Ilhas de
       Cabo Verde - 1810*. Lisbon: Anais do Conselho Ultra-
       marino, Parte Official, Serie II, 1860 e 1861.

Ramos, Artur
1951   *The Negro in Brazil*. Washington: Associated Pub-
       lishers.

Rancière, Jacques
1974   *La Leçon d'Althusser*. Paris: Gallimard.

Rehm, Barbara
1975   A Study of the Cape Verdean *Morna* in New Bedford,
       Massachusetts. Unpublished Master's Thesis, Depart-
       ment of Music, Brown University, Providence, RI.

Reyes, João da Silva
1797   *Ensaio Filosófico e Politico Sobre as Ilhas de Cabo
       Verde*. Caixa No. 731, Pacotilha 2, Documento No. 57.
       Rio de Janeiro: Arquivo Nacional, Secção de Admin-
       istraçao.

Ribeiro, Orlando
1956   As Ilhas de Cabo Verde no Principio do Século XIX.
       Garcia da Horta IV:607-33. Lisbon.

1960   *A Ilha do Fogo e as Suas Erupções*. Lisbon: Junta de
       Investigações do Ultramar, Memórias, Série Geográ-
       fica.

Roberts, George
1968   Account of a Voyage to the Islands of the Canaries, Cape de Verde, and Barbadoes, in 1721. In *A New General Collection of Voyages and Travels*. Thomas Astley, ed.; John Green, compiler. Pp. 599–627. London: F. Cass.

Rodney, Walter
1967   *West Africa and the Atlantic Slave-Trade*. Nairobi: East African Publishing House.

1970   *A History of the Upper Guinea Coast: 1584-1800*. Oxford: Clarendon Press.

Romano, Luis
1975   *Famintos*. Lisbon: Nova Aurora.

Rose, J. Holland, A.P. Newton and E.A. Benians
1929   *The Cambridge History of the British Empire*. Cambridge: Cambridge University Press.

Sanjek, Roger
1971   Brazilian Racial Terms: some aspects of meaning and learning. *American Anthropologist* 73:1,126–43.

Santos, Edmundo Daniel Climaco dos
1979   Angola: Colonialisme et Développement. Unpublished Master's Thesis, Department of Sociology, University of Montréal, Montréal, Québec, Canada.

Saul, John
1979   The Dialectic of Class and Tribe. In *State and Revolution in East Africa*. John Saul, ed. Pp. 391–421. New York: Monthly Review Press.

Sena, Manuel Roaz Lucas de
1818   *Dissertacão Sobre As Ilhas de Cabo Verde*. Manuscrito azul no. 248 (Inédito). Lisbon: Academic das Ciências.

Sennett, Richard and Jonathan Cobb
1973   *The Hidden Injuries of Class*. New York: Vintage.

Serviços de Estatística
1939   *Colónia de Cabo Verde Annuario Estatístico*. Praia, Cabo Verde.

1943   *Colónia de Cabo Verde Annuario Estatístico*. Praia, Cabo Verde.

1946   *Colónia de Cabo Verde Annuario Estatístico*. Praia, Cabo Verde.

1947   *Colónia de Cabo Verde Annuario Estatístico*. Praia, Cabo Verde.

Silva, Adriano Duarte
 1929 A Instrucção Pública em Cabo Verde. Centro de
      Estudos Politicos e Sociais *Boletim Geral do Ultra-
      mar* 46:172-75. Lisbon: Imprensa Nacional.

Silva, Balthasar Lopes da
 1956 *Cabo Verde Visto par Gilberto Freyre*. Praia, Cabo
      Verde: Imprensa Nacional.

 1957 *O Dialecto Crioulo de Cabo Verde*. Lisbon: Agência
      Geral do Ultramar.

Sousa, Henrique Teixeira de
 1958 Sobrados, Lojas e Funcos. *Claridade* 8:2-8.

 1963 As Doenças de Fome. *Cabo Verde*, May, pp. 20-24.

 1974 *Ilheu da Contenda*. Lisbon: Editorial do Século.

Spradley, James P.
 1979 *The Ethnographic Interview*. New York: Holt, Rine-
      hart and Winston.

Sturtevant, William C.
 1964 Studies in Ethnoscience. *American Anthropologist*
      66(3), pt. 2:2:99-131.

Szwed, John
 1975 Race and the Embodiment of Culture. *Ethnicity*
      2:19-33.

Taft, Donald
 1923 *Two Portuguese Communities in New England*. Studies
      in History, Economics and Public Law, No. 241. New
      York: Columbia University Press,

Tannenbaum, Frank
 1946 *Slave and Citizen*. New York: Knopf.

Teixeira, Antonio José and Louis Augusto Grandvanor Barbosa
 1958 *A Agricultura do Arquipelago de Cabo Verde*. Lisbon:
      Junta de Investigações do Ultramar.

Tenreiro, Francisco
 1961 *A Ilha de São Tomé*. Lisbon: Junta de Investigações
      do Ultramar, Memória No. 24.

Thomas, Charles W.
 1969 *Adventures and Observations on the West Coast of
[1960] Africa and Its Islands: Historical and Descriptive
      Sketches of Madeira, Canary, Biafra and Cape Verde
      Islands*. New York: Negro Universities Press.

Tyak, David B.
 1952 Cape Verdeans in the United States. Unpublished
      Senior Honors Thesis, Harvard University, Cambridge,
      MA.

Wax, Rosalie
  1960   Twelve Years Later: Analysis of Field Experiences.
          In *Human Organization Research*. Richard Adams and
          Jack Priess, eds. Pp. 166-78. Homewood, IL: Dorsey
          Press.

  1971   *Doing Fieldwork: Warnings and Advice*. Chicago:
          University of Chicago Press.

Whitten, Norman E., Jr. and Szwed, John F.
  1970   *Afro-American Anthropology: Contemporary Perspec-
          tive*. New York: Free Press.

Williams, James A.
  1929   England and the Opening of the Atlantic. In *The
          Cambridge History of the British Empire*. J. Holland
          Rose, A.P. Newton, and E.A. Benians, eds. Pp. 22-51.
          Cambridge: Cambridge University Press.

Williams, Thomas R.
  1967   *Field Methods in the Study of Culture*. New York:
          Holt, Rinehart and Winston.

Winstanley, Derek
  1976   Climatic Changes and the Future of the Sahel. In
          The Politics of National Disaster. Michael H.
          Glantz, ed. Pp. 189-213. New York: Praeger.

NOTES: n *refers to footnotes. Only the most important Crioulo words are indexed. Authors who have been cited throughout the book, i.e., more than 20 times, have the notation "cited through-out" after their names, rather than page numbers.*

Abolition of slavery, 48, 64-65, 70, 75, 84, 87-89, 93
Afonso V, Don, 32
Afonso, Diogo, 31
Africa, vii, 27, 151. See also Africans
  emigrants to Cabo Verde, 23, 24, 26, 31
  Portuguese colonies, 127, 128, 129-34, 135, 136, 140
  trade, 32, 36
  war with Portugal, vii, 3, 9, 11, 18, 127, 138-39, 143, 152
African Squadron, 48, 60, 71n4
Africans. See also Africa
  cultural traits, 24, 91n1, 139, 166-67
  language, 23
  perceived inferiority, 7, 104, 105, 142, 152, 155
  physical features, 93, 101, 102, 114, 151, 164
  slaves, vii, 37
Agar, Michael H. (cited), 2. 3, 4, 7, 8, 11, 13n6
Agriculture, 19, 20-21, 22, 31, 56, 75, 121
Albouy, Yves (cited), 56, 57
Alentejo, Portugal, 24
Alexander VI, Pope, 103
Algarve, Portugal, 24
Almada, Dulce (cited), 19, 148, 157n7
Almada, André Alvares de, 132-33, 157n7
Althusser, Louis, 107
American African Squadron, 48, 60, 71n4
Andrade, E. Silva (cited), 165
Andréini, Jean Claude (cited), 132
Angola, vii, 21, 43, 48, 140, 165
  colonatos, 133-34
  education, 135
  labor migration, 65, 71n7, 83
  mulattoes, 82
  Portuguese colonialism, 104
  relationship with Cabo Verde, 133-34
  slavery, 64, 87
  war, 130, 138, 144
Angolan Labor Institute, 157n2
Animal hides, 19, 25, 47, 49, 53n19, 59
Animals, 21, 38, 47, 57, 59
  textile designs, 44
Anne, Saint, 120
Anthropological research, 2-12
Antilles, 38
Araujo, Norman (cited), 133, 136
Arguim, Mauritania, 32, 40
Asad, Talal (cited), 2, 13n5
Assimilados, 128-31, 134, 157n1, 163, 165
Atlantic Islands (Duncan), 15
Azevedo, Thales (cited), 161
Azores, 31, 32, 38, 51n1, 51n3, 70
  emigrants, 1, 2, 26

Badius, 66, 141-44, 151, 155, 158n12
Bahia, Brazil, 160
Bailyn, Bernard (cited), 38
Bambara, 23
Banton, Michael (cited), 106, 162, 163
Barbados, 38
Barbosa, Jorge, 148; cited, ix
Barbosa, Louis Augusto Grandvanor (cited), 57
Barcelos, Cristiano José de Sena, cited throughout

Barlavento, 19, 26, 47, 56, 66, 142
Barnes, John (cited), 11, 13n8
Barreira, Balthazar, 58-59
Barreto, João (cited), 131, 133
Barros, Dona Isabel de, 76-77
Barros, Simão (cited), 45, 47, 49
Barter, 39, 44, 52n11, 52n13
Barthes, Roland (cited), 106
Bastide, Roger (cited), 92n9, 114, 161
Belgium, 74, 147
Bender, Gerald J. (cited), 129, 129, 133, 134, 157n1, 157n2, 165
Bendix, Reinhard (cited), 165
Bennett, Norman R. (cited), 18, 51n1
Berlin Conference, 132
Berreman, Gerald D. (cited), 2, 3
Blacks
  in Brazil, 82, 163-64
  in Cabo Verde, 104, 107
    festas, participants in, 117, 145
    indigenas, 128-29, 130
    lançados, 33
    manumission, 84, 86
    racial categories, 82-83, 92n11, 95-96, 160
    social classes, 94, 95
    stereotypes, 106, 122, 152
  in the United States, 129, 164, 166, 167
Black, John William (cited), 18, 23, 32, 33, 34, 35, 36, 39, 51n5
Blumer, Herbert (cited), 106
Boa Vista, 25, 49, 67, 68, 77
  geography, 19-20
  statistics, 171
  trade, 19, 47
Boston, Massachusetts, 1, 39, 47, 52n9, 52n17, 53n19
Bottomore, Tom (cited), 165
Boulenger, Bruno (cited), 56, 57
Boxer, Charles (cited), 80, 81-82, 104
Brace, C. Loring (cited), 73
Branco, 171
Branco, Castelo, 40-41
Brásio, Antonio (cited), 59, 84
Brava, 5, 16, 23, 25, 57, 82, 94
  badius, 142
  Crioulo dialect, 71n5
  emigration, 3, 6, 48, 65, 115, 122, 125n9, 137
  famine, 63
  festas, 118, 120, 121, 122, 126n13
  geography, 15, 20-22
  history, 26, 29n5
  racial categories, 96-97, 116
  racial classification, 98-99
  religion, 4, 144, 146
  slaves, 76, 77
  statistics, 171
Brazil, vii, 18, 21, 32, 36, 46, 53n21
  abolition of slavery, 88
  immigrants, 24
  language, 151
  mulattoes, 82
  race relations, 73, 74, 83, 93, 159-64
  racial categories, 96-97, 159-64
  racial classification, 98, 99, 102, 161
  racial ideology, viii, 162-64
  racial terminology, 7, 160-64, 169n2

Brazil *(continued)*
  slavery, 37, 42, 74, 75, 76, 77, 79,
    80
  social classes, 112, 163-64
  trade, 21, 40, 49
Bridge, Horatio (cited), 52n18, 60, 71n4
Brooks, George E., Jr. (cited), 18, 19,
    22, 25, 29n3, 39, 47, 48, 51n1,
    51n3, 71n3
Brown, Richard (cited), 13n7
Bryson, R.A. (cited), 57
Bulola River, 133

Cabo Verde: Uma Sociedade Escravocrata
    (Carreira), 49, 51n1, 39
Caboverdeano, 1
Cabral, Amilcar, 132, 151; cited, 141,
    154, 155-56
Cabral, Nelson E. (cited), 128, 136, 137,
    139, 141, 142, 143, 144, 145, 146,
    147, 148, 153
Cacao, 56, 64, 65, 83, 130, 142
Cacheu, Guinea, 36, 40, 41
Caetano, Marcelo, vii, 42, 73, 147,
    158n10; cited, 103, 128-29
Canada, 12n
Canizade, 110, 117, 119
Cannibalism, 59
Cape Verdean Solidarity Institute, 154
Caribbean, 26, 76, 102, 148
Carreira, António, cited throughout
Carreira, Diego, 29n7
Carvalho, Eduardo de, 72n10
Carvalho, Joachim Paiva de, 66, 72n10
Casmiro, António, 25, 29n9
Catholic Church, 4, 26, 145, 146. *See
    also* Clergy, *Festas*
  in Brazil, 79
  in Guinea, 132
  slaves and, 24, 74-75, 78-79, 84, 88
Censorship, 128, 136, 139
Certeza, 136
Cesaire, Aime, 27
Chabal, Patrick (cited), 132, 154, 156
Chad, 71n1
Chelmiki, José Carlos Conrado de (cited),
    24, 75, 80, 91n3, 92n14, 105, 135,
    151
Cholera, 77
Church of the Nazarene, 4, 116, 144, 146
Cid, Paula, 65
Cima, 171
Civil War (American), 49, 70
Claridade, 136
Clergy, 82, 100, 143, 146
  corruption, 144, 157n5
  education and, 132
  festas, 121
  slavery and, 78, 79, 80-81, 92n10
  trade, 49, 157n6
Climate, 18, 21, 22-23, 26, 31, 56-58,
    75, 131
Clothing, 39, 45-46, 48, 94
Coal, 46
Cobb, Jonathan (cited), 165
Coffee, 20-21, 49, 64, 83
Cohen, David, 25
Cohn, Michael (cited), 16
Colonatos, 133-34
Colonial Act of 1930, 128
Committee of Trade (London), 52n16
Company of Cacheu, 41
Company of Cacheu and Cabo Verde, 41
Company of Grao Pará and Maranhão, 42-
    45, 59, 84
Conakry, 132
Congregation of the Holy Spirit, 143

Conklin, Harold L. (cited), 169n1
Connecticut, 138
*Contribution to the Critique of Political
    Economy* (Marx), 125n8
Costa, Fernando Correira da (cited),
    16
Costa, Fontura da, 128, 135, 136
Cotton, 32, 43-45, 52n11, 88
Creole language, vii, 1, 26
Crioulo language, 23, 29n1, 35, 105,
    121, 167
  dialects, 6, 17, 19, 71n5, 87, 142
  relationship to Portuguese, 1-2,
    104, 125n3, 148-51
  restrictions in use, 138, 139, 141
  use by slaves, 37, 51n6, 76
Crise, 55-56, 58, 59, 61, 63, 64, 68
Cuba, 89, 95, 112
Culture, 17, 127, 134, 162, 165, 166
  Portuguese colonialism and, 103-7,
    138-51
  role in national liberation, 154,
    155
Cunha, J.M. da Silva, 103, 104, 129,
    140
Curaçao, 148
Currency, 39, 43
Curtin, Philip D. (cited), 53n20
Cutileiro, José (cited), 107

Dakar, 65
Dances, 110, 111
Darwinism, 134
Dampier, Captain, 16, 19, 39
Davis, David Brion (cited), 89
Death rituals, 45
Decraene, Phillippe (cited), 68, 135
Degler, Carl (cited), 74, 79, 80, 83,
    89
DGS, 138, 158n10
Direcçao Geral da Segurança, 138,
    158n10
Discrimination, 12, 82, 95, 161-67
Disease, 58, 59, 68-69, 77. *See also*
  names of specific diseases,
    e.g., malaria
Djunga. *See* Martins, João Cleofas
Donnan, Elizabeth (cited), 51n7,
    52n13, 52n16, 52n17
Dow, George Francis (cited), 38
Drake, Francis, 36
Drought, 11, 15, 19, 21, 55-70
  economics, 94, 153
  history, 18, 32, 49, 71n2
  slaves, 76, 88, 91n8
  trade, 45, 47
DuBois, W.E. Burghardt (cited), 48
Duffy, James (cited), 81, 87, 129,
    133
Dujardin, Richard C. (cited), 13n1
Dumont, René (cited), 156
Duncan, T. Bentley, cited throughout
Dutch West India Company, 40
Dyes, 42, 44

East Indies, 18, 36, 46
Economic history. *See* History,
    economic
Edgerton, Robert B. (cited), 2, 4, 7
Education, 17, 91n5, 128, 130, 133,
    134-38, 140, 165
  control by Portugal, 11, 73, 139
  Crioulo, use of, 149, 151
  in Guinea, 132
Elizabeth I, Queen, 52n12
Elkins, Stanley (cited), viii, 74,
    79, 89, 161

Emigration, vii, 6, 48, 85, 135, 147
  aid to Cabo Verde, 49, 60, 94, 154
  labor recruitment, 65-66
  language, effect on, 71n5
  social classes, effect on, 122
  state-directed, 64, 69
  statistics, 172
  to the United States, 1, 3, 13n1,
    17, 70, 144, 159, 164-67
    fees, 65
    folklore, 138
    marriage, 115, 125n9
    social classes, 137
Erosion, 58
European Economic Community, 153
Evora family, 26

Famine, 24, 52n15, 55-90, 108, 113,
    130, 137, 144, 153
  emigration, 35, 133
  migration, 19, 21, 26, 47, 55
  slaves, 38, 77, 85
Famintos (Romano), 59
Fanon, Frantz (cited), 27, 102
Farim River, 133
Feasts. See Festas.
Fernandes, Florestan (cited), 112,
Festas, 161, 162, 163
Ferreira, Eduardo de Sousa (cited),
    104, 128, 132, 134, 135, 140,
    146
Ferreira, Manuel (cited), 162, 163
    76, 87, 117-22, 125n10, 125n11,
    125-26n12, 126n13, 145, 166
  Crioulo, use of, 150
  social classes, 110
Firth, Raymond (cited), 2, 9-10
Flanders, 34, 44
Fogo, 20, 36, 51n4, 58, 153, 167
  agriculture, 75
  badius, 142
  drought, 57
  labor recruitment, 66, 150
  land grants, 75, 82, 91n2
  medical care, 69
  mulattoes, 82
  racial categories, 116
  slavery, 26, 76, 77, 84, 86, 88
  social classes, 95, 98, 110, 115,
    119
  statistics, 171
  trade, 45
  volcano, 15, 16, 21
  weaving, 44
Folk ritual, 116-22, 139, 142
Folk tales, 137-38
Fonseca, Humberto Duarte (cited), 56-
    57
Fonseca, Oliviera de, 77
Food, 50, 94-95
  famine, 59, 64, 68
  imported, 31-32, 153
  trade, 48
Foreign aid, 55, 153-54
Fox Point, Providence, Rhode Islands,
    1
Frake, Charles O. (cited), 169n1
France, 25, 29n3, 53n21, 131, 147
Freyre, Gilberto (cited), 73-74, 79,
    80, 88, 91n1, 114, 161
Fula, 23
Furna, Brava, 21, 26, 55, 62

Galvão, Henrique (cited), 72n9
Gambia, 39, 71n3
Gambia River, 35
The 'Gees, (Melville), 13n3

Genealogy, 99, 100, 105
Genovese, Eugene D. (cited), 78, 79,
    88, 89, 147
Geography, vii, 15-29, 86, 146
Gestapo, 158n10
Goffman, Erving (cited), 102, 103
Gold Coast, 40
Gomes, Bernadim, 34
Gomes, Fernando, 32, 40
Gonçalves, José Júlio (cited), 128
Goodenough, Ward H. (cited), 169n1
Goree, 29n3
Gough, Kathleen (cited), 8
Government, 42, 94, 153
Gramsci, Antonio (cited), 141, 147,
    155
Grande, 171
Great Britain, 25, 29n3, 52n12, 74
  aid, 60
  trade, 39, 46-49, 131, 153
Gregory II, Pope, 80
Guadeloupe, 27
Guillaumin, Colette (cited), 106, 122,
    125n7
Guinea, 52n12, 53n21, 82, 152, 155,
    157n5
  education, 132, 135
  language, 139, 151
  relationship with Cabo Verde, 131-34
  trade, 35, 37, 41, 42, 44, 45, 49
  war, 138, 147
Guinea-Bissau, 27, 40, 46, 132, 154,
    157n6
Gulf of Guinea, 48, 83
Gutkind, Peter (cited), 6
Gutterres, Jorge de Brito (cited), 16

Haiti, 97
Hamilton, Russell G. (cited), 136
Harris, Marvin, cited throughout
Henry, Frances (cited), 6, 10-11
Henry the Navigator, Prince, 31, 74
History, vii, 31-32
History, economic, 31-50, 88
Hitler Youth, 146
Hodges, Samuel, 60, 71n3
Hoetink, H. (cited), 74, 79-80, 92n9,
    102
Holland, 115, 125n9, 147, 148
Hymes, Dell (cited), 98, 169n1

Ianni, Octavio, 161, 163-64
Ilheu da Contenda (Sousa), 72n11
India, 11, 34, 36, 51n5
Indígenas, 65, 128-30, 132
Infant mortality, 68
Innes, Harold (cited), 52n8
Islam, 23, 132
James, Saint, 145
Jamieson, E. Franklin (cited), 38
Japan, 26, 50
Jesus, 25, 33
Joao V, Dom, 87
John the Baptist, Saint, 118, 125n11,
    126n13
Jose I, Dom, 42
Labelle, Micheline (cited), 97
Labor and laborers, 56, 70, 83, 145,
    154
  communal, 154, 158n13
  migration during famine, 63-67, 69-
    70, 71n7, 72n9, 130, 142
Lacoste-Dujardin, Camille (cited), 5
Lagos, Nigeria, 6
Lançados, 33-35, 82, 84, 133, 139n
  slaves, 37, 85, 131
Land grants, 75-76, 82, 91n2, 91n3, 91n6

Landlords, 26, 68, 75-76, 87, 106, 132, 150
  festas, 117, 145
  mulattoes, 82, 83
  racial categories, 105
  sharecropping, 94
  slavery, 78, 85-86, 88, 93
  social classes, 95, 107, 108, 109, 111, 115, 142
Langness, L.L. (cited), 2, 4, 7
Language, 148-51, 159-61, 169n1
  as cultural control, 140-41
Lebu, 23
Legum, Colin (cited), 158n14
Lenço, 104-5
Leprosy, 58, 66, 69
Lessa, Almerindo (cited), 23
Lewis, I.M. (cited), 10, 13n5
Lima, José Joaquim Lopes de (cited), 19, 24, 29n5, 48, 75-76, 91n5, 105, 135, 149
Line of Demarcation, 103
Lipset, Seymour (cited), 165
Lounsbury, Floyd G. (cited), 169n1
Lusotropicalism, 73-74, 123, 161
Lyall, Archibald (cited), 46

Macchiocchi, Maria-Antoinetta (cited), 141
Macedo, José de (cited), 158n9
Machado, Deirdre A. Meintel (cited), 1, 2, 97, 141, 158n12
Madeira, 31, 32, 38, 51n1, 51n3, 116
  emigrants, 2, 24, 26
Magalhães, A., 157-58n8
Maio, 16, 19, 26, 41, 57
  medical care, 68
  slaves, 77
  statistics, 171
  trade, 38, 39, 47, 49, 52n8, 52n10, 52n17
Malaria, 21, 66, 131, 143, 145
Mali, 71n1
Mandinka, 23, 44, 132
Manumission, 26, 74, 78, 84-86, 88, 89
Map, xi
Mariano, Gabriel (cited), 81
Marinho, Joachim Perreira, 91n3
Marques, A.H. de Oliveira (cited), 31, 72n9, 128n, 129, 135, 136, 146, 158n10
Marriage, 75, 80, 93, 100, 109, 112-16, 143, 161
  emigrants, 125n9, 167
  mulattoes, 83
  pirates, 29n6
  slaves, 77, 78, 84, 92n13
Martinez-Allier, Verena (cited), 95, 112
Martinique, 27
Martins family, 85
Martins, João Cleofas (cited), 60, 64, 69, 91n4, 157n4
Martins, Manuel Antonio, 39, 42, 71n3
Martins, Ovidio, 148
Marx, Gary (cited), 167
Marx, Karl (cited), 125n8
Maryland, 38
Masefield, John (cited), 16, 19, 39
Massachusetts, 138
Mathilde (schooner), 63
Mauritania, 71n1
McManus, Edgar J. (cited), 38
Medical care, 17, 68-69, 95, 143
Medina family, 24
Meintel, Deirdre A. (cited), 23, 70, 148

Melville, Herman, 13n3
Memmi, Albert (cited), 104
Mendes, Alphonso, 157n2
Migrações nas Ilhas de Cabo Verde (Carreira), 13n4
Migration, 22, 26, 56, 70, 71n7
  famine, 19, 21, 49, 55
  state-directed, 63-67
Miguelistas, 25
Military, 87, 131, 137, 148, 157n4
Mindelo, São Vicente, 10, 15, 16, 20, 148
  cemeteries, 25, 48
  education ,37
  migration, 19, 26
  religion, 146
  social classes, 111
  trade, 46, 47, 153
Minter, William (cited), 72n9
Mintz, Sidney (cited), 26, 89, 92n9
Miscegenation, 26, 74, 79-84, 89, 101-2
Missionaries, 75, 131, 133, 143, 144, 145
  slavery, 78, 79, 84
Missionary Statute of 1941, 128
A Modern Slavery (Nevinson), 66
Mónica, Maria Filomena (cited), 135, 140, 157-58n8
Monopoly companies, 35, 41-43
Monteiro, Felix, 121; cited, 29n4, 98, 143
Monteiro, Júlio, Jr. (cited), 144, 145, 146
Moone, Janet R. (cited), 6
Moreira, Adriano, 138
Mörner, Magnus (cited), 80
Morocco, 25
Morris, Patrick, 11
Mota, Avelino Teixeira da (cited), 29n7
Mottin, Marie-France (cited), 156
Mozambique, 3, 43, 140, 157n2
  indígenas, 129
  labor migration, 65, 71n7
  slavery, 87
  war, 138
mulattoes, vii, 80, 81-84, 86, 89, 91n4, 107, 132, 161
  African, 35
  festas, 117
  lançados, 33-34
  military, 87
  racial categories, 95
  slavery, 74, 85
  social classes, 108, 110, 115, 122
  stereotypes, 152
Music, 6, 25, 46, 137, 151, 166
  Crioulo, use in, 149, 150
  festas, 79, 117
Muslim, 23
Mussolino, Benito, 158n10

Nantucket, 1
Navigation, 16, 19
Nazarenes, 4, 116, 144, 146
Netherlands, 40, 50, 76, 165-66
Nevinson, Henry Wood (cited), 66
New Bedford, Massachusetts, 1, 2, 13n1
  whaling museum, 16
New England, viii, 60
  textile industry, 1
  trade, 38, 42
New England Merchants in Africa (Bennett and Brooks), 51n1
Newfoundland, 39
Newport, Rhode Island, 1

Niger, 71n1
Nogueira, Oracy (cited), 106, 162, 163
Noli, Antonio da, 31, 32
Nôs Vida, 166
Nova Sintra, Brava, 3, 21, 62

O Arquipelago, 138
Oliveira, Jorge Eduardo da Costa
    (cited), 16
OPEC, 153
Orchil, 42-43
Organic Charter of 1933, 128
Overseas Council Report of 1670, 40

PAIGC, 11, 128, 132, 141, 147, 151, 154
Panos, 44-46, 119
Papels, 45
Papiamento, 148
Pares, Richard (cited), 38
Parsons, Elsie Clews (cited), 138
Partido Africano da Independencia de
    Cabo Verde. *See* PAIGC
Peabody Museum, 71n3
Pellagra, 69
Pernambuco, Brazil, 40, 80
Perry, Matthew, 18, 48, 71n4
Peter, Saint, 125-26n12
Philip, Saint, 46, 117-19
PIDE, 138, 147, 158n10
Pinto, Serpa, 60
Pirates, 18, 36, 53n21, 76, 86
  marriage, 29n6
  settlers, 23
Pitt-Rivers, Julian (cited), 107
Platzer, David (cited), 16
Platzer, Michael K.H. (cited), 1
Police, 127, 138, 144. *See also* DGS,
    PIDE
  brutality, 94, 106, 130, 142, 145-46
  control by Portugal, 11
  Portuguese, 147-48
Policia International e da Defesa do
    Estado, 138, 147, 158n10
Pollution, 57
Pombal, Marquês de, 42, 80
Population, 23-26
  statistics, 171
Porto, Vitoriano do, 81
Porto Inglês, Maio, 39
Portuense, Padre Vitoriano, 131, 157n5
Portugal, 3, 9, 11, 21
  acquisition of Cabo Verde, 31
  African colonies, 127-34
  aid to Cabo Verde, 59-60, 63, 64, 68,
    152, 164
  colonialism, 3, 73-74, 103, 104, 127-
    34, 163
  cultural controls in Cabo Verde, 138-
    51
  currency in Cabo Verde, 39
  education, 136, 137, 140
  emigrants, 1, 2, 24
  Guinea, 40-41
  Revolution of 1820, 87
  trade, 44-50
  war in Africa, vii, 3, 9, 11, 18,
    138-39, 143, 152
Portuguese language, 29n1, 121, 125n2,
    159, 167
  relationship to Crioulo, 1-2, 104,
    125n3, 148-51
  use encouraged in Cabo Verde, 131,
    139, 140-41
Powdermaker, Hortense (cited), 2, 5-6,
    9
Praia, Santiago, 10, 16, 138, 148
  cemeteries, 25, 48

migration, 19, 64
religion, 146
Priests. *See* Clergy
Primogeniture, 75
Príncipe, 56, 64, 65, 66, 142
  emigration from Cabo Verde, 172
Providence, Rhode Island, 1, 2, 3,
    13n1
Provision of 1792, 92n10
Public works projects, 63-64, 68
Pusitch, Antônio, 85, 135

Rabat, Morocco, 25
Race relations, viii, 6, 73-74, 79-
    89, 93-96, 159-67
Race Relations (Banton), 162
Race Relations in the Portuguese Empire
    (Boxer), 81
Racial categories, 5-6, 7, 73, 82-83,
    92n11, 93, 95-101, 105, 123n3,
    159-64
  festas, 117
  marriage, 114, 116
  social classes, 108
  stereotypes, 106
  valuation, 102
Racial classification, ix, 2, 13n2,
    73, 98-103, 161-64
Racial ideology, 7, 12, 73, 93, 101-
    23, 127-31, 151-53, 165-67
  Brazilian, viii, 162
Racial terminology, 7-8, 93, 96-98,
    101, 108, 125n3, 159-64
Ramos, Artur (cited), 76, 91n7
Ramos, Tony, 126n14
Rancière, Jacques (cited), 107, 125n8
Raso, 171
Rebelados, 143-46
Reforestation, 58
Religion, 4, 6, 26, 78-79, 91n2, 142,
    143, 144-46. *See also* Catholic
    Church, Clergy, *Festas*
  Portuguese colonialism, 103, 104,
    127, 129
  slavery, 74-75, 76, 86
Revolution of 1820 (Portugal), 87
Reyes, João da Silva (cited), 47
Rhode Island, 52n13, 128
Rhodes-Livingston Institute, 13n7
Rhodesia, 9, 13n7
Ribeira Grande, Santiago, 36, 41,
    157n5
Ribeiro, Orlando (cited), 25, 29n5,
    32, 56, 57, 58, 60, 75, 85, 135
Rickets, 69
Rio Nuno, Guinea, 44
Roberts, George (cited), 16
Rodney, Walter (cited), 23, 34, 37,
    131, 157n6
Romano, Luis (cited), 59
Rose, J. Holland (cited), 52n12
Royal African Company, 52n16
Royal Mail Steam Packet Company, 46

Sahel, 56-57, 71n1
Sal, 15, 19, 31, 39, 49
  statistics, 171
Salazar, Antonio de Oliveira
  censorship, 66, 136
  colonialism, 128, 145
  colonatos, 133
  education, 135, 140
  indígenas, 65
  PIDE, 158n10
  racial ideology, 73, 94, 127
  religion, 144
  tabanca, 139, 143

Salem, Massachusetts, 21n3
Salgado, Antonio, 42
Salt, 31, 68
  trade, 19, 39, 42, 47, 49, 52n8-
  11, 52n17
Sanjek, Roger (cited), 96, 97, 160,
  169n1, 169n2
Santa Cruz (feast), 87, 120-22
Santa Luzia, 171
Santa Maria, Zuzarte de, 81
Santana (feast), 120-22
Santiago, 16, 20, 21, 24, 51n3, 131,
  132, 167
  agriculture, 75
  badius, 141-42
  drought, 57
  famine, 59, 64, 133
  labor recruitment, 66
  land grants, 75, 82, 91n2, 91n6
  landlords, 68, 94, 142
  mulattoes, 82
  peasant uprising, 128, 142
  pirates, 53n21
  religion, 139, 143, 144, 157n5
  slavery, 23, 31-38, 51n6, 76, 84,
  86, 87, 88
  social classes, 25
  statistics, 171
  strategic importance, 138
  trade, 45, 52n17
  weaving, 46
Santo Antão, 20, 23, 25, 29n6, 94
  drought, 67
  medical care, 68
  slaves, 76, 86
  statistics, 171
Santos, Edmundo Daniel Climaco dos
  (cited), 104
São Felipe, Fogo, 16, 26, 51n4
  famine, 61
  festas, 119, 120, 125-26n12
São Nicolau, 20, 23, 25, 29n6
  drought, 57, 67
  education, 133
  famine, 59
  medical care, 68
  slaves, 76
  statistics, 171
São Paulo, Brazil, 112
São Tomé, 18, 56, 80, 150
  labor and laborers, 56, 64, 65-66,
  130, 142
  migration from Cabo Verde, 70, 192
  mulattoes, 81, 83, 84
São Vicente, 15, 20, 132
  education, 133, 135
  famine, 68
  migration, 26
  statistics, 171
  strategic importance, 138
  trade, 46
Saul, John (cited), 154
Seca, 55-56
Sena, Manuel Roaz Lucas de (cited),
  78
Senegal, 23, 37, 71n1, 151, 155, 165
Sennett, Richard (cited), 165
Settlers, 23-25, 26, 31
Sexual relations, 5, 74, 81, 112-14
Sharecropping, 44, 87, 94, 108,
  158n14
  freed slaves, 85-86, 88, 89
Sickle-cell anemia, 131
Sierra Leone, 23, 35, 37
Silva, Balthasar Lopes da (cited),
  19, 91n1, 128, 135, 148
Silva, Duarte, 136

Sinogoga, Santo Antão, 25
Slavery, 12, 18, 31-50, 73-89, 93-96,
  129, 131. *See also* Abolition of
  slavery; Slaves
Slavery (Elkins), viii, 89
Slaves, 21, 31-50, 53n20, 66, 70, 73-89,
  142. *See also* Slavery
  African, vii, 23, 26
  tabanca, 145
  marriage, 92n13
  religion, 24
  categories, 51n6
Sleeping sickness, 66
Smallpox, 59, 77
Smuggling, vii, 25, 40-41, 50, 80
Soares, Mario, 25
Social classes, 4, 66, 95, 98, 107-23,
  127
  education, 137
  festas, 46
  Jews, 25
  landlords, 142
  petty bourgeoisie, 155-56
  racial categories, 162-67
  women, 5, 8
Sociedade Geral, 50
Sociolinguistics, 6, 135
Somalia, 10
Sotavento, 19, 56, 98
Sousa, Henrique Teixeira de (cited),
  72n11, 83, 98
South Africa, 74, 81
Spain, 44, 103
Spinola, António da, 147
Spradley, James P. (cited), 8
Stereotypes, 17, 73, 106-7, 122, 151-53,
  154-55
Stoughton, Massachusetts, 71n3
Strategic importance, vii, 3, 9, 18, 138
Sturtevant, William C. (cited), 169n1
Sugar, 31, 51n3, 68, 77, 89
Sunspots, 56
Surinam, 76
Swan, Samuel, 18
Syphilis, 66
Szwed, John (cited), 96, 105, 106, 119

Tabanca, 142-43, 144, 145, 150-51
Tannenbaum, Frank (cited), 74, 79, 161
Tantum, Brava, 62
Tarrafal, Santiago, 46, 147
Tavares, Eugenio, 25, 148, 149
Teixeira, Antonio José (cited), 57
Tenreiro, Francisco (cited), 64, 66, 67,
  83, 84, 92n11
Textiles, 52n15
  imports, 34
  New England, 1
  trade, 37, 42, 43-46, 49, 52n16, 52n17
Thomas, Charles W. (cited), 48, 49, 71n4
Tikopia, 9
Tobacco, 38, 47
Tomas, Americo, 105
Tortugas, 52n8
Torture, 66, 72n10, 76-77, 91n7, 158n10
Trade, 18, 19, 37-50, 52n8-11, 52n16,
  52n17
  Brazil, 21, 32
  food, 31-32
  Great Britain, 131, 153
  Guinea, 35-36
  lançados, 33-35
Tratado breve dos rios de Guiné (Almada), 133
Trinidad, 10, 11
Tuberculosis, 66
Tucoro, 23
Tunisia, 104

Tyak, David B. (cited), 17

United States
  aid during famine, 59-60, 63, 153
  Blacks, 129, 164, 166, 167
  Cabo Verdean immigrants. *See*
    Emigration
  race relations, 159-61, 164
  racial categories, viii, 159, 160,
    162
  racial classification, ix, 13n2
  slavery, 53n20, 74, 81, 88, 89
  stereotypes, 106
  trade, 45, 46-49, 50, 52n10
University of Dakar, 155
Upper Volta, 71n1

Varnhagen, Francisco Adolpho de
    (cited), 24, 80, 91n3, 91n5,
    92n14, 105, 135, 151
Vegetation, 15, 19, 20, 31-32, 57
Vernon, Samuel, 52n13
Vernon, William, 52n13
Vieira, Antonio, 82
Virginia, 38
Volcanoes, 16, 21, 26, 57, 91n2
Voting, 130
Voz de Cabo Verde, 148

Wages, 68, 130
Waldo, Samuel, 52n17
Walsingham (ship), 41
War of 1812, 47
Ware, Enoch, 29n3
Wax, Rosalie (cited), 2, 5, 6
Weaving, 23, 24, 44-46, 52n13, 77
Webster-Ashburton Treaty, 48
West Indies, 26, 38
Whaling, viii, 1, 16, 18, 47-49, 70
Whitten, Norman E., Jr. (cited), 96
Williams, Thomas R. (cited), 2, 3,
    9, 11
Wilson, Godfrey, 13n7
Winstanley, Derek (cited), 56, 57
Winthrop's Journal (Jamieson), 38, 39
Witchcraft, 76, 105
Wolof, 23, 31, 44
Women
  anthropologists, 5, 10
  religion, role in, 143
  singers, 117-18, 120
  smoking pipes, 7, 104
  social classes, 5, 8, 109, 11-12
The World the Portuguese Created (Freyre),
    74
World War II, 73

*Yankee Traders, Old Coasters and African
    Middlemen* (Brooks), 51n1

Note on the Author

Deirdre Meintel was born in California and has lived in
various parts of the midwestern United States and in
Galveston, Texas. She studied for the B.A. at Catholic University of America and received the Ph.D. from Brown University in 1978. For the last ten years, she has made her home
in Montreal, Québec. At present she divides her time between
teaching and co-directing a research project on immigrant
women workers.